Contents

A note on how to use this book

While the author and publisher acknowledge that names may vary widely on spellings and pronunciations, names have been arranged by common spellings and first initial only. Alternative first initial spellings are listed under their relative letter, but spelling variations with the same first initial are listed only once, under the most common spelling.

10,000
baby names

choose from the latest and best baby names

Holly Ivins

white
LADDER

Acknowledgements

Thank you to Victoria Oundjian and Robin Boothroyd, and to everyone at Crimson Publishing.

This edition first published in Great Britain 2010 by

Crimson Publishing, a division of Crimson Business Ltd
Westminster House
Kew Road
Richmond
Surrey
TW9 2ND

A catalogue record for this book is available from the British Library.

ISBN 978 1 90541 063 7

Printed and bound by Legoprint SpA, Trento

1

How to choose a name

Top tips on choosing a name

- **Fall in love with the name(s) you've chosen.** If you plough through hundreds of pages of names in this book and none of them jump off the page at you, then you probably haven't found the right one yet. Likewise, if a relative, friend, or even your spouse suggests a name and you wrinkle your nose every time you hear it, it's not the name for your baby.

> You will want to pick a name that you can shout with confidence across the school playground, or hear with pride when they graduate from university. Pick a name which makes you smile because if you love it, hopefully your child will too.

- **Research.** You've already started the process of researching which name to pick simply by buying this book, but there are ways to expand the process if you wish to. The internet can be a fantastic way to look up meanings in more depth, or to find out if your baby's name is becoming more or less popular through the years. This is particularly useful if you want to avoid a situation where your daughter has the same name as three other children in her class, or if you don't want your son to be teased because his name sounds rude in another language. Other ways to do research include making lists of names you hear during the run-up to the birth, going back into history to find names of great cultural importance, or finding a meaning you like and linking a name to it. The name Helen, for example, means 'light', but there are a great many variations of it, including Aileen, Eleanor, Helena and Lena. Therefore, if you like the idea of naming your daughter 'light' but aren't keen on Helen, researching other variations might just lead you to the perfect one.

- **Don't listen to other people.** Sometimes, grandparents and friends will offer 'advice' during this time which may not always be welcome. This is worth bearing in mind if you've fallen in love with a name and it's either slightly unusual or doesn't follow the set pattern your partner's family have used for the last 50 years. Sharing your choice of name with other people can lead them to criticise it, which you'd probably rather not hear if you've got your heart set on it. Also, if you're bucking with tradition and don't plan on calling your newborn after their great-great-great-Grandfather, keeping it a secret until after the birth and registration can work to your advantage. Trust your own instincts and remember: no-one will really care once they see your baby. Its name will simply be its name.

Jack has remained the top boys' name for 15 years in a row.

- **Find a name with meaning.** A lot of parents want to find a name for their baby that means something. If you're interested in history you might try naming your daughter after queens of England (Elizabeth, Mary or Victoria) in the hope that it will fill your child's soul with a sense of pride and importance. This can inspire your child to try to live up to their name's reputation. Having a name which has a back story helps your child understand their significance in the world, so whether you name them after a religious saint or prophet, an important political figure or a hero in a Greek tragedy, ensure they know where their name comes from. They may just be inspired to be as great as their namesake.

- **Have fun.** Picking out names should be a fun process. Laughing at the ones you'd never dream of choosing can really help you narrow it down to the ones you would. You can also experiment with different spellings, pronunciations or variations of names you like, or go to places where you might feel inspired.

Some of the best names come from the worlds of nature and literature, so why not go down to your local garden centre or library and have fun with the classic, cute and downright silly words you find there?

- **Expand your mind.** Don't rule out the weird ones just yet! As a teenager I went to school with a girl named Siam. Her parents had conceived her on a honeymoon trip to

Thailand and given her the country's old name as a result. She loved growing up and having an unusual name, as I'm sure Ireland Baldwin (Alex Baldwin and Kim Basinger's son) and Rumer Willis (Demi Moore and Bruce Willis' daughter) do too. Also, don't be afraid to play around with spellings and pronunciations, even if the results are a little less than conformist. The name Madison, for example, could be spelt Maddison, Madyson, Maddiesun or even Maddeesunn if you so choose, although you might want to be careful you don't saddle your child with an impossible name to spell, pronounce *and* fit onto a passport application form.

- **Try it out.** While you're pregnant, talk to your baby and address it using a variety of your favourite names to see if it responds. There are numerous stories of names being chosen because the baby kicked when it was called Charlie or Aisha, but was suspiciously silent when it was called Dexter or Mildred, so see if it has a preference! You can also try writing names down and sticking them to your fridge, or saying one out loud enough times to see if you ever get sick of it. That name you picked out when you were eight and always said you'd name your first child, for example, might not sound so appropriate now you're an adult and have to name a human being for real.

- **What if you can't agree?** This is probably the trickiest problem in the baby-naming process to solve. It's wise to research a number of names you and your partner are both interested in and make a point of discussing your reasons for liking or disliking them long before the baby is due to be born. The labour and delivery room is probably not the best time to argue as you'll both be tired, emotional and at least one of you will be in pain. Avoid sticking to your guns on a name one of you really isn't happy with because it might lead to resentment down the line, with your baby caught in the middle. You could try compromising and picking two middle names so you both have a name in there you love, or you could each have five names you're allowed to 'veto' but no more. You could also try making contractions out of names you both like, such as Anna and Lisa (Annalisa) or James and Hayden (Jayden). Whichever way you go about it, it is important that you both eventually agree on the name you are giving your baby, even if it means losing out on that one you've had your heart set on for a while.

- **Look at foreign names.** Looking at names popular in other countries may provide just the inspiration you need. You could decide to use a foreign spelling of a name you like to make your choice that bit more unusual, such as Natalia instead of Natalie, or it might turn you on to a name you hadn't considered yet. Jorge might not suit your baby, but George could.

- **Look to the future.** One important aspect of naming your child is thinking ahead to their future. Will the name you've chosen stand the test of time? Will names popular in 2010 remain popular in 2035? Will they be able to confidently enter a room and give a crucial business presentation with an awkward or unpronounceable name? Will they be able to hand their business card over to a potential client without that client looking bemused? Even on a smaller scale, can they survive the potential minefields of primary and secondary school with a name that could be easily shortened to something embarrassing? You need to consider how your child will cope with that name as an adult. While this seems a very long way off now, it is important. Introducing themselves as Professor Xavier to a group of university deans might raise a few smirks among knowing *X-Men* fans, as would any unusual or trendy name which has lost its shine by the time your child is an adult. Would you want to try catching criminals as Police Officer Apple Blossom or have other politicians take you seriously with a name like MP Lil' Kim Scarlett? You don't want to give your child a name which they just cannot live with for the rest of their life, so make your choice based on what's appropriate for a child as well as an adult.

- **Involve siblings.** If you have children already, you should try to get them involved in the naming process too. Many older siblings find new names hard to remember or pronounce and your baby could end up with a nickname before you know it. Many people find that the nickname given to them by siblings can stick, so their family will forever call them 'Tree' instead of Teresa or 'Non' for Jonathan.

If your baby has an older sibling, try talking to them about their new brother or sister using the name you've chosen so you can discover how their imagination might choose to interpret it.

If your other children are slightly older they might provide the valuable insight that they have a friend at school who gets teased for having an unfortunate nickname derived from the name you've chosen.

Banned names

The following names were all banned by registration officials in New Zealand:

Cinderella Beauty Blosson	Stallion
Fat Boy	Talula Does The Hula From
Fish and Chips (twins)	Hawaii
Keenan Got Lucy	Twisty Poi
Sex Fruit	Yeah Detroit

New Zealand law prevents parents from giving their children names which would cause offence or are more than 100 characters long.

These names, however, were all permitted by the same officials:

All Blacks	Midnight Chardonnay
Benson and Hedges (twins)	Number 16 Bus Shelter
Ford Mustang	Spiral Cicada
Kaos	Superman (changed from 4real)
Masport and Mower (twins)	Violence

Other countries also have restrictions when it comes to choosing names:

- In France, names must come from an approved list.
- The UK only bars names which are deemed to be offensive.
- Portugal, Spain, Argentina and Germany also have an approved list of names for parents to choose from.

Nicknames

Nicknames are an unavoidable part of the history of names. Even seemingly simple names which do not lend themselves to being shortened can be subject to it: Prince Harry's real name, for example, is actually Henry, but he has been referred to as Harry since birth.

Nicknames can range from the common – Mike from Michael, Sam from Samantha – to the trendy, funny or downright insulting. Everyone knows countless Richards who refuse to be called 'Dick' or the Francescas who prefer 'Fran' over 'Fanny'.

With all this said however, it is perfectly possible to choose a name which you know has an unfortunate nickname associated with it but for it to not bother you. If you don't encourage the use of nicknames when your child is young, chances are one won't stick when they're older either. Most people who had an embarrassing nickname as a child generally don't introduce themselves by that name, meaning their adult friends don't call them that.

Another way to avoid embarrassing nicknames is to select one for your child that you actually like so that others don't even get a mention. Call your daughter Elizabeth by Liz, Lizzie or Libby if you don't like Betty or Beth, and no-one will even consider the alternatives.

You can pre-empt problem nicknames to some extent by saying the name you've chosen out loud and trying to find rhymes for it. This is a clever way to avoid playground chants and nursery rhyme-type insults, such as Andy Pandy or Looby Lou. It's a sad truth though that children will rhyme anything with anything else if they can, so while you might wish to take playground chants into account during your naming process, don't be too concerned about them. Most children are subjected to it at some point and emerge unscathed.

> A Chinese couple were prevented from naming their child '@' in 2007, despite their reasoning that it was simply a modern choice of name in this technological age.

Using family names

Some families have a strong tradition of using names that come from their family tree. There are instances where naming your son Augustine VIII is simply not an option; it's a rule. Or perhaps you like the idea of your son or daughter being named after the parent of the same sex and so you simply have to add 'Junior' (Jr.) to the end of a name you already know and love.

There are obviously pros and cons with using family names:

- Pro: Your child will feel part of a strong tradition, which will create a sense of security for them and help make them feel a complete member of the family.
- Pro: If you're having a problem selecting a name you and your partner both agree on, this is a very simple solution and will make your new child's family very happy.
- Con: You might not actually like the name that's being passed down. Naming your child the 12th Thumbelina in

a row might not actually hold the same attraction for you as for the generation before you.

- Con: Another drawback could be if the cultural associations with that name have changed in your lifetime and it is no longer appropriate.

One way to navigate around choosing a family name is to compromise. You could use the name as a middle name, or refer to your baby by a nickname instead. You could also suggest using a name from the other partner's family: if the name comes from your side, try finding one you like from the other side. If their argument is for tradition then this is an astonishingly effective counter-argument.

Whatever you decide about using family names, just remember that this is *your* baby. Just as your parents got to decide what they named you, you get to decide this. If family and friends are disappointed, don't be alarmed. Once the baby is here they will only see how much she has her grandmother's nose, or his grandfather's ears, and the name will become far less important.

Initials

What surname will your baby have? Does its first letter lend itself easily to amusing acronyms already, and would choosing certain forenames only exacerbate the problem? If your child will inherit a double-barrelled surname this becomes a bigger consideration still, as there are more amusing four letter words than there are three. Parents who are considering a name like Andrew Steven Smith should consider what these initials will spell before making their final decision!

It's worth taking the time to think about acronyms of initials in the real world too, such as how credit cards display names or seeing your child's name written out on a form. Nobody should have to go through life known as Earl E. Bird, I. P. Freely or S. Lugg because their parents didn't think that far ahead. For a wonderful selection of these types of names, tune in to *The Simpsons* and observe Bart's prank phone calls to Moe's Tavern.

Amusing initials

Earl E. Bird	S. Lugg
Kay F. Cee	Warren T.
I. P. Freely	I.C. Blood
Al E. Gador	H. I. Vee
Angie O. Graham	Gene E. Yuss

Your surname

Connected to your child's potential new initials is their new surname. Whether they are receiving their name from their mother, father or a hyphenated combination of both, matching an appropriate first name to their surname is an important undertaking. Try to avoid forenames which might lead to unfortunate phrases when combined with certain surnames to prevent a lifetime of embarrassment for your child. The best way to work out if this might happen is to write down all the names you like alongside your child's last name and have someone else read them out loud. This second pair of eyes and ears might just spot something you didn't.

Unfortunate forename/surname combinations

Anna Sasin	Isabella Horn
Barb Dwyer	Jenny Taylor
Barry Cade	Justin Time
Ben Dover	Mary Christmas
Duane Pipe	Oliver Sutton
Ewan Carr	Paige Turner
Grace Land	Russell Sprout
Harry Rump	Stan Still
Hazel Nutt	Teresa Green

There is also the danger of your child being subjected to having a Spoonerism made out of their name, where the first letters or syllables get swapped around to form new words. An unfortunate and recent example of this would be Angelina Jolie and Brad Pitt's daughter Shiloh, whom they named Shiloh Jolie-Pitt to avoid the inevitable Shiloh Pitt Spoonerism. Try to avoid making the same mistake!

Quirky names and stereotypes

There are lots of disadvantages to having a quirky name, but there are plenty of advantages too. For one thing, your child's name will never be forgotten by other people, and if they do something influential with their life their name could become inspirational for other parents to name their children. On the other hand, a quirky name often requires a quirky personality. If you don't think your genes could stand up to a name like Satchel or Kerensa, perhaps it's time to think of one a little more run-of-the-mill.

A quirky name often says more about the parents than the child, whose own personalities may affect the personality of their child in a significant way. A conventional family who name their baby John will probably find he becomes a conventional child, whereas a quirky family who name their baby Zanzibar will find he develops a quirky personality. The name itself is not the leading factor; it's the quirky or conventional behaviour encouraged by the parents who chose the name that is.

It is not true that babies are as influenced by their names as people believe. There is no scientific evidence to say that names dictate who we become, which means that you cannot give your child a perfect or imperfect name, whichever one you finally pick.

What is usually the case is that people make assumptions about a name and that person's personality lives up to or fails those expectations. A boy named William might be expected to be intelligent, whereas one named Attila will be viewed automatically as a bully. A girl named Norma might be told her name is too old for her and one named Honey might be told it's too young. None of these assumptions, however, will change the personality of your child one iota, so if you want to choose a quirky name for them feel free to do so.

Assumptions about names

Research has shown that most people do make assumptions based on a person's name. A 2009 survey of 3,000 teachers found that 49% of teachers make assumptions about their pupils based on their name. One in three admitted that certain names spell a troublemaker to them, including Callum, Brandon, Chelsea and Aleisha, while the names Christopher, Edward, Rebecca and Charlotte were assumed to belong to brighter children. Of course these assumptions vanish as soon as teachers meet their pupils but you know what they say about first impressions!

Names from fictional characters

The one type of quirky name you may wish to pause and consider is that of fictional characters. Your baby is highly likely to be exposed to cartoons before they start school, so they will have their name associated with whatever their peers have read or seen. A boy named Barney or Fred, for example, might be teased for having the same name as a giant purple dinosaur or a Stone Age cartoon character. A girl named Ariel or Belle might be expected to behave like a little princess, while one named Dorothy might be constantly asked if she wants to go home…

While avoiding any kind of possible connection to a fictional character is nigh on impossible, you can help make things easier for your child by educating them about their namesake and encouraging them to read more about them. Stay up-to-date with new cartoons and children's characters to prepare both yourself and your child for toddlerdom and childhood. That way they can be proud of their name and have ammunition if things get rough in the playground.

Spellings and pronunciation

Once you've finally agreed upon a name, it's time to consider how you wish it to be spelt and pronounced. Some parents take great joy in experimenting with unusual variations of traditional names, while others prefer for names to be instantly recognisable. The only advice here is to use caution in your experiments. There are many anecdotal tales of parents seeing or hearing pretty names in the hospital during delivery and choosing them for their children, only to find out later they were medical terms and therefore completely inappropriate as names. Even spelling or pronouncing them differently won't be of much use once they're old enough to know the meaning behind them.

Obviously medical terms as names are a little extreme, but the choices you make regarding spelling and pronunciation are really important. Try to avoid making a common name too long or too unusual in its spelling as this will be the first thing your child learns how to write. They will also be subjected to constant corrections during their lifetime, as other people misspell or mispronounce their name in ever more frustrating patterns.

Make sure the name isn't so long that it won't fit on forms

or name badges as they'll simply stop using it and take on a nickname instead.

Substituting the odd 'i' for a 'y' isn't too bad, but turning the name Jonathan into Jonnaythanne doesn't do anyone any favours.

Middle names

The use of middle names is generally acknowledged to be standard practice in the UK these days. In fact, it has become fairly uncommon to name a child *without* a middle name, although there are cultures where this is still the case. A middle name can have just as much of an impact as a forename so your choice for your own baby should be made as carefully as their first name.

You may have already decided what middle name to give your child due to tradition or culture, in which case the following advice may be moot. In Spanish cultures, for example, middle names are often the mother's surname or another name to promote that matriarchal lineage. Similarly, parents who have not taken each other's surnames or are not married may choose to give their child one surname as a middle name and one as a last name so both parents are represented. Other traditions may use an old family name, passed down to each first-born son or daughter to encourage a sense of family pride and history. A decision about what middle name to pass on may have therefore already been made for you, even before your own birth.

If you are choosing a middle name there are some common trends to help you narrow it down.

- **Opposite-length names**. It has become very popular to give a child either a long forename and short middle name, or a short forename and long middle name. If this idea attracts you, consider using syllables to give you an idea of length and combinations.

- **Name from the family tree**. Honouring your ancestors is another popular trend. Parents are frequently looking back to their own lineage for interesting, unusual or inspirational names, or to honour the memory of a beloved family member.

- **Unusual names**. Along with a wider variety of first names in recent years (Ruby, Amelia and Mia have all climbed the Top 20 charts over the last five years, replacing the standard Emily, Chloe and Megan), parents are choosing more unusual middle names too. This would make sense, as a child named Bronte or Keilyn probably needs a fairly uncommon middle name to balance it out. Alternatively, as middle names are far less frequently used, this is an opportunity for parents to have an unusual name included that they wouldn't perhaps use otherwise. If their child grows up not to like it they have the option of only using their initial, or simply dropping it from daily use altogether.

- **Common names**. As a last resort, if you find you are struggling to pick a middle name you could always pick a traditionally used one – if it ain't broke... For girls, Anne, Marie, May and Rose have all been strikingly popular in recent years and the same is true for Andrew, David, James and Thomas for boys.

As with first names, middle names can have hilarious con-sequences if not thought about carefully. It's worth writing down your favourite combinations and saying them out loud to make sure you're not making inadvertently calling your child 'mayonnaise' (or May Ann Naze).

Of course, you don't have to narrow down middle name choices to just one. It is becoming more and more common to have several middle names, particularly if parents like more than one or want to include a family name as well. Be careful not to have too many though, as this makes life very difficult when filling out official forms or enrolling your child in school. Most institutions only recognise one middle name, and some only recognise a middle initial.

The Glastonbury teenager named **Captain Fantastic Faster Than Superman Spiderman Batman Wolverine Hulk And The Flash Combined**, changed his name from George Garratt in 2008. He claims to have the longest name in the world. If he does then he replaces Texan woman **Rhoshandiatellyneshiaunneveshenk Koyaanisquatsiuth Williams**, whose 57-letter length name pales in comparison to Captain's 81.

One last thing to bear in mind when choosing a middle name is that many people actually choose to go by this name instead of their forename. Celebrities often do this, such as Brad Pitt whose real name is William Bradley Pitt, but it is just as common for non-celebrities too. In fact, you probably know someone in your family or workplace that has always been known as Ed or Sam when their name is actually James Edward Jones or Felicity Samantha Taylor. You might even choose to do this with your own child, particularly if you're using a family name and adding Jr. to the title. It might be easier to call James Jones Jr. Ed, if only to make it clear who you're telling off at the dinner table!

The science of baby naming

Whether you agree with it or not, there is a certain science to naming babies. Even at the very basic level of choosing a name you like the sound of, the science is there.

Some experts have noted that parents who choose inspirational names for their offspring (Destiny, Serenity, Unique) or names of products they aspire to own (Armani, Jaguar, Mercedes) are projecting a future onto their child for them to aspire to. After all, the idea of a Mercedes working at a local fast-food restaurant isn't nearly as attractive as one who works as a lawyer or artist.

While parents are often cautioned or even discouraged from picking wild and crazy names for their babies (think about Petal Blossom Rainbow, Jamie Oliver's third daughter) there isn't actually any scientific evidence to suggest that children are hindered in any way by them. There seems to be more evidence to suggest that the stories behind names are more important.

Children who are told they have inherited an ancestor's name or that of an influential character from history seem to be more driven and focused than children who are told disappointingly, 'We just liked the sound of it'. As a parent, therefore, it seems it's okay to pick an unusual name if you have the story or anecdotal evidence to back it up.

Another thing to consider about the science of baby naming is how your child's name will be perceived by the outside world. Typically, judgements are passed on names before a person is met, such as at job interviews or in school. This does have the potential to hold back your child, although there is conflicting evidence to say that once someone is met in person, assumptions and stereotypes are wiped away.

> Personality and character have a far greater influence than name alone and after a while, a name becomes just a name.

It is wise to be cautious though, particularly if the name you're considering is extremely controversial. In the United States in December 2008 there was a case of a supermarket bakery refusing to ice the words 'Happy Birthday, Adolf Hitler' onto a three year old's birthday cake, despite never having met the child it was intended for. The parents were able to eventually fulfil the order at another shop, but as a result of the publicity surrounding the event Social Services were called in to assess the child's home and Adolf, along with his siblings JoyceLynn Aryan Nation and Honszlynn Hinler Jeannie, were taken into care.

Controversial names adopted by real people

Adolf Hitler	Judas
Allah	Lolita
Beelzebub	Lucifer
Desdemona	Stalin
Jezebel	Voldemort

If your child will be given a name from an ethnic or cultural heritage, there is often a fear that this will potentially hold them back. Many children from a Chinese heritage, for example, choose to adopt a Western name while at school rather than have countless teachers and classmates mispronounce or make judgements about their name.

Another example would be strong Islamic names (think Ahmed, Mohammed or Neha), which given the current political climate, some children and teenagers fear could prevent them from being treated fairly at school or in their first job. This is not to say that these names should not be used, as it is the fault of prejudiced people passing judgements on your child's name rather than the fault of the name itself. In fact, the greater the diversity of names and cultures represented by them, the greater the chance of society's acceptance overall.

Naming twins, triplets and more

If you have discovered you are expecting multiples, congratulations! Naming multiples needn't be any different to naming a single child... unless you want it to be. You could stick to the same process as everyone else, and pick an individual name for each individual child, or you could go with a theme. Try anagrams or names in reverse, or give each child the same initials. You could even do this if you're not expecting multiples, like the Duggar family of Arkansas, USA, who have given each of their 18 children the initial 'J'.

A palindrome name is a name which is spelt the same backwards and forwards, as with Bob, Elle, Eve and Hannah.

Twin names with the same meaning

Bernard and Brian (strong)
Daphne and Laura (laurel)
Deborah and Melissa (bee)
Dorcas and Tabitha (gazelle)
Elijah and Joel (God)
Eve and Zoe (life)
Irene and Salome (peace)
Lucius and Uri (light)
Lucy and Helen (light)
Sarah and Almira (princess)

Of course, when all's said and done you can just stick to giving each child a name unique to them. For triplets, quads and more this is probably an easier choice than twisting your head around three names with the same meaning, or trying to create four anagrams you like for all of your babies. Some parents do like to use a theme though, such as matching initials or names that go down the alphabet (think Alastair, Benjamin, Christopher and David).

How do you find eight names?

'Octomom' Nadya Suleman had the difficult task of naming eight babies at once. She settled on Maliah and Nariah for the two girls and McCai, Isaiah, Jeremiah, Jonah, Jeremiah, Makai and Noah for the boys.
The babies all share the middle name Angel though so that might make it easier to call them inside for dinner!

2

Boys' Names

A **Boys' names**

Aaban
Muslim, meaning 'angel'.

Aabha
Indian, meaning 'light'.

Aabharan
Hindi, meaning 'treasure' or 'jewel'.

Aadi
Sanskrit, meaning 'first' or 'most important'.

Aahil
Muslim, meaning 'prince'.

Aakesh
Indian, meaning 'lord of the sky'.

Aalam
African, meaning 'world' or 'universe'.

Aarif
Arabic, meaning 'expert'.

Aaron
Hebrew, meaning 'mountain of strength'.

Aasaf
African, meaning 'clear'.

Aba
Turkish, meaning 'father'.

Abacus
(alt. Abacas, Abakus)
Greek, meaning 'a mathematical possibility'.

Abaddon
Israeli, meaning 'destroyer'.

Aban
Persian, meaning 'clearer'.

Abasi
Egyptian, meaning 'male'.

Abbott
(alt. Abbe, Abbot, Abott)
Anglo-Saxon, meaning 'father of the abbey'.

Abdhi
Hebrew, meaning 'my servant'.

Abdiel
Biblical, meaning 'servant of God'.

Abdul
Arabic, meaning 'servant'. Often followed with a suffix indicating who Abdul is the servant of (ie Abdul-Basit, servant of the creator).

Abdullah
Arabic, meaning 'servant of God'.

Abe
Hebrew, from Abraham, meaning 'father'.

Abel
Hebrew, meaning 'breath' or 'breathing spirit'. Associated with the Biblical son of Adam and Eve who was killed by his brother Cain.

Abelard
German, meaning 'resolute'.

Aberforth
Gaelic, meaning 'mouth of the river Forth'. Name of Dumbledore's brother in the Harry Potter books.

Abheek
Indian, meaning 'fearless'.

Abhishek
Indian, meaning 'bath for a deity' or 'anointing'.

Abir
(alt. Abeer)
Hebrew, meaning 'strong'.

Abner
Biblical Hebrew, meaning 'father of light'.

Abraham
(alt. Abe, Avram, Ibrahim)
Hebrew, meaning 'father of many'. Associated with the biblical figure of Abraham and Abraham Lincoln the American president during the Civil War.

Absalom
(alt. Absalon)
Hebrew, meaning 'father/leader of peace'.

Acacio
Greek origin, meaning 'thorny tree'. Now widely used in Spain.

Ace
English, meaning 'number one' or 'the best'.

Achebe
Nigerian, Surname of famous writer Chinua Achebe.

Achilles
Greek, Mythological hero of the Trojan war, whose heel was his only weak spot.

Achim
Hebrew, meaning 'God will establish' or Polish, meaning 'The Lord exalts'.

Aciano
(alt. Acyano)
Spanish, meaning 'like the blue-bottle flower'.

Acilino
Latin, meaning 'eagle'.

Ackerley
Old English, meaning 'oak meadow'. Often used as surname, many similarly spelt variants.

Adal
German, meaning 'one of honourable character'.

Adalberto
Germanic/Spanish, meaning
'nobly bright'.

Adam
Hebrew, meaning 'man' or
'earth'. First man to walk the
earth, accompanied by Eve.

Adão
Variant of Adam, meaning 'earth'.

Addison
Old English, meaning 'son of
Adam'. Also used as a female
name in the USA.

Ade
African, meaning 'peak' or
'pinnacle'.

Adel
Hebrew, meaning 'God is
everlasting'.

Adelard
Teutonic, meaning 'brave' or
'noble'.

Adelbert
Old German form of Albert.

Aden
Gaelic, meaning 'fire'.

Adetokunbo
Yoruba, meaning 'the crown
came from over the sea'.

Adin
Hebrew, meaning 'slender'
or 'voluptuous'. Also Swahili,
meaning 'ornamental'.

Adio
African, meaning 'devout'.

Aditya
Sanskrit, meaning 'belonging to
the sun'.

Adlai
Hebrew, meaning 'God is just', or
sometimes 'ornamental'.

Adler
Old German, meaning 'eagle'.

Adley
English, meaning 'son of Adam'.

Admon
Hebrew origin, variant of Adam
meaning 'earth'. Also the name of
a red peony.

Adolph
Old German, meaning 'noble
majestic wolf'. The popularity of
the name plummeted after the
Second World War, for obvious
reasons.

Adonis
Phoenician, meaning 'Lord'.

Adrian
Latin origin, meaning 'from
Hadria', a town in Northern Italy.

Adriel
Biblical Hebrew, meaning 'of
God's flock'.

Adyn
(alt. Adann, Ade, Aden)
Irish, meaning 'manly'.

Aeneas
Greek/Latin origin, meaning 'to
praise'. Name of the hero who
founded Rome in Virgil's Aeneid.

A

Aeson
Greek origin, father of Jason.

Afif
(alt. Afeef, Afief, Afeif)
Arabic, meaning 'pure'.

Afonso
Portuguese, meaning 'eager noble warrior'.

Agamemnon
Greek. Figure in mythology, commanded the Greeks at the siege of Troy.

Agathon
Greek, meaning 'good' or 'superior'.

Agha
(alt. Aaghaa)
African, meaning 'master'.

Agustin
Latin/Spanish meaning 'venerated'.

Ahab
Hebrew, meaning 'father's brother'. Pleasant way to address an uncle.

Ahijah
Biblical Hebrew, meaning 'brother of God' or 'friend of God'.

Ahmed
Arabic/Turkish, meaning 'worthy of praise'.

Ahsan
(alt. Ahson, Ahsun, Ahsin)
Arabic, meaning 'merciful'.

Aidan
Gaelic, meaning 'little fire'.

Aidric
Old English, meaning 'oaken'.

Aiken
(alt. Aikin, Aicken, Aickin)
English, meaning 'sturdy'.

Ainsworth
(alt. Answorth, Annsworth, Ainsworthe)
English, meaning 'of Anne's domain'.

Airyck
Old Norse, from Eric, meaning 'eternal ruler'.

Ajani
African, meaning 'he fights for what he is'. Also Sanskrit, meaning 'of noble birth'.

Ajax
Greek, meaning 'mourner of the Earth'. Another Greek hero from the siege of Troy.

Ajay
Indian, meaning 'unconquerable'.

Akeem
Arabic, meaning 'wise or insightful'.

Akio
Japanese, meaning 'bright man'.

Akira
Japanese, meaning 'intelligent'.

Akiva
Hebrew, meaning 'to protect' or 'to shelter'.

Akmal
(alt. Aqmal, Akmall, Acmal)
Arabic, meaning 'perfect man'.

Akon
American, made popular by
the famous rapper charting in
2008/2009.

Aksel
Hebrew/Danish, meaning 'father
of peace'.

Aladdin
Arabic, meaning 'servant of
Allah'. Popular Disney character.

Alamar
(alt. Alamarr, Alemar, Alomar)
Arabic, meaning 'encased in
gold'.

Alan
(alt. Allan, Allen, Alun)
Gaelic, meaning 'rock'.

Alaric
Old German, meaning 'noble
regal ruler'.

Alastair
(alt. Alasdair, Allister)
Greek/Gaelic, meaning
'defending men'.

Alban
Latin, meaning 'from Alba'. Also
the Welsh and Scottish Gaelic
word for 'Scotland'.

Alberic
Germanic, meaning 'Elfin king'.

Albert
Old German, meaning 'noble,
bright, famous'.

Albin
Latin, meaning 'white'.

Albus
Latin, variant of Albin meaning
'white'. Also the Christian
name of Albus Dumbledore,
headmaster of Hogwarts School
in the Harry Potter books.

Alden
Old English, meaning 'old friend'.

Aldis
English, meaning 'from the old
house'.

Aldo
Italian origin, meaning 'old' or
'elder'.

Aldric
English, meaning 'old King'.

Alec
(alt. Alek)
English, meaning 'defending
men'.

Aled
Welsh, meaning 'child' or
'offspring'.

Aleron
(alt. Aileron, Alerun, Ailerun)
Latin, meaning 'child with wings'.

Alessio
Italian, meaning 'defender'.

Alexander
(alt. Alex)
Greek origin, meaning 'defending
men'.

Alexei
Russian origin, meaning 'defender'.

Alfred
(alt. Alfi, Alf)
English, meaning 'elf' or 'magical counsel'.

Alfonso
Germanic/Spanish, meaning 'noble and prompt, ready to struggle'.

Alford
Old English, meaning 'old river/ford'.

Algernon
French origin, meaning 'with a moustache'.

Ali
Arabic, meaning 'noble, sublime'.

Allison
English, meaning 'noble'.

Alois
German, meaning 'famous warrior'.

Alok
Indian, meaning 'cry of triumph'.

Alon
Jewish, meaning 'oak tree'.

Alonso
(alt. Alonzo)
Germanic, meaning 'noble and ready'.

Aloysius
Italian saint's name, meaning 'fame and war'.

Alpha
First letter of the Greek alphabet.

Alphaeus
Hebrew origin, meaning 'changing'.

Alpin
Gaelic, meaning 'related to the Alps'.

Alter
Yiddish, meaning 'old man'.

Alton
Old English, meaning 'old town'.

Alva
Latin, meaning 'white'.

Alvie
German, meaning 'army of elves'.

Alvin
English, meaning 'friend of elves'.

Alwyn
Welsh, meaning 'wise friend'. May also come from the River Alwen in Wales.

Amachi
African, meaning 'who knows what God has brought us through this child'.

Amadeus
Latin, meaning 'God's love'.

Amadi
African, meaning 'appeared destined to die at birth'.

Amado
Spanish, meaning 'God's love'.

Amador
Spanish, meaning 'one who loves'.

Amari
Hebrew, meaning 'given by God'.

Amarion
Arabic, meaning 'populous, flushing'.

Amasa
Hebrew, meaning 'burden'.

Ambrose
Greek, meaning 'undying, immortal'.

Americo
Germanic, meaning 'ever-powerful in battle'.

Amias
Latin, meaning 'loved'.

Amil
African, meaning 'effective'.

Amir
Hebrew, meaning 'prince' or 'treetop'.

Amit
Hindu, meaning 'friend'.

Ammon
Egyptian, meaning 'the hidden one'.

Amory
German/English, meaning 'work' and 'power'.

Amos
Hebrew, meaning 'encumbered' or 'burdened'.

Anakin
American, meaning 'warrior'. Made famous by Anakin Skywalker in the *Star Wars* films.

Ananias
Greek/Italian, meaning 'answered by the Lord'.

Anastasius
Latin, meaning 'resurrection'.

Anat
Jewish, meaning 'water spring'.

Anatole
Greek, meaning 'cynical but without malice'.

Anders
Greek, meaning 'lion man'.

Anderson
English, meaning 'male'.

Andrew
(alt. Andreas)
Greek, meaning 'man' or 'warrior'.

Androcles
Greek, meaning 'glory of a warrior'.

Angel
Greek, meaning 'messenger'.

Angus
Scottish, meaning 'one choice'.

Anil
Sanskrit, meaning 'air' or 'wind'.

Anselm
German, meaning 'helmet of God'.

A

Anson
English, meaning 'son of Agnes'.

Anthony
English, from the old Roman
family name.

Antwan
Old English, meaning 'flower'.

Apollo
Greek, meaning 'to destroy'.
Greek god of the sun.

Apostolos
Greek, meaning 'apostle'.

Ara
Armenian. Ara was a legendary
king.

Aragorn
Literary, used by Tolkien in The
Lord of the Rings trilogy.

Aram
Biblical, meaning 'Royal
Highness'.

Aramis
Latin, meaning 'swordsman'.

Arandu
Place in Pakistan, meaning 'little
garden'.

Archibald
(alt.Archie)
Old German, meaning 'genuine/
bold/brave'.

Ardell
Latin, meaning 'eager/burning
with enthusiasm'.

Arden
Celtic, meaning 'high'.

Ares
Greek, meaning 'ruin'. Son of
Zeus and Greek god of war.

Ari
Hebrew, meaning 'lion' or 'eagle'.

Arias
Germanic, meaning 'lion'.

Aric
English, meaning 'merciful ruler'.

Ariel
Hebrew, meaning 'lion of God'.
One of the Archangels, Angel of
healing and new beginnings.

Arild
Old Norse, meaning 'battle
commander'.

Aris
Greek, meaning 'best figure'.

Ariston
Greek, meaning 'the best'.

Aristotle
Greek, meaning 'best'. Famous
philosopher.

Arjun
Sanskrit, meaning 'white'.

Arkady
Greek, region of central Greece.

Arlan
Gaelic, meaning 'pledge' or
'oath'.

Arlis
Hebrew, meaning 'pledge'.

Arlo
Spanish, meaning 'barberry tree'.

Armand
Old German, meaning 'soldier'.

Armani
Same origin as Armand, meaning 'soldier'. Nowadays closely associated with the Italian designer.

Arnaldo
Spanish, meaning 'eagle power'.

Arnav
Indian, meaning 'the sea'.

Arnold
Old German, meaning 'eagle ruler'.

Arrow
English, from the common word denoting weaponry.

Art
Irish, name of a warrior in Irish mythology, Art Oenfer (Art the lonely).

Arthur
(alt. Artie, Artis)
Celtic, probably from 'artos', meaning 'bear'. Made famous by the tales of King Arthur and the Knights of the Round Table.

Arvel
From the Welsh 'Arwel', meaning 'wept over'.

Arvid
English, meaning 'Eagle in the woods'.

Arvind
Indian, meaning 'red lotus'.

Arvo
Finnish, meaning 'value' or 'worth'.

Arwen
Welsh, meaning 'fair' or 'fine'.

Asa
Hebrew, meaning 'doctor' or 'healer'.

Asante
African, meaning 'thank you'.

Asher
Hebrew, meaning 'fortunate' or 'lucky'.

Ashley
Old English, meaning 'ash meadow'.

Ashok
Sanskrit, meaning 'not causing sorrow'.

Ashton
English, meaning 'settlement in the ash-tree grove'.

Aslan
Turkish, meaning 'lion'. Strongly associated with the lion from C.S. Lewis' *The Lion, The Witch, and The Wardrobe*.

Asriel
Biblical origin, meaning 'help of God'.

Astrophel
Latin, meaning 'star lover'.

Athanasios
Greek origin, meaning 'eternal life'.

Atílio
Portuguese, meaning 'father'.

Atlas
Greek, meaning 'to carry'. In Greek mythology Atlas was a Titan forced to carry the weight of the heavens.

Atlee
Hebrew, meaning 'God is just'.

Atticus
Latin, meaning 'from Athens'.

Auberon
Old German, meaning 'Royal bear'.

Aubrey
Old German, meaning 'power'.

Auden
Old English, meaning 'old friend'.

Audie
Old English, meaning 'noble strength'.

Augustas
(alt. Augustus)
Latin, meaning 'venerated'.

Aurelien
French, meaning 'golden'.

Austin
Latin, meaning 'venerated'. Also city in the state of Texas in America.

Avi
Hebrew, meaning 'father of a multitude of nations'.

Avery
(alt. Avrie, Averey, Averie)
English, meaning 'wise ruler'.

Avon
(alt. Avun, Aven, Avan)
Celtic, meaning 'river'.

Awnan
Irish, meaning 'little Adam'.

Axel
Hebrew, meaning 'father is peace'. Made famous by Guns 'n Roses frontman Axl Rose.

Ayers
(alt. Ayer, Aires, Aire)
English, meaning 'heir to a fortune'.

Ayo
(alt. Ayoe, Ayow, Ayowe)
African, meaning 'joyous'.

Azad
African, meaning 'free'.

Azarel
Hebrew, meaning 'helped by God'.

Azaryah
Hebrew, meaning 'helped by God'.

Azriel
Hebrew, meaning 'God is my help'.

Azuko
African, meaning 'past glory'.

B Boys' names

Baback
Persian, meaning 'little father'.

Baden
German origin, meaning 'battle'.

Badru
African, meaning 'birth at the full moon'.

Baeddan
Welsh, meaning 'boar'.

Bailey
English, meaning 'bailiff'.

Baird
Scottish, meaning 'poet' or 'one who sings ballads'.

Bakari
Swahili, meaning 'hope' or 'promise'.

Baker
English, from the word baker.

Baldwin
Old French, meaning 'bold, brave friend'.

Balin
Old English. Balin was one of the Knights of the Round Table.

Balint
Hungarian, meaning 'health'.

Balthazar
Babylonian, meaning 'protect the King'.

Balvinder
Hindu, meaning 'merciful, compassionate'.

Banagher
Irish, meaning 'pointed hill'.

Banner
American, meaning 'flag'.

Bannon
Irish, descendant of O'Banain. Also a river in Wales.

Bansi
Indian, meaning 'flute'.

Banyan
English, coming from the tree of the same name.

Bao
Vietnamese, meaning 'to order'.

Baqer
Arabic, meaning 'a man of knowledge'.

Barack
African, meaning 'blessed'. Made popular by US President Barack Obama.

Barbod
Persian, meaning 'guitar'.

Barclay
Old English, meaning 'birch tree meadow'.

Bardia
Persian, meaning 'lofty'.

Bardolph
English, meaning 'clever wolf'.

Barid
Persian, meaning 'messenger'.

Barke
African, meaning 'blessing'.

Barker
Old English, meaning 'shepherd'.

Barnaby
(alt. Barney)
Greek, meaning 'son of consolation'.

Barnard
English, meaning 'strong as a bear'.

Barney
(alt. Barny)
English, alternative of Barnaby meaning 'son of consolation'.

Baron
Old English, meaning 'young warrior'.

Barrett
English, meaning 'strong as a bear'.

Barron
Old German, meaning 'old clearing'.

Barry
Irish Gaelic, meaning 'fair haired'. Also a town in South Wales, made popular by the BBC television series *Gavin & Stacey*.

Bart (from Bartholomew)
Hebrew, meaning 'son of the farmer'. Made popular by the famous American TV character Bart Simpson.

Barto
Spanish, meaning 'bright'.

Barton
Old English, meaning 'barley settlement'.

Baruch
Hebrew, meaning 'blessed'.

Names of composers

Benjamin (Britten)
Edward (Elgar)
Claude (Debussy)
George (Gershwin)
Igor (Stravinsky)
Ludwig (van Beethoven)
Philip (Glass)
Ralph (Vaughan Williams)
Richard (Wagner)
Wolfgang (Amadeus Mozart)

Barzillai
Hebrew, meaning 'my iron'.

Bascom
Old English, meaning 'from Bascombe' (in Dorset).

Bash
Turkish, meaning 'chief'.

Bashir
Arabic, meaning 'well-educated' and 'wise'.

Basil
Greek, meaning 'royal, kingly'.

Basim
Arabic, meaning 'smile'.

Bast
Persian, meaning 'shelter'.

Bastien
Greek, meaning 'revered'.

Batu
Mongolian, meaning 'loyal'.

Baxter
Old English, meaning 'baker'.

Bayard
French, meaning 'auburn haired'.

Bayle
American, meaning 'beautiful'.

Bayo
Nigerian, meaning 'to find joy'.

Baz
Irish Gaelic, meaning 'fair-haired'.

Bazyli
Polish, meaning 'king'.

Beagan
Scottish, meaning 'little'.

Beale
English, meaning 'handsome'.

Beau
French, meaning 'handsome'.

Beck
Old Norse, meaning 'stream'.

Beckett
Old English, meaning 'beehive' or 'bee cottage'. Associated with the Irish writer Samuel Beckett.

Beckham
English, meaning 'homestead by the stream'. Made famous by David and Victoria Beckham.

Bede
English, meaning 'saint of scholars'. Associated with The Venerable Bede, author of *The Ecclesiastical History of the English People*.

Bedros
Greek, meaning 'stone'.

Behitha
Native American, meaning 'eagle child'.

Béla
Hungarian, meaning 'within'.

Belarius
Shakespearean, meaning 'a banished Lord'.

Belay
African, meaning 'superior'.

B

Belen
Spanish, meaning 'Bethlehem'.

Bello
Italian, meaning 'beautiful'.

Bem
African, meaning 'peace'.

Ben
Hebrew, alternative of Benjamin or Benedict.

Benard
French, meaning 'courageous bear'.

Bendek
Polish, meaning 'blessed'.

Benjamin
(alt. Ben)
Hebrew, meaning 'son of the South'.

Benedict
Latin, meaning 'blessed'.

Benicio
Spanish, meaning 'benevolent'.

Benigno
Italian, meaning 'kind'.

Benito
Italian, alternative of Benedict.

Benjiro
(alt. Benjyro)
Japanese, meaning 'a lover of peacefulness'.

Benjy
Hebrew, alternative of Benjamin.

Bennett
French/Latin, vernacular form of Benedict, meaning 'blessed'.

Benny
Hebrew, meaning 'son on my right hand'.

Beno
Hebrew, meaning 'son'.

Benoit
French form of Benedict, meaning 'blessed'.

Benson
English, meaning 'son of Ben'. Also linked to the town of Benson in Oxfordshire.

Bentley
Old English, meaning 'bent grass meadow'.

Benton
Old English, meaning 'town in the bent grass'.

Berg
German, meaning 'mountain'.

Famous writers

Charles (Dickens)
George (Orwell)
Graham (Greene)
Ian (Flemming)
Mark (Twain)
Martin (Amis)
Oscar (Wilde)
Salman (Rushdie)
Truman (Capote)
Walter (Scott)

Beriah
Biblical, meaning 'in fellowship' or 'in envy'.

Berke
(alt. Berkeley, Berkely, Berkly)
English, meaning 'birch tree'.

Bern
(alt. Bernt, Berny)
French, meaning 'courageous'.

Bernard
(alt. Bernie)
Germanic, meaning 'strong, brave bear'.

Berry
Old English, meaning 'berry'.

Bert
(alt. Bertram, Bertrand)
Old English, meaning 'illustrious'.

Berton
Old English, meaning 'bright settlement'.

Bevan
Welsh, meaning 'son of Evan'.

Bevis
English, meaning 'dear son'.

Beynon
Welsh, meaning 'Eynon's son'.

Bhavya
Indian, meaning 'large' or 'elegant'.

Biagio
Italian, meaning 'limping'.

Bidaban
Native American, meaning 'start of dawn'.

Bien
Vietnamese, meaning 'ocean'.

Bijan
Persian, meaning 'hero'.

Bilal
Arabic, meaning 'wetting, refreshing'.

Bill
(alt. Billy)
English, from William, meaning 'determined' or 'resolute'.

Bima
(alt. Bimo)
Indonesian, meaning 'brave'.

Bingham
(alt. Bin, Binn, Bing)
English, meaning 'from Binna's people's farm'.

Binh
Vietnamese, meaning 'full of peace'.

Birch
Old English, meaning 'bright' or 'shining'.

Birger
Norwegian, meaning 'rescue'.

Birgungi
African, meaning 'bringer of positive things'.

Bishop
Old English, meaning 'bishop'.

Bjorn
Old Norse, meaning 'bear'.

Bladen
Hebrew, meaning 'hero'.

Blaine
Irish Gaelic, meaning 'yellow'.

Blair
English, meaning 'plain'.

Blaise
French, meaning 'lisp' or 'stutter'.

Blake
Old English, meaning 'dark, black'.

Blakeney
English, meaning 'black island'. Also the surname of the protagonist in *The Scarlet Pimpernel*, Sir Percival Blakeney.

Blas
(alt. Blaze)
German, meaning 'firebrand'.

Bo
Scandinavian, short form of Robert, meaning 'bright fame'.

Boaz
Hebrew, meaning 'swiftness' or 'strength'.

Bob
(alt. Bobby)
From Robert, meaning 'bright fame'.

Boden
(alt. Bodie)
Scandinavian, meaning 'shelter'.

Bogumil
Slavic, meaning 'God favour'.

Bohdan
Slavic, meaning 'proud ruler'.

Bola
(alt. Bolah, Boli)
American, meaning 'careful'.

Bolivar
Spanish, meaning 'the bank of the river'.

Bomani
(alt. Boman)
African, meaning 'warrior'.

Bond
Old English, meaning 'peasant farmer'.

Bonner
English, meaning 'gentle'.

Booker
(alt. Book, Booki, Bookie, Booky)
English, meaning 'book lover'.

Booth
(alt. Boot, Boothe, Boothie, Bootsie)
German, meaning 'protective'.

Bordan
(alt. Bordee, Boden)
English, meaning 'from the boar'.

Borg
(alt. Borge, Borgh)
Scandinavian, meaning 'castle'. Also the surname of the famous Swedish tennis player, Björn Borg.

Boris
Slavic, meaning 'battle glory'.

Bosley
(alt. Boslee, Boslie, Bosly)
English, meaning 'copse'.

Bosten
English, meaning 'town by the woods'.

Botolf
(alt. Botof)
English, meaning 'wolf'.

Bowen
Welsh, meaning 'son of Owen'.

Boyce
(alt. Boice, Boy, Boyce)
French, meaning 'one who defends'.

Boyd
Scottish Gaelic, meaning 'yellow'.

Brad
(alt. Bradley)
Old English, meaning 'broad' or 'wide'.

Bradan
(alt. Braden)
English, meaning 'one who is open-minded'.

Brady
Irish, meaning 'large-chested'.

Bradyn
Gaelic, meaning 'descendant of Bradan'.

Bram
Gaelic, meaning 'raven'.

Brand
English, meaning 'fiery'.

Brandon
Old English, meaning 'gorse'.

Brandt
Old English, meaning 'beacon'.

Brandy
English, name of the liqueur.

Brannon
Gaelic, meaning 'raven'.

Branson
English, meaning 'son of Brand'.

Brant
Old English, meaning 'hill'.

Braulio
Greek, meaning 'shining'.

Bravillo
(alt. Braville)
Spanish, meaning 'brave'.

Braxton
(alt. Brackston, Braxsten, Brax)
English, meaning 'worldly'.

Braydon
(alt. Braedon, Brayden, Braydun)
English, meaning 'effective'.

Brendan
Gaelic, meaning 'prince'.

Brennan
Gaelic, meaning 'teardrop'.

Brenton
English, from Brent, meaning 'hill'.

Brett
English, meaning 'a Breton'.

Brewster
(alt. Brew, Brewer)
English, meaning 'a brewer'.

Breyen
(alt. Brey, Breyan)
Irish, meaning 'strong'.

B

Brian
Gaelic, meaning 'high' or 'noble'.

Brice
Latin, meaning 'speckled'.

Brier
French, meaning 'heather'.

Brock
Old English, meaning 'badger'.

Broderick
English, meaning 'ruler'.

Brody
Gaelic, meaning both 'ditch' and 'brother'.

Brogan
Irish, meaning 'sturdy shoe'.

Bronson
(alt. Brondson, Bronsan, Bronsen)
English, meaning 'the son of Brown'.

Bronwyn
Welsh, meaning 'white breasted'.

Brook
English, meaning 'stream'.

Bruce
Scottish, meaning 'high' or 'noble'.

Brumley
(alt. Brum)
French, meaning 'smart'.

Bruno
Germanic, meaning 'brown'.

Brutus
(alt. Bruto)
Latin, meaning 'dim-witted'. The name of Julius Caesar's assassin.

Bryant
English variant of Brian, meaning 'high' or 'noble'.

Bryce
Scottish, meaning 'of Britain'.

Brycen
Scottish, meaning 'son of Bryce'.

Bryden
Irish, meaning 'strong one'.

Bryson
Welsh, meaning 'descendant of Brice'.

Bubba
American, meaning 'boy'.

Buck
American, meaning 'goat' or 'deer'.

Bud
(alt. Buddy)
American, meaning 'friend'.

Buell
(alt. Bue)
German, meaning 'hill'.

Buford
(alt. Bueford, Bufe, Buforde)
English, meaning 'industrious'.

Bulat
(alt. Bulatt)
Russian, meaning 'possessor of great strength'.

Bunard
(alt. Bunerd, Bunn)
English, meaning 'good'.

Bundar
(alt. Bundor, Bundur, Bundir)
Arabic, meaning 'a man who is both rich and intelligent'.

Bunmi
(alt. Bunmie, Bunmy, Bunmey)
Arabic, meaning 'gift'.

Burdett
Middle English, meaning 'bird'.

Burgess
(alt. Burges, Burgiss, Berge)
English, meaning 'businessman'.

Burke
French, meaning 'fortified settlement'.

Burl
French, meaning 'knotty wood'.

Burnis
English, meaning 'near the brook'.

Burt
(alt. Bert, Burtie, Burty)
English, meaning 'shining'.

Busby
(alt. Busbee, Busbi, Buzbie)
Scottish, meaning 'artist'.

Buster
(alt. Bustah)
American, meaning 'fun'.

Buzz
American, shortened form of Busby. Associated with the astronaut Buzz Aldrin.

Bwana
(alt. Bwanah)
Swahili, meaning 'gentleman'.

Byram
(alt. Byrem, Byrie, Byrim)
English, meaning 'crafty'.

Byrne
(alt. Birne, Byrn, Byrny)
English, meaning 'loner'.

Byron
Old English, meaning 'barn'. Made famous by the poet Lord Byron.

Names of comedians

David (Mitchell, Walliams)
Eddie (Izzard)
Eric (Morecambe)
Ken (Dodd)
John (Cleese)
Matt (Lucas)
Paul (Merton)
Ronnie (Barker, Corbett, Wise)
Russel (Brand)
Tommy (Cooper)

C Boys' names

Cable
American, meaning 'rope'.

Cabot
Old English, meaning 'to sail'.

Cache
American, meaning 'storage place'.

Cadarn
(alt. Cadern, Cadorn, Cadurn)
Welsh, meaning 'one who has great strength'.

Cadby
(alt. Cadbey, Cadbee, Cadbie)
English, meaning 'soldier's colony'.

Cadda
(alt. Cada, Caddah, Cadah)
English, meaning 'military man'.

Caddock
(alt. Caddoc, Caddok, Caddog)
Welsh, meaning 'eager for battle'.

Cade
(alt. Caden)
English, meaning 'round/lumpy'.

Cadence
Latin, meaning 'with rhythm'.

Cadmus
Greek, meaning 'of the east'. Mythology has Cadmus as the founder of the doomed city Thebes.

Cadogan
Welsh, meaning 'battle glory and honour'.

Caedmon
Celtic, meaning 'wise warrior'.

Caelan
Gaelic, from St. Columba.

Caerwyn
(alt. Carwyn, Gerwyn)
Welsh, meaning 'white fort' or 'settlement'.

Caesar
Latin, meaning 'head of hair'. Made famous by the first Roman emperor Julius Ceasar.

Caetano
Portuguese, meaning 'from Gaeta, Italy'.

Cagney
Irish, meaning 'successor of the advocate'.

Cahya
Indonesian, meaning 'light'.

Caiden
Arabic, meaning 'companion'.

Caillou
French, meaning 'pebble'.

Cain
Biblical, brother of Abel.

Cainan
Biblical, meaning 'possessor' or 'purchaser'.

Cairo
Egyptian city.

Cais
Vietnamese, meaning 'rejoices'.

Cal
Short form of names beginning Cal-.

Calder
Scottish, meaning 'rough waters'.

Caleb
Hebrew, meaning 'dog'.

Calen
From Caleb, meaning 'dog'.

Calhoun
Irish, meaning 'slight woods'.

Calix
Greek, meaning 'very handsome'.

Callahan
Irish, meaning 'contention' or 'strife'.

> **English cricketers**
> Andrew/Freddie (Flintoff)
> Darren (Gough)
> David (Gower)
> Geoffrey (Boycott)
> Graham (Gooch)
> Ian (Botham)
> Kevin (Pieterson)
> Michael (Atherton, Vaughan)
> Mike (Gatting)
> Phil (Tuffnel)

Callum
Gaelic, meaning 'dove'.

Calvin
French, meaning 'little bald one'.

Camara
African, meaning 'teacher'.

Camden
Gaelic, meaning 'winding valley'. Also an area of North West London.

Cameron
Scottish Gaelic, meaning 'crooked nose'.

Camillo
Latin, meaning 'free born' or 'noble'.

Campbell
Scottish Gaelic, meaning 'crooked mouth'.

Canaan
Biblical, meaning 'to be humbled'.

Candido
Latin, meaning 'candid' or 'honest'.

Cannon
French, meaning 'of the church'.

Canton
French, 'dweller of corner'. Also name given to areas of Switzerland.

Canute
(alt. Cnut, Cnute)
Scandinavian, meaning 'knot'.

Caolan
(alt. Caolen, Caolin, Caolyn)
Irish, meaning 'thin man'.

Capp
(alt. Cap, Capps, Caps)
French, meaning 'chaplain'.

Cappy
Gypsy Italian, meaning 'lucky'.

Carden
Old English, meaning 'wood carder'.

Cardew
(alt. Cardou, Cardu, Cardoo)
Celtic, meaning 'black castle'.

Carel
French, meaning 'strong'.

Carey
Gaelic, meaning 'love'.

Cargan
(alt. Cargen, Cargon, Cargun)
Gaelic, meaning 'little rock'.

Carl
Old Norse, meaning 'free man'.

Carlin
Gaelic, meaning 'small victor' and German, meaning 'man'.

Carlisle
English, meaning 'child of the walled city'.

Carlo
Italian form of Carl, meaning 'free man'.

Carlos
Spanish form of Carl, meaning 'free man'.

Carlton
Old English, meaning 'free peasant settlement'.

Carmelo
Latin, meaning 'garden' or 'orchard'.

Carmen
Latin/Spanish, meaning 'song'.

Carmichael
Gaelic, meaning 'Michael's follower'.

Carmine
Latin, meaning 'song'.

Carnell
English, meaning 'defender of the castle'.

Carrick
(alt. Carick, Carik, Caric)
Irish, meaning 'of the rocks'.

Carson
(alt. Carsten)
Scottish, meaning 'marsh-dwellers'.

Carter
Old English, meaning 'transporter of goods'.

Cary
Old Celtic river name. Also means 'love'. Made popular by the screen actor, Cary Grant.

Case
(alt. Casey)
Irish Gaelic, meaning 'alert' or 'watchful'.

Cash
Latin, shortened form of Cassius, meaning 'vain'.

Casimer
Slavic, meaning 'famous destroyer of peace'.

Cason
Latin, from Cassius, meaning 'empty' or 'hollow'.

Casper
Persian, meaning 'treasurer'.

Caspian
From the Caspian Sea.

Cassidy
Gaelic, meaning 'curly haired'.

Cassius
(alt. Cassio)
Latin, meaning 'empty, hollow'.

Catahecassa
Native American, meaning 'black hoof'.

Cathal
Celtic, meaning 'battle rule'.

Cato
Latin, meaning 'all-knowing'.

Catori
(alt. Catorie, Catory, Catorey)
Native American, meaning 'holy man'.

Cayden
American, meaning 'warrior'.

Cecil
Latin, meaning 'blind'.

Cedar
English name of evergreen trees.

Cedric
Welsh, meaning 'spectacular bounty'.

Celestino
Spanish/Italian, meaning 'heavenly'.

Celesto
(alt. Celestino, Celindo)
Latin, meaning 'heaven sent'.

Cerone
French, meaning 'serene'.

Chace
(alt. Chase, Chaise, Chaice,)
English, meaning 'huntsman'.

Chad
(alt. Chadrick)
Old English, meaning 'warlike, warrior'.

Chai
(alt. Chaika, Chaim, Chayim)
Hebrew, meaning 'life giver'.

Chalil
(alt. Halil, Hallil)
Hebrew, meaning 'flute'.

Chaim
Hebrew, meaning 'life'.

Champion
English, from the word 'champion'.

Chance
English, from the word 'chance'.

Chandler
Old English, meaning 'candle maker and seller'.

Chang
Chinese, meaning 'free'.

Charaka
Hindi, meaning 'traveller'.

Charles
Old German, meaning 'free man'.

Charlie
Old German, alternative of Charles meaning 'free man'.

Charro
(alt. Charo, Charroh)
Spanish, meaning 'wild lively cowboy'.

Chaska
Native American name usually given to first son.

Chaucer
English, meaning 'distinguished'. Made famous by Geoffrey Chaucer, the author of the Canterbury Tales.

Chaviv
(alt. Habib, Haviv)
Hebrew, meaning 'beloved'.

Chayne
(alt. Chane, Channe, Chay)
Scottish, meaning 'swagger'.

Che
Spanish, shortened form of Jose. Made famous by Che Guevara.

Chesley
Old English, meaning 'camp on the meadow'.

Chester
Latin, meaning 'camp of soldiers'.

Chevalier
French, meaning 'valiant'.

Chevy
(alt. Chev, Chevi, Chevie)
French, meaning 'clever'. Made famous by the American comedian Chevy Chase.

Chilton
(alt. Chillton, Chilly, Chilt)
English, meaning 'tranquil'.

Chima
Old English, meaning 'hilly land'.

Christian
English, from the word Christian.

Christophe
French variant of Christopher, meaning 'bearing Christ inside'.

Christopher
Greek, meaning 'bearing Christ inside'.

Chuck
(alt. Chuckey, Chuckie, Chucky)
German, meaning 'rash'.

Cian
Irish, meaning 'ancient'.

Ciar
(alt. Keir)
Irish, meaning 'dark'.

Ciaran
Irish, meaning 'black'.

Cicero
Latin, meaning 'chickpea'. Also the name of the famous Roman philosopher and orator.

Cid
(alt. Ciddy, Cyd, Sid)
Spanish, meaning 'leader'.

Cillian
(alt. Cillin, Killian, Kilian)
Irish, meaning 'war conflict'.

Cimarron
City in western Kansas.

Ciprian
Latin, meaning 'from Cyprus'.

Ciro
Spanish, meaning 'sun'.

Claiborne
(alt. Claiborn, Claibourn, Claibourne)
French and German, meaning 'border with clover'.

Clancy
Old Irish, meaning 'red warrior'.

Clarence
Latin, meaning 'one who lives near the river Clare'.

Clark
Latin, meaning 'clerk'.

Claude
(alt. Claudie, Claudio, Claudius)
Latin, meaning 'lame'.

Claus
Variant of Nicholas, meaning 'people of victory'.

Clay
English, from the word clay.

Cleary
Gaelic, meaning 'scholar'.

Clement
(alt. Clem)
Latin, meaning 'merciful'.

Cleo
Greek, meaning 'glory'.

Cleon
(alt. Kleon)
Greek, meaning 'glorious'. A famous Athenian statesman and Peloponnesian War strategist.

Cletus
Greek, meaning 'illustrious'.

Cliff
(alt. Clifford, Clifton)
English, from the word 'cliff'.

Clint
(alt. Clinton)
Old English, meaning 'fenced settlement'.

Clive
English, meaning 'cliff'.

Clydai
Welsh, meaning 'fame'.

Clyde
Scottish, from the river in Glasgow.

Coby
(alt. Cody, Colby)
Irish, son of Oda.

Colby
(alt. Cole)
Norse, meaning 'dark country'.

Colden
Old English, meaning 'dark valley'.

Cole
Old French, meaning 'coal black'.

Coley
Old English, meaning 'coal black'.

Colin
Gaelic, meaning 'young creature'.

Colson
Old English, meaning 'coal black'.

Colter
Anglo-Saxon, meaning 'colt herder'.

Colton
English, meaning 'swarthy'.

Columbus
Latin, meaning 'dove'.

Colwyn
Welsh place name.

Coman
(alt. Comen, Comin, Comon)
Arabic, meaning 'noble'.

Comanche
(alt. Comanch, Komanche)
Native American, meaning 'tribe'.

Conall
(alt. Conal)
Scottish, meaning 'highly respected'.

Conan
Gaelic, meaning 'wolf'.

Conley
Gaelic, meaning 'sensible'.

Connell
(alt. Connolly)
Irish, meaning 'high' or 'mighty'.

Connor
(alt. Conrad, Conroy)
Irish, meaning 'lover of hounds'.

Conrad
(alt. Con, Conrade, Konrad)
German, meaning 'optimist'.

Conroy
(alt. Con, Conn, Connie)
Gaelic, meaning 'wise'.

Constant
(alt. Constantine)
English, from the word constant.

Conway
(alt. Con, Connie, Konway)
Irish, meaning 'watchful'.

Cooper
Old English, meaning 'barrel
maker'.

Corban
Hebrew, meaning 'dedicated and
belonging to God'.

Corbett
(alt. Corbin, Corby)
Norman French, meaning 'young
crow'.

Cordell
Old English, meaning 'cord
maker'.

Corey
Gaelic, meaning 'hill hollow'.

Corin
Latin, meaning 'spear'.

Corliss
(alt. Corlis, Corlyss, Corlys)
English, meaning 'benevolent'.

Cormac
Gaelic, meaning 'impure son'.

Cornelius
(alt. Cornell)
Latin, meaning 'horn'.

Cort
(alt. Corte, Court, Kort)
German, meaning 'expressive'.

Cortez
Spanish, meaning 'courteous'.

Corwin
Old English, meaning 'heart's
friend' or 'companion'.

Cory
(alt. Coarie, Corey, Kohryi)
Latin, meaning 'entertaining'.

Cosimo
(alt. Cosme, Cosmo)
Italian, meaning 'order' or
'beauty'.

Costas
(alt. Costa, Costah)
Greek, meaning 'constant'.

Coty
French, meaning 'riverbank'.

Coulter
English, meaning 'young horse'.

Courtney
Old English, meaning 'domain of
Curtis'.

British heroes

Adam (Smith)
Alexander (Graham Bell)
Charles (Darwin)
Christopher (Columbus)
David (Lloyd George)
Francis (Drake)
Horatio (Nelson)
Robert (Scott aka Captain
Scott)
Walter (Raleigh)
Winston (Churchill)

Cowan
Gaelic, meaning 'hollow in the hill'.

Cowell
(alt. Kowell)
English, meaning 'honest'.

Coyle
(alt. Coile)
Gaelic, meaning 'combat flower'.

Craig
Welsh, meaning 'rock'.

Crawford
(alt. Crafe, Craford, Craw)
English, meaning 'flowing'.

Creed
(alt. Crede, Creede, Kreed)
American, meaning 'believer'.

Crispin
Latin, meaning 'curly haired'.

Croix
French, meaning 'cross'.

Cruz
Spanish, meaning 'cross'. Made famous by David and Victoria Beckham's son.

Cullen
(alt. Culen, Cullan, Kullen)
Irish, meaning 'beautiful'.

Cuong
Vietnamese, meaning 'healthy' or 'prosperous'.

Curran
Gaelic, meaning 'dagger' or 'hero'.

Curtis
(alt. Curt)
Old French, meaning 'courteous'.

Cutler
Old English, meaning 'knife maker'.

Cy
(alt. Cye, Si)
Greek, meaning 'shining'.

Cybard
French, meaning 'leader'.

Cynfor
Welsh, meaning 'great ruler'.

Cyprian
English, meaning 'from Cyprus'.

Cyril
Greek, meaning 'master' or 'Lord'.

Cyrus
Persian, meaning 'Lord'.

Czeslaw
(alt. Slav, Slavek)
Polish, meaning 'admirable'.

D Boys' names

Dabeet
(alt. Dabeat, Dabiet, Dabyt)
Indian, meaning 'warrior'.

Dabi
(alt. Dabee, Dabie, Daby)
Hebrew, meaning 'beloved'.

Dabir
Persian, meaning 'teacher'.

Dabney
English, meaning 'from Aubigny'.

Dace
(alt. Daece, Daice, Dayce)
French, meaning 'noble born'.

Dacia
Latin, meaning 'from Dacia'.

Daemyn
American, meaning 'loyal'.

Dagen
(alt. Dagon, Dagun, Daegan)
Irish, meaning 'black-haired'.

Dagwood
(alt. Dagwode)
English, meaning 'from the
shining forest'.

Dahy
(alt. Dahee, Dahi, Dahie)
Irish, meaning 'quick'.

Dai
Japanese, meaning 'large'.

Daichi
Japanese, meaning 'great
wisdom'.

Dailey
(alt. Daley, Daly, Daely)
Gaelic, meaning 'from the
assembly'.

Dainan
(alt. Daenan, Daenen, Daenin)
Australian, meaning
'kindhearted'.

Daire
(alt. Daer, Daere, Dair)
Irish, meaning 'wealthy'.

Daisuke
Japanese, meaning 'lionhearted'.

Dakari
African, meaning 'happy'.

Dakota
Native American, meaning
'allies'.

Dalai
Indian, meaning 'peaceful'.

Dale
Old English, meaning 'valley'.

Dalil
(alt. Daleel, Daleil, Daliel)
Arabic, meaning 'a guide'.

Dallin
English, meaning 'dweller in the valley'.

Dalton
English, meaning 'town in the valley'.

Daly
Gaelic, meaning 'assembly'.

Damarion
Greek, meaning 'gentle'.

Damaris
(alt. Damariss, Damarys, Damaryss)
Greek, meaning 'gentle one'.

Damek
Slavic, meaning 'earth'.

Damerae
(alt. Damarai, Damarae, Damaray)
Jamaican, meaning 'joyous'.

Damian
(alt. Damon)
Greek, meaning 'to tame/subdue'.

Damisi
(alt. Damisea, Damisee, Damisey)
African, meaning 'cheerful'.

Dane
Old English, meaning 'from Denmark'.

Dang
Vietnamese, meaning 'praiseworthy'.

Daniel
(alt. Dan, Danny)
Hebrew, meaning 'God is my judge'.

Dante
Latin, meaning 'lasting'. Famous as the name of the Italian 13th century poet Dante Alighieri.

Danso
(alt. Dansoe, Dansow, Dansowe)
African, meaning 'reliable'.

Danuta
Polish, meaning 'a present from God'.

Dafydd
Welsh, meaning 'beloved'. Made famous by the character in the BBC television series *Little Britain*.

Darbrey
(alt. Darbree, Darbri, Darbry)
Irish, meaning 'free man'.

Darby
Irish, meaning 'without envy'.

Darcy
Gaelic, meaning 'dark'. Associated with Jane Austen's Mr. Darcy, and the parody of this character in *Bridget Jones' Diary*.

Dareh
Persian, meaning 'circle'.

Darra
(alt. Darrah)
Irish, meaning 'fruitful'.

D

Darrell
(alt. Daryl)
Old English, meaning 'open'.

Dario
(alt. Darius)
Greek, meaning 'Kingly'.

Darnell
Old English, meaning 'the hidden spot'.

Darragh
Irish, meaning 'dark oak'.

Darren
(alt. Darrian)
Gaelic, meaning 'great'.

Darrick
Old German, meaning 'power of the tribe'.

Darshan
Hindi, meaning 'vision'.

Dartagnan
(alt. D'Artagnan)
French, meaning 'a leader'.
The protagonist of *The Three Musketeers* by Alexandre Dumas.

Darvell
(alt. Darvel, Darvele, Darvell)
French, meaning 'eagle town'.

Darwin
Old English, meaning 'dear friend'.

Dasan
Native American, meaning 'chief'.

Dash
(alt. Dashawn)
American, meaning 'enlightened one'.

Dashiell
French, meaning 'page boy'.

David
(alt. Dave, Davey, Davie)
Biblical, meaning 'beloved'.

Davion
American, meaning 'one who is loved'.

Davis
Old English, meaning 'son of David'.

Davu
(alt. Davoo, Davou, Davue)
African, meaning 'beginning'.

Dawar
(alt. Dawarr)
Arabian, meaning 'wanderer'.

Dawson
Old English, meaning 'son of David'.

Dax
(alt. Daxton)
French origin, was once a town in southwestern France. Now associated with the *Star Trek* character.

Dayakar
Indian, meaning 'kind'.

Dayal
Indian, meaning 'kind'.

D

Soap characters

Alf (*Home and Away*)
Ashley (*Coronation Street*)
Bradley (*Eastenders*)
Charlie (*Casualty*)
Harold (*Neighbours*)
Karl (*Neighbours*)
Ken (*Coronation Street*)
Grant (*Eastenders*)
Phil (*Eastenders*)
Tyrone (*Coronation Street*)

Dayton
Old English, meaning 'David's place'.

De
Vietnamese, meaning 'royalty'.

Deacon
(alt. Deacan, Deakon, Deecon)
Greek, meaning 'dusty'. Also a ministerial assistant in the Christian Church.

Dean
Old English, meaning 'valley'.

Declan
Irish, meaning 'full of goodness'.

Dedric
Old English, meaning 'gifted ruler'.

Deepak
(alt. Deepan)
Indian, meaning 'illumination'.

Dehateh
Native American, meaning 'enlightened'.

Del
(alt. Delano, Delbert, Dell)
Old English, meaning 'bright shining one'.

Delaire
English, meaning 'from the air'.

Delaney
(alt. Delany, Delanee, Delanie)
Irish, meaning 'dark challenger'.

Delbert
English, meaning 'noble'.

Delmar
(alt. Delmarr, Delmor, Delmore)
French, meaning 'of the sea'.

Delmon
(alt. Delmun, Delmen, Delmin)
English, meaning 'of the mountain'.

Delroy
(alt. Delray, Delrick, Delcoi)
French, meaning 'king'.

Dembe
(alt. Dembi, Dembie, Demby)
African, meaning 'peaceful'.

Demetrius
Greek, meaning 'harvest lover'.

Demissie
(alt. Demissi, Demissy, Demissee)
African, meaning 'destroyer'.

Demos
(alt. Demus, Demmos, Demmus)
Greek, meaning 'of the people'.

Dempsey
Irish, meaning 'proud'.

Denby
(alt. Denbey, Denbi, Denbee)
Scandinavian, meaning 'from the village of the Danes'.

Denham
(alt. Denholm)
Old English, meaning 'valley settlement'.

Dennis
(alt. Denny, Denton)
English, meaning 'follower of Dionysius'.

Denton
English, meaning 'from the town in the valley'.

Denver
Town in Colorado, USA.

Denzil
English, town in Cornwall.

Deo
Greek, meaning 'like a God'.

Deon
Greek, meaning 'of Zeus'.

Derek
English, meaning 'power of the tribe'.

Derenik
Armenian, meaning 'monk'.

Dermot
Irish, meaning 'free man'.

Desmond
Irish, meaning 'from south Munster'.

Destin
French, meaning 'destiny'.

Deunoro
Spanish, meaning 'saint'.

Devan
(alt. Devyn)
Irish, meaning 'poet'.

Devlin
Irish, meaning 'descendant from the unlucky one'.

Dewei
Chinese, meaning 'great principle'.

Dewey
Welsh origin, from Dewi (David).

Dexter
(alt. Dex)
Latin, meaning 'right-handed'.

Dhaval
Sanskrit, meaning 'white'.

Dhiren
Indian, meaning 'strong'.

Diallo
African, meaning 'bold'.

Dick
(alt. Dickie, Dickon)
From Richard, meaning 'powerful leader'.

Dieter
German, meaning 'the people's army'.

D

Didier
French, meaning 'much desired'.

Diego
Spanish, meaning 'supplanter'.

Dietrich
Old German, meaning 'power of the tribe'.

Diggory
English, meaning 'dyke'.

Dilbert
English, meaning 'day-bright'.

Dimitri
(alt. Dimitrios, Dimitris)
Greek, meaning 'Prince'.

Dinesh
Sanskrit, meaning 'of the sun'.

Dino
Diminutive of Dean, meaning 'valley'.

Dion
Greek, short form of Dionysius.

Dirk
Variant of Derek, meaning 'power of the tribe'.

Divakar
Sanskrit, meaning 'the sun'.

Dixon
English, meaning 'Richard's son'.

Dmitriy
(alt. Dmitri)
Russian, meaning 'fruit of the earth'.

Dobbin
Diminutive of Robert, meaning 'bright fame'.

Dolan
Irish, meaning 'dark haired'.

Dominic
Latin, meaning 'Lord'.

Donahue
Irish, meaning 'brown haired leader'.

Donald
(alt. Donal, Don, Donaldo)
Gaelic, meaning 'great chief'.

Donato
Italian, meaning 'gift'.

Dong
Vietnamese, meaning 'winter'.

Donnell
(alt. Donnie, Donny)
Gaelic, meaning 'world fighter'.

Donovan
Gaelic, meaning 'dark-haired chief'.

Olympians

Chris (Hoy)
Colin (Jackson)
Jesse (Owens)
Jonathan (Edwards)
Ian (Thorpe)
Mark (Spitz)
Matthew (Pinsent)
Michael (Johnson, Phelps)
Steve (Redgrave)
Usain (Bolt)

Doran
Gaelic, meaning 'exile'.

Dorian
Greek, meaning 'descendant of Doris'.

Dorsey
From the French D'Orsay.

Douglas
(alt. Dougal, Dougie)
Scottish, meaning 'black river'.

Doyle
Irish, meaning 'foreigner'.

Draco
Latin, meaning 'dragon'. Made popular by the character Draco Malfoy in the *Harry Potter* novels.

Drake
Greek origin, meaning 'dragon'.

Drew
Shortened form of Andrew, meaning 'man' or 'warrior'.

Dryden
English, meaning 'dry town'.

Duane
Irish, meaning 'little dark one'.

Dubois
French, meaning 'woodcutter'.

Dudley
Old English, meaning 'people's field'. Also a town in Yorkshire, and the name of Harry Potter's cousin.

Duer
Celtic, meaning 'heroic'.

Duff
Gaelic, meaning 'swarthy'.

Duke
Latin origin, meaning 'leader'.

Dumi
African, meaning 'inspirer'.

Duncan
Scottish, meaning 'dark warrior'.

Dusan
Slavic, meaning 'heavenly spirit'.

Dustin
(alt. Dusty)
French origin, meaning 'brave warrior'.

Duy
Vietnamese, meaning 'save'.

Dwayne
Irish Gaelic origin, meaning 'swarthy'.

Dwight
Flemish, meaning 'blond'.

Dwyer
Gaelic, meaning 'dark wise one'.

Dyami
Native American, meaning 'eagle'.

Dylan
(alt. Dillan, Dillon)
Welsh, meaning 'son of the sea'.

Dzigbode
African, meaning 'patience'.

E Boys' names

Eachan
(alt. Eachann, Echan, Echann)
Irish, meaning 'horseman'.

Eadburt
(alt. Eadbert, Eadbirt, Eadbyrt)
English, meaning 'wealthy'.

Eagan
(alt. Eegan, Eagen, Eagon)
Irish, meaning 'fiery'.

Eagle
Native American, meaning 'like
the Eagle'.

Eamon
(alt. Eames)
Irish, meaning 'wealthy
protector'.

Ean
(alt. Eyan, Eyon, Eian)
Gaelic, alternative of John.

Earl
(alt. Earle, Errol)
English, from the word Earl.

Earnan
(alt. Earnen, Earnin, Earnun)
Irish, meaning 'knowing'.

Earnest
English, meaning 'earnest'.
Famously used by Oscar Wilde in
The Importance of Being Earnest.

Earvin
(alt. Earven, Earvan, Earvyn)
English, meaning 'friend of the
sea'.

Ebb
Short form of Ebenezer, meaning
'stone of help'.

Eben
(alt. Eban, Ebon, Ebin)
Hebrew, meaning 'solid as a
rock'.

Ebenezer
Hebrew, meaning 'stone of
help'. Associated with the literary
character Scrooge from Dickens's
novel A Christmas Carol.

Eckerd
(alt. Ekerd, Eckherd, Eckhert)
German, meaning 'sacred'.

Ed
(alt. Edd, Eddie, Eddy)
Shortened form of Edward,
meaning 'wealthy guard'.

Edan
Irish, meaning 'little fire'.

Edel
(alt. Edlin, Edell, Edlen)
German, meaning 'noble one'.

Eder
(alt. Edar, Edir, Edur)
Hebrew, meaning 'one of the flock'.

Edgar
(alt.Elgar)
Old English, meaning 'wealthy spear'.

Edison
English, meaning 'son of Edward'.

Edmar
(alt. Edmarr, Eddmar, Eadmar)
English, meaning 'wealthy sea'.

Edmund
English, meaning 'wealthy protector'.

Edom
Hebrew, meaning 'red'.

Edric
Old English, meaning 'rich and powerful'.

Edsel
Old German, meaning 'noble'.

Edward
(alt. Eduardo)
Old English, meaning 'wealthy guard'.

Edwin
English, meaning 'wealthy friend'.

Eero
Scandinavian, meaning 'ruler'.

Effiom
(alt. Effyom, Efyom, Effeom)
African, meaning 'like a crocodile'.

Efrain
Hebrew, meaning 'fruitful'.

Efron
(alt. Ephron)
Hebrew, meaning 'like a songbird'.

Egan
Irish, meaning 'fire'.

Egerton
(alt. Egertun, Edgertun, Edgartun)
English, meaning 'from the town on the edge'.

Egil
(alt. Egyl, Eigil, Eigyl)
Scandinavian, meaning 'sword's point'.

Egor
(alt. Eigor, Eygor)
Russian, meaning 'farmer'.

Ehren
German, meaning 'honourable'.

Ehud
Hebrew, meaning 'beloved'.

Eilif
(alt. Elif, Eilyf, Elyf)
Norse, meaning 'immortal'.

Eimhin
(alt. Eimhyn, Eimarr, Eimar)
Irish, meaning 'swift'.

Einar
Old Norse, meaning 'battle leader'.

Eisa
(alt. Eisah, Eissa, Eissah)
Arabic, alternative of Jesus.

Eko
Indonesian, meaning 'first child'.

Ekram
Indian, meaning 'honour'.

Eladio
Greek, meaning 'Greek'.

Elam
Hebrew, meaning 'eternal'.

Elbert
Old English, meaning 'famous'.

Elbis
(alt. Elbys, Elbiss, Elbyss)
American, meaning 'exalted'.

Elchanan
(alt. Elhanan, Elhannan, Elchannan)
Hebrew, meaning 'God is gracious'.

Eldon
Old English, meaning 'Ella's hill'.

Eldred
Old English, meaning 'old venerable counsel'.

Eldridge
(alt. Eldrege, Eldrege, Eldrige)
German, meaning 'wise ruler'.

Elek
(alt. Elec, Eleck)
Hungarian, alternative of Alexander.

Elgin
Old English, meaning 'high minded'.

Eli
(alt. Eliah)
Hebrew, meaning 'high'.

Elias
(alt. Elijah)
Hebrew, meaning 'the Lord is my God'.

Elijah
(alt. El, Eli, Elija)
Hebrew, meaning 'God is my lord'.

Elio
Spanish origin, meaning 'the Lord is my God'.

Eliseo
(alt. Elizeo)
Spanish, meaning 'daring'.

Ellery
Old English, meaning 'elder tree'.

Elliott
Variant of Elio, meaning 'the Lord is my God'.

Ellis
Welsh variant of Elio, meaning 'the Lord is my God'.

Ellison
English, meaning 'son of Ellis'.

E

Elmer
(alt. Elmo)
Old English, meaning 'noble'.

Elmo
(alt. Ellmo, Elmoh)
Greek, meaning 'gregarious'.

Elon
Hebrew, meaning 'oak tree'.

Elroy
French, meaning 'king'.

Elsu
Native American, meaning 'flying falcon'.

Elton
Old English, meaning 'Ella's town'.

Elvin
English, meaning 'elf-like'.

Elvis
Figure in Norse mythology. Made famous by the singer Elvis Presley.

Ely
English, meaning 'height'.

Emanuel
Hebrew, meaning 'God is with us'.

Emeric
German, meaning 'work rule'.

Emerson
English, meaning 'son of Emery'.

Emery
English, meaning 'work leader'.

Emile
(alt. Emiliano, Emilio)
Latin, meaning 'eager'.

Emlyn
Welsh, name of town, Newcastle Emlyn, in West Wales.

Emmett
English origin, meaning 'universal'.

Emrys
Welsh, meaning 'immortal'.

Enapay
Native American, meaning 'courageous'.

Eneco
Spanish, meaning 'fiery one'.

Enoch
Hebrew, meaning 'dedicated'.

Enrico
(alt. Enrique)
Form of Henry, meaning 'home ruler'.

Enzo
Italian, short for Lorenzo, meaning 'laurel'.

Eoghan
(alt. Eoin)
Irish form of Owen, meaning 'well born' or 'noble'.

Eoin
Irish, meaning 'God is gracious'.

Ephraim
Hebrew, meaning 'very fruitful'.

E

Ephron
(alt. Effron)
Biblical, meaning 'dust'.

Erasmo
(alt. Erasmus)
Greek, meaning 'to love'.

Eric
Old Norse, meaning 'ruler'.

Ernest
(alt. Ernesto, Ernie, Ernst)
Old German, meaning 'serious'.

Eron
Hebrew, meaning 'enlightened'.

Eros
Greek, meaning 'God of love'.

Errol
English, meaning 'boar wolf'.

Erskine
Scottish, meaning 'high cliff'.

Erwin
Old English, meaning 'boar friend'.

Eryx
Greek, meaning 'boxer'.

Esteban
(alt. Estevan, Estevao)
Spanish, meaning 'crown'.

Ethan
(alt. Etienne)
Hebrew, meaning 'long lived'.

Ethelred
English, meaning 'noble counsel'.

Eugene
Greek, meaning 'well-born'.

Evan
Welsh, meaning 'God is good'.

Everard
Old English, meaning 'strong boar'.

Everett
English, meaning 'strong boar'.

Ewald
(alt. Ewan, Ewell)
From Owen, meaning 'well born' or 'noble'.

Ewelani
Hawaiian, meaning 'chief of celestial descent'.

Eyad
Arabic, meaning 'support'.

Eyal
Hebrew, meaning 'courage'.

Ezekiel
Hebrew, meaning 'God will strengthen you'.

Ezhno
Native American, meaning 'he walks alone'.

Ezra
Hebrew, meaning 'helper'.

F

Boys' names

Fa
Chinese, meaning 'growth'.

Faaiz
Arabic, meaning 'successful'.

Faas
Latin, meaning 'rescued'.

Fab
Latin, meaning 'a bean'.

Faber
(alt. Fabir)
Latin, meaning 'a blacksmith'.

Fabian
(alt. Fabien, Fabio)
Latin, meaning 'one who grows beans'.

Fabrice
(alt. Fabrizio)
Latin origin, meaning 'works with his hands'.

Fabron
(alt. Faber, Fabre, Fabbro)
French, meaning 'blacksmith'.

Fachnan
(alt. Fachtna, Faughnan)
Irish, meaning 'malicious'.

Fadi
(alt. Fadie, Fady, Fadey)
Arabic, meaning 'saviour'. This is the Arabic name for Jesus.

Fafnir
(alt. Fafner, Fafnor, Fafnur)
Norse, a mythological dragon.

Fagin
(alt. Fagan, Feagan, Fegan)
Irish, meaning 'rural'. The name of the head pickpocket in *Oliver Twist*.

Fahd
(alt. Fahad)
Arabic, meaning 'panther'.

Fai
Chinese, meaning 'beginning'.

Faine
(alt. Fain, Fane)
English, meaning 'full of joy'.

Fairburn
Teutonic, meaning 'handsome'.

Fairchild
(alt. Fairbairn)
Teutonic, meaning 'blond child'.

Fairhold
Teutonic, meaning 'powerful'.

Faisal
Arabic, meaning 'resolute'.

Faivish
Greek, meaning 'bright'.

Faizon
(alt. Fayzon, Faezon, Faizun)
Arabic, meaning 'understanding'.

Fajr
Arabic, meaning 'rise'.

Falak
Indian, meaning 'sky'.

Falan
Indian, meaning 'fruitful'.

Falco
(alt. Falcon, Falconer, Falke)
Latin, meaning 'falconer'.

Falk
German, meaning 'hawk'.

Fallon
(alt. Fallun, Fallan, Fallin)
Irish, meaning 'ruler'.

Falguni
Hindi, meaning 'born in the month of Falgun'.

Faolan
Irish, meaning 'wolf'.

Faris
(alt. Farris)
Arabic, meaning 'horseman'.

Faron
Spanish, meaning 'pharaoh'.

Farrah
English, meaning 'ironsmith'.

Farrell
Gaelic, meaning 'hero'.

Farug
Arabic, meaning 'distinguisher'.

Faulkner
Latin, from 'falcon'.

Faustino
Latin, meaning 'fortunate'.

Favian
Latin, meaning 'wise'.

Favre
(alt. Fabre, Faivre, Faure)
French, meaning 'ironworker'.

Fawzi
Arabic, meaning 'victorious'.

Faxon
English, meaning 'hair'.

Febronio
(alt. Febroneo, Febrono, Febroniyo)
Spanish, meaning 'bright'.

Fedele
Spanish, meaning 'faithful'.

Feeny
(alt. Feeney, Feichìn)
Irish, meaning 'raven'.

Feivel
(alt. Feival, Feivol, Feivil)
Hebrew, meaning 'brilliant'.

Fela
(alt. Felah, Fella, Fellah)
African, meaning 'a man who is warlike'. The name of the famous Nigerian musician Fela Kuti.

Felix
(alt. Felice)
Italian/Latin, meaning 'happy'.

Felipe
(alt. Filippo)
Spanish, meaning 'lover of horses'.

Felton
English, meaning 'town by a field'.

Fennell
Latin, name of vegetable.

Fenwick
Teutonic, meaning 'marshlands'.

Feoras
Irish, meaning 'rock'.

Ferdinand
(alt. Fernando)
Old German, meaning 'bold voyager'.

Fergus
(alt. Ferguson)
Gaelic, meaning 'supreme man'.

Ferran
German, meaning 'peaceful'.

Ferris
Gaelic, meaning 'rock'. The name of the classic cult hero in the film *Ferris Bueller's Day Off*.

Fflamddwyn
Welsh, meaning 'flame bearer'.

Fiachra
Irish, meaning 'raven'.

Fidel
Latin, meaning 'faithful'.

Fielding
(alt. Fieldyng, Feldyng)
English, meaning 'of the field'.

Fiero
(alt. Fyero)
Spanish, meaning 'fiery man'.

Filbert
(alt. Filberte, Filberto, Philibert)
German, meaning 'brilliant'.

Filmore
(alt. Fillmore, Fylmer)
English, meaning 'famous'.

Finbar
Gaelic, meaning 'fair head'.

Finch
English, taken from the bird of the same name.

Finian
Gaelic, meaning 'fair'.

Finlay
(alt. Finley, Finn)
Gaelic, meaning 'fair haired courageous one'.

Finn
(alt. fin, Fingal, Fingall, Fionn)
Alternative of Finian and Finnegan.

Finnegan
Gaelic, meaning 'fair'.

Fintan
Gaelic, meaning 'little fair one'.

F

Fiorello
(alt. Fiore)
Italian, meaning 'little flower'.

Fisher
(alt. Fish, Fischer, Fisscher, Visscher)
English, meaning 'fisherman'.

Fisseha
African, meaning 'happiness'.

Fitzroy
English, meaning 'the king's son'.

Fitzwilliam
English, meaning 'William's son'. Famously associated with Fitzwilliam Darcy in *Pride and Prejudice*.

Flan
(alt. Flann, Flannery, Flanagan)
Irish, meaning 'ruddy'.

Flavio
Latin, meaning 'yellow hair'.

Fleming
(alt. Flemming, Flemyng)
English, meaning 'from Flanders'.

Fletcher
(alt. Fletch, Fletche, Flecher)
English, meaning 'arrow maker'.

Flint
(alt. Flynt, Flintt, Flyntt)
English, meaning 'from the stream'.

Florencio
(alt. Florentino)
Latin, meaning 'from Florence'.

Florian
(alt. Florin)
Slavic/Latin, meaning 'flower'.

Floyd
Welsh origin, meaning 'grey haired'.

Flynn
Gaelic, meaning 'with a ruddy complexion'.

Fodor
(alt. Fodur, Fodir, Fodyr)
Hungarian, meaning 'curly-haired'.

Folke
(alt. Fulke, Fulker, Volker)
Norse, meaning 'people'.

Foley
(alt. Foly, Folee, Foleigh)
English, meaning 'one who is creative'.

Fonda
Spanish, meaning 'profound'.

Forbes
(alt. Forbs, Forb, Forbe)
Gaelic, meaning 'of the field'.

Ford
(alt. Forde, Forden, Fordon)
English, meaning 'inhabitant of the ford'.

Forrest
(alt. Forest, Forester, Forrester)
English, alternative of Foster, meaning 'woodsman'.

F

Fortney
(alt. Forteney, Forteny, Fourtney)
Latin, meaning 'strong'.

Fortunato
Italian, meaning 'lucky'.

Foster
Old English, meaning
'woodsman'.

Fotini
(alt. Fotis)
Greek, meaning 'light'.

Francesco
(alt. Francis, Francisco)
Latin, meaning 'from France'.

Frank
(alt. Frankie, Franklin, Franz)
Middle English, meaning 'free
landholder'.

Fraser
Scottish, meaning 'of the forest
men'.

Fred
(alt. Freddie, Frederick)
Old German, meaning 'peaceful
ruler'.

Freemont
English, meaning 'freedom
mountain'.

Frey
Scandinavian, meaning 'lord'.

Frick
(alt. Fryck, Frik, Fryk)
English, meaning 'vigorous'.

Frigyes
Hungarian, meaning 'peaceful
leader'.

Frode
(alt. Froad, Froade)
Norse, meaning 'wise'.

Fromel
(alt. Fromell, Fromele, Fromelle)
Hebrew, meaning 'outgoing'.

Froyim
(alt. Froiim)
Hebrew, meaning 'kind'.

Fry
(alt. Frye, Fryer)
English, meaning 'father's son'.

Fu
Chinese, meaning 'wealthy'.

Fukuda
Japanese, meaning 'from the
field'.

Fulbright
(alt. Fullbright, Fulbrite, Fullbrite)
English, meaning 'brilliant'.

Fuller
English, meaning 'cloth stretcher'.

Fullerton
English, meaning 'from Fuller's
town'.

Furman
Old German, meaning 'ferryman'.

Fydor
(alt. Faydor, Fedor, Fydor)
Russian alternative of Theodore,
meaning 'God's gift'.

Fyfe
(alt. Fife, Fyffe)
Scottish, meaning 'from Fifeshire'.

G Boys' names

Gaagii
(alt. Gaagi, Gagii, Gagi)
Native American, meaning 'like the raven'.

Gabai
Hebrew, meaning 'delightful'.

Gabbana
(alt. Gabana, Gabanah, Gabanna)
Italian, meaning 'creative man'.

Gabbo
(alt. Gabbow)
Old English, meaning 'joke'.

Gabe
Shortened form of Gabriel, meaning 'hero of God'.

Gable
French, alternative of Gabriel. Made famous by actor Clark Gable.

Gabino
Latin origin, meaning 'God is my strength'.

Gabriel
Hebrew, meaning 'hero of God'. One of the Archangels.

Gace
(alt. Gayce, Gayse, Gaece)
French, meaning 'pledge'.

Gad
(alt. Gadi, Gadie, Gady)
Hebrew, meaning 'good fortune' and Native American, meaning 'juniper tree'.

Gael
English, old reference to the Celts.

Gaetano
Italian, from the name of a region in Southern Italy.

Gaerwn
Welsh, meaning 'white fort'.

Gaffney
(alt. Gaffni, Gaffnie, Gaffnee)
Irish, meaning 'like a calf'.

Cahuj
African, meaning 'hunter'.

Gaillard
(alt. Gaillard, Gaillhard, Gaillhardt)
English, meaning 'brave'.

Gaines
(alt. Gains, Gayne, Gaynes)
English, meaning 'acquires'.

Gaius
(alt. Gaeus)
Latin, meaning 'rejoicing'.

Gal
Hebrew, meaning 'of the rolling waves'.

Galahad
English, meaning 'noble'.

Galen
Greek origin, meaning 'healer'.

Galileo
Italian, meaning 'from Galilee'.

Gallagher
Irish, meaning 'eager helper'.

Gallatin
(alt. Gallatyn, Gallaten, Gallatun)
American, meaning 'of the river'.

Galloway
(alt. Galoway, Gallowaye, Galowaye)
Latin, meaning 'from Gaul'.

Galton
(alt. Galt, Galten)
English, meaning 'a rented domain'.

Galvin
Irish, meaning 'sparrow'.

Gan
Chinese, meaning 'wanderer'.

Gandhi
Indian, meaning 'sun'.

Ganesh
Hindi, meaning 'Lord of the throngs'. One of the Hindu deities.

Gannon
Irish, meaning 'fair skinned'.

Garan
Welsh, meaning 'stork'.

Gareth
(alt. Garth)
Welsh, meaning 'gentle'.

Garfield
Old English, meaning 'spear field'. Also the name of the cartoon cat.

Garland
English, as in 'garland of flowers'.

Garner
Latin, meaning 'to gather grain'.

G

Literary names

Christopher (*Now We Are Six*, A. A. Milne)
Danny (*Danny, the Champion of the World*, Roald Dahl)
Dorian (*The Picture of Dorian Gray*, Oscar Wilde)
Faust (*Faust*, Wolfgang von Goethe)
Heathcliff (*Wuthering Heights*, Emily Brontë)
Horatio (*Hamlet*, William Shakespeare)
Ishmael (*Moby-Dick*, Herman Melville)
Oliver (*Oliver Twist*, Charles Dickens)
Mowgli (*The Jungle Book*, Rudyard Kipling)
Tom (*Tom Jones*, Henry Fielding)

G

Garnet
English, a precious stone, red in colour.

Garrett
English, alternative of Gerard.

Garrick
(alt. Garek, Garick, Garik)
English, meaning 'rules with a spear'.

Garrison
English, meaning 'Garret's son'.

Garron
(alt. Garran, Garren, Garrin)
Gaelic, meaning 'gelding'.

Garry
(alt. Gary, Geary)
Old English, meaning 'spear'.

Garth
(alt. Garthe, Gart, Garte)
Norse, meaning 'enclosure'.

Garuda
Indian, meaning 'king of birds'.

Gaspar
(alt. Gaspard)
Persian, meaning 'treasurer'.

Gaston
From the region in the south of France.

Gaubert
French, meaning 'bright sovereign'.

Gavin
(alt. Gawain)
Scottish/Welsh, meaning 'little falcon'.

Gavriel
(alt. Gavril, Gavryel, Gavrill)
Hebrew, meaning 'God is my strength'.

Gedaliah
(alt. Gedalia, Gedalya)
Hebrew, meaning 'made great by Jehovah'.

Geert
(alt. Geart, Geerte, Gearte)
German, meaning 'strong and brave'.

Gefen
(alt. Geffen, Gefni, Gefnie)
Hebrew, meaning 'from the vine'.

Gene
Shortened form of Eugene, meaning 'well-born'.

Genet
(alt. Genat, Genit, Genut)
African, meaning 'from Eden'.

Genkei
Japanese, meaning 'honoured'.

Gennaro
Italian, meaning 'of Janus'.

Gentian
(alt. Genshian)
Latin, meaning 'blue flower'.

Geoffrey
Old German, meaning 'peace'.

Geona
Italian, meaning 'dove'.

George
(alt. Giorgio)
Greek, meaning 'farmer'.

Gera
Latin, meaning 'brother'.

Gerald
(alt. Geraldo, Gerard, Gerhard)
Old German, meaning 'spear ruler'.

Gerlach
(alt. Gerlaich)
Scandinavian, meaning 'spear thrower'.

Geronimo
Italian origin, meaning 'sacred name'.

Gerry
English, meaning 'independent'.

Gershom
(alt. Gersh, Gersham, Gershon)
Hebrew, meaning 'stranger'.

Gert
Old German, meaning 'strong spear'.

Gervase
Old German, meaning 'with honour'.

Giacomo
Italian, meaning 'God's son'.

Gibor
(alt. Gibbor)
Hebrew, meaning 'strong'.

Gibson
English, meaning 'son of Gilbert'.

Gideon
Hebrew, meaning 'tree cutter'.

Gifford
(alt. Giffard, Giffered, Gyfford)
Old English, meaning 'puffy face'.

Gilad
(alt. Giladi, Gilead)
Hebrew, meaning 'camel hump'.

Gilbert
(alt. Gilberto)
French, meaning 'bright promise'.

Gilby
(alt. Gil, Gillby, Gilley)
Irish, meaning 'blond boy'.

Giles
Greek, meaning 'small goat'.

Gili
(alt. Gil, Gilam, Gilon)
Hebrew, meaning 'joy'.

Gilmore
(alt. Gillie, Gillmore, Gilmour)
Irish, meaning 'Virgin Mary devotee'.

Gino
Italian, meaning 'well born'.

Giovanni
Italian form of John, meaning 'God is gracious'.

Giri
(alt. Girie, Giry, Girey)
Indian, meaning 'from the mountain'.

Giulio
Italian, meaning 'youthful'.

Giuseppe
Italian form of Joseph, meaning 'Jehovah increases'.

G

Gizmo
(alt. Gismo, Gyzmo, Gysmo)
American, meaning 'playful one'.

Glaisne
(alt. Glaisny, Glaisney, Glaisnie)
Irish, meaning 'serene'.

Glen
English, from the word 'glen'.

Glyn
Welsh form of Glen.

Godfrey
German, meaning 'peace of God'.

Godric
(alt. Godrick, Godrik, Godryk)
English, meaning 'rules with God'.

Goku
Japanese, meaning 'of the sky'.

Goliath
Hebrew, meaning 'exile'. Biblical character, the giant killed by David.

Gomda
(alt. Gomdah)
Native American, meaning 'of the wind'.

Gomer
Hebrew, meaning 'to complete'.

Gonzalo
(alt. González, Gonzo, Gonzolito)
Spanish, meaning 'saved from combat'.

Goodwin
(alt. Goodwinn, Goodwen, Goodwyn)
English, meaning 'beloved friend'.

Gordon
Gaelic, meaning 'large fortification'.

Goren
(alt. Gorin, Goryn, Goran)
Hebrew, meaning 'of the granary'.

Gottlieb
German, meaning 'good love'.

Gower
Area on the Welsh coast.

Grady
(alt. Gradey)
Irish, meaning 'industrious'.

Graeme
(alt. Graham)
English, meaning 'gravelled area'.

Granger
(alt. Grainger, Grange)
English, meaning 'granary worker'.

Grant
English, from the word 'grant'.

Granville
English, meaning 'gravely town'.

Gray
(alt. Grey)
English, from the word 'gray'.

Grayson
English, meaning 'son of gray'.

Green
English, from the word 'green'.

Greg
(alt. Gergorio, Gregory, Grieg)
English, meaning 'watcher'.

Gregor
Greek, alternative of Gregorios.

Griffin
English, from the word 'griffin'.

Grover
English, meaning 'inhabites near a grove of trees'.

Guido
Italian, meaning 'guide'.

Guillaume
French form of William, meaning 'strong protector'.

Gulliver
English, meaning 'glutton'.

Gunther
German, meaning 'warrior'.

Guri
Hebrew, meaning 'lion cub'.

Gurpreet
Indian, meaning 'love of the teacher'.

Gustave
(alt. Gus)
Scandinavian, meaning 'royal staff'.

Guthrieb
(alt. Guthrey, Guthry)
Scottish, meaning 'windy place'.

Guy
English, from the word 'guy'.

Guyapi
(alt. Guyapie, Guyapy, Guyapey)
Native American, meaning 'candid one'.

Gwalchmai
Welsh, meaning 'battle hawk'.

Gwill
(alt. Gwil, Gwyll, Gwyl)
American, meaning 'one who has dark eyes'.

Gwydion
(alt. Gwydeon, Gwydionne, Gwydeonne)
Welsh, a mythological magician.

Gylfi
(alt. Gylfie, Gylfee, Gylfi)
Scandinavian, meaning 'king'.

Gwyn
Welsh, meaning 'white'.

Famous male singers

Cliff (Richard)
Dean (Martin)
Frank (Sinatra)
Freddie (Mercury)
John (Lennon)
Lionel (Richie)
Marvin (Gaye)
Michael (Bublé)
Morrissey
Tom (Jones)

H Boys' names

Haakon
(alt. Hakon)
Scandinavian, meaning 'highborn'.

Habakkuk
(alt. Habacuc, Habbakuk)
Hebrew, meaning 'embrace'.

Habib
Arabic, meaning 'beloved one'.

Hackett
(alt. Hacket, Hackit, Hackitt)
German, meaning 'small hacker'.

Haden
(alt. Haiden)
English, meaning 'hedged valley'.

Hades
Greek, meaning 'sightless'. Name of the underworld in Greek mythology.

Hadley
(alt. Hadlee, Hadleigh, Hadly)
English, meaning 'meadow of heather'.

Hadrian
From Hadria, a north Italian city.

Hadriel
(alt. Hadyrel, Hadriell, Hadryell)
Hebrew, meaning 'brilliance of God'.

Hadwin
Old English, meaning 'friend in war'.

Hagan
(alt. Egan)
Irish, meaning 'small fire'.

Haidar
(alt. Haider, Hayder, Haidor)
Arabic, meaning 'lion'.

Haig
Armenian, meaning 'legend' or 'of the field' and English, meaning 'covered with hedges'. The English version is often used as a surname.

Haines
(alt. Hainey, Hanes, Haynes)
German, meaning 'a cottage covered in vines'.

Hakan
Native American, meaning 'fire' or Turkish, meaning 'leader'.

Hakeem
Arabic, meaning 'wise and insightful'.

Hal
(alt. Hale, Hallie)
English, nickname for Henry, meaning 'home ruler'.

Halden
(alt. Hadan, Haldane)
Scandinavian, meaning 'half Dane'.

Hale
(alt. Haile, Hal, Hayle)
English, meaning 'hero'.

Haley
(alt. Haly, Haleigh, Hayley)
English, meaning 'hay field' or Irish, meaning 'original'.

Hali
Greek, meaning 'sea'.

Halim
Arabic, meaning 'gentle'.

Hall
(alt. Heall)
Anglo-Saxon, meaning 'dweller of an estate'.

Hallam
(alt. Hallem, Hallim, Hallum)
English, meaning 'valley'.

Halliwell
English, meaning 'from the holy source'.

Halton
English, meaning 'manor' or 'estate'.

Ham
(alt. Hamm)
Hebrew, meaning 'hot'. Short form of Hamilton.

Hamal
(alt. Amahl, Amal, Hamahl)
Arabic, meaning 'lamb'.

Hamid
Arabic, meaning 'praiseworthy'.

Hamill
(alt. Hamel, Hamell, Hammill)
English, meaning 'scarred'.

Hamilton
Old English, meaning 'flat topped hill'.

Hamish
Scottish form of James, meaning 'he who supplants'.

Hamlet
(alt. Hamlett, Hammet, Hamlit)
German, meaning 'village'. A variation of the Danish Amleth, and often associated with Shakespeare's tragedy *Hamlet*.

Hamlin
(alt. Hamlyn, Hamblin)
German, meaning 'little homebody'.

Hammond
(alt. Hammund, Hammend, Hammand)
German, meaning 'guardian of the home'.

Hampton
English, meaning 'settlement'. It is also a place name.

Hampus
Swedish form of Homer, meaning 'pledge'.

Hamza
Arabic, meaning 'lamb'.

Han
(alt. Hannes, Hans)
Scandinavian, meaning 'the Lord is gracious'.

Hanan
Hebrew, meaning, 'gracious'.

Handel
German, a variation of John.

Hani
(alt. Hanie, Hany, Hanee)
Arabic, meaning 'joyful'.

Hania
(alt. Haniah, hanya, Hanyah)
Native American, meaning 'spirit soldier'.

Hanif
(alt. Haneef, Haneaf, Haneif)
Arabic, meaning 'devout'.

Hank
German, meaning 'home ruler'. Form of Henry.

Hansel
German, meaning 'the Lord is gracious'.

Hanson
(alt. Hansen, Hanssen, Hansun)
Scandinavian, meaning 'Han's son'.

> **TV personality names**
> Andrew (Marr)
> Bruce (Forsyth)
> Graham (Norton)
> Griff (Rhys Jones)
> Jeremy (Clarkson, Kyle, Paxman)
> Jonathan (Ross)
> Michael (Parkinson)
> Richard (Hammond)
> Trevor (McDonald)
> Vernon (Kay)

Hansraj
Hindi, meaning 'king of the swans'.

Hardy
English, meaning 'tough'.

Harland
Old English, meaning 'army land'.

Harlan
English, meaning 'dweller by the boundary wood'.

Harley
Old English, meaning 'hare meadow'.

Harlow
(alt. Harlowe, Harlo, Harloe)
English, meaning 'warriors on the hill'.

Harmon
Old German, meaning 'soldier'.

Harold
Scandinavian, meaning 'army ruler'.

Haroun
Arabic, alternative of Aaron.

Harper
(alt. Harpur)
English, meaning 'harpist'.

Harrison
(alt. Harris, Harriss, Harrisson)
English, meaning 'Harry's son'.

Harry
Old German, meaning 'home ruler'. Alternative form of Henry.

Hart
Old English, meaning 'stag'.

Hartley
(alt. Hartlea, Hartlee, Hartleigh)
English, meaning 'deer field'.

Haru
Japanese, meaning 'spring child'.

Haruki
Japanese, meaning 'shining'.

Harvard
English, meaning 'guardian'.

Harvey
Old English, meaning 'strong and worthy'.

Hasan
(alt. Hussein, Hasani, Husain)
Arabic, meaning 'good'.

Haskell
Hebrew, meaning 'intellect'.

Hassan
Arabic, meaning 'handsome'.

Hayden
(alt. Haden, Haydon, Haydun)
English, meaning 'hedged valley'.

Haydn
Old English, alternative of Hayden, meaning 'hedged valley'. Also German, meaning 'heathen'.

Heart
English, from the word 'heart'.

Heath
English, meaning 'heath' or 'moor'.

Heathcliff
English, meaning 'cliff near a heath'. Made famous by Emily Bronte's novel *Wuthering Heights*.

Heber
Hebrew, meaning 'partner'.

Hector
Greek, meaning 'steadfast'.

Heldrado
German, meaning 'soldiers' councillor'.

Henry
(alt. Hendrik, Hendrix)
Old German, meaning 'home ruler'.

Henson
English, meaning 'son of Henry'.

Herbert
(alt. Herb, Bert)
Old German, meaning 'illustrious warrior'.

Heriberto
Italian variant of Herbert,
meaning 'illustrious warrior'.

Herman
(alt. Herminio, Hermon)
Old German, meaning 'soldier'.

Hermes
Greek, meaning 'messenger'.

Herschel
Yiddish, meaning 'deer'.

Hewitt
(alt. Hewet, Hewett, Hewit)
German, meaning 'intelligent'
or Anglo-Saxon, meaning 'little
Hugh'.

Hezekiah
Biblical, meaning 'God gives
strength'.

Hideki
Japanese, meaning 'excellent
trees'.

Hideo
Japanese, meaning 'excellent
name'.

Hiero
Greek, meaning 'holy'.

Hilario
Latin, meaning 'cheerful, happy'.

Hilary
English, meaning 'cheerful'.

Hillel
Hebrew, meaning 'greatly
praised'.

Hilliard
Old German, meaning 'battle
guard'.

Hilton
Old English, meaning 'hill
settlement'.

Hinto
Native American, meaning 'blue
haired'.

Hiram
Hebrew, meaning 'exalted
brother'.

Hiro
Spanish, meaning 'sacred name'.

Hiroshi
Japanese, meaning 'generous'.

Hirsch
Yiddish, meaning 'deer'.

Hobart
English, meaning 'bright and
shining intellect'.

Hodge
English, meaning 'son of Roger'.

Hogan
Gaelic, meaning 'youth'.

Hokaratcha
Native American, meaning 'pole
cat'.

Holden
English, meaning 'deep valley'.

Hollis
Old English, meaning 'holly tree'.

Homer
Greek, meaning 'pledge'.

Honorius
Latin, meaning 'honourable'.

Horace
Latin, name of the Roman poet.

Houston
Old English, meaning 'Hugh's town'. Also city in the state of Texas, USA.

Howard
Old English, meaning 'noble watchman'.

Howell
Welsh, meaning 'eminent and remarkable'.

Hoyt
Norse, meaning 'spirit' or 'soul'.

Hristo
From Christo, meaning 'follower of Christ'.

Hubbell
(alt. Hubble)
English, meaning 'brave hearted'.

Hubert
German, meaning 'bright and shining intellect'.

Hudson
Old English, meaning 'son of Hugh'.

Hugh
Old German, meaning 'soul, mind and intellect'.

Humbert
Old German, meaning 'famous giant'. Be warned: it's the name and surname of the paedophile protagonist of Vladimir Nabokov's Lolita.

Humphrey
Old German, meaning 'peaceful warrior'.

Hunter
English, from the word 'hunter'.

Hurley
Gaelic, meaning 'sea tide'.

Huxley
Old English, meaning 'Hugh's meadow'.

Huy
Vietnamese, meaning 'glorious'.

Hyrum
Hebrew, meaning 'exalted brother'.

Uncommon three syllable names

Alastair
Arnaldo
Barnaby
Dominic
Elliot
Ferdinand
Jefferson
Jeremy
Prospero
Sebastian

Boys' names

Iago
Spanish, meaning 'he who supplants'.

Ian
(alt. Ion)
Variant of John, meaning 'God is gracious'.

Ianto
Welsh, meaning 'gift of God'.

Iassen
(alt. Issan, Iassin, Iasson)
Bulgarian, meaning 'of the ash tree'.

Ibaad
Arabic, meaning 'a believer in God'.

Ibu
Japanese, meaning 'creative'.

Ibrahim
Arabic, meaning 'father of many'.

Ichabod
Hebrew, meaning 'glory is good'.

Ichiro
Japanese, meaning 'first born son'.

Idan
Hebrew, meaning 'place in time'.

Idris
Welsh, meaning 'fiery leader'.

Ifan
Welsh variant of John, meaning 'God is gracious'.

Ifor
Welsh, meaning 'archer'.

Igashu
(alt. Igasho)
Native American, meaning 'seeker'.

Ignace
(alt. Iggy, Ignase)
French, meaning 'one who is fiery'.

Ignacio
Latin, meaning 'ardent' or 'burning'.

Ignatius
(alt. Ignac, Ignace, Ignacius)
Alternative of Ignacio, meaning 'ardent' or 'burning'.

Ignatz
German, meaning 'fiery'.

Igor
Russian, meaning 'Ing's soldier'.

Ikaika
Hawaiian, meaning 'strong'.

Ike
Hebrew, short for Isaac, meaning 'laughter'.

Iku
Japanese, meaning 'nourishing'.

Ilan
Hebrew, meaning 'tree'.

Ilario
(alt. Iara, Ilari, Ilarion)
Latin, meaning 'cheerful'.

Ilias
Variant of Hebrew Elijah, meaning 'the Lord is my God'.

Ilya
(alt. Ilia, Illya)
Alternative of Elijah, meaning 'the Lord is my God'.

Imad
Arabic, meaning 'support'.

Imanol
Hebrew, meaning 'God is with us'.

Immanuel
(alt. Imannuel, Imanoel, Imanuel)
German alternative of Emanuel, meaning 'God is with us'.

Imre
(alt. Imric, Imrie, Omri)
Hungarian, meaning 'strength'.

Inali
Native American, meaning 'black fox'.

Indiana
Latin, meaning 'from India'. Also a state in the US.

Indigo
English, describing a deep blue colour.

Ingram
(alt. Ingamar, Inglis, Ingmar)
German, meaning 'angel' or 'raven'.

Ingo
Danish, meaning 'meadow'.

Inigo
Spanish, meaning 'fiery'.

Iniko
Nigerian, meaning 'troubled time'.

Innis
Irish, meaning 'isle'.

Ioan
(alt. Iancu, Ion, Ionel)
Romanian alternative of John, meaning 'the Lords is gracious'.

Ioannis
Greek, meaning 'the Lord is gracious'.

Iolo
Welsh, meaning 'worthy lord'.

Ioviano
Native American, meaning 'yellow hawk'.

Ipo
Hawaiian, meaning 'sweetheart'.

Old name, new fashion?

Bertie
Edgar
Gilbert
Hector
Horatio
Jasper
Norbert
Percival
Tarquin
Winston

Ira
Hebrew, meaning 'full grown and watchful'.

Irem
Turkish, meaning 'garden in heaven'.

Irvin
(alt. Irving, Irwin)
Gaelic, meaning 'green and fresh water'.

Irwin
(alt. Erwin, Erwyn, Irwinn)
English, meaning 'a boar friend'.

Isaac
(alt. Isaak)
Hebrew, meaning 'laughter'.

Isadore
(alt. Isidore, Isidro)
Greek, meaning 'gift of Isis'.

Isai
(alt. Isaiah, Isaias, Izaiah)
Arabic, meaning 'protection and security'.

Isaiah
Hebrew, alternative of Isai, meaning 'God is salvation'.

Isandro
Spanish, meaning 'liberator'.

Iser
Yiddish, meaning 'God wrestler'.

Ishaan
(alt. Ishan)
Hindi, meaning 'sun'.

Ishedus
Native American, meaning 'on top'.

Ishmael
(alt. Ismael)
Hebrew, meaning 'God listens'.

Ismet
Turkish, meaning 'honour'.

Israel
Hebrew, meaning 'God perseveres'. Also the name of the country.

Issachar
(alt. Isachar, Yisachar, Yissachar)
Hebrew, meaning 'his reward will come'. One of Jacob's 12 sons who founded the 12 tribes of Israel in the Bible.

Istvan
Hungarian variant of Stephen, meaning 'crowned'.

Itachi
Japanese, meaning 'weasel'.

Itai
Hebrew, meaning 'the Lord is with me'.

Itamar
(alt. Itamarr, Ittamarr, Ithamar)
Hebrew, meaning 'of the palm island'.

Itotia
Aztec, meaning 'dance'.

Iulian
(alt. Iulien,Iiulio, Iuleo)
Romanian, meaning 'youthful'.

Iuwine
(alt. Iuwin, Iuwinn, Iuwinne)
Anglo-Saxon, meaning 'beloved friend'.

Iva
Japanese, meaning 'yew tree'.

Ivan
Hebrew, meaning 'God is gracious'.

Ivanhoe
Russian origin, meaning 'God is gracious'. Also the name of a novel by Walter Scott.

Ives
Scandinavian, meaning 'archer's bow'.

Ivey
English, variant of Ivy.

Ivo
From the French yves, meaning 'yew tree'.

Ivor
Scandinavian, meaning 'yew'.

Ivory
English, from the word ivory.

Ivrit
Hebrew, meaning 'the Hebrew language'.

Ivy
English, meaning 'like the evergreen vining plant'.

Iwatoke
Native American, meaning 'serpent'.

Ixtli
Aztec, meaning 'face'.

Iyar
(alt. Iyyar, Iye, Iyyer)
Hebrew, meaning 'in the light'.

Iye
Native American, meaning 'from the smoke'.

Izaan
(alt. Izan, Izane, Izain)
Arabic, meaning 'obedient one'.

Izaiah
Hebrew, alternative of Isaiah, meaning 'God is salvation'.

Izar
Basque, meaning 'star'.

Ize
Native American, meaning 'the sun'.

Izel
Aztec, meaning 'unique'.

J Boys' names

Ja
African, meaning 'magnetic'.

Jabal
Indian, meaning 'one who is attractive'.

Jabari
Swahili, meaning 'valiant'.

Jabbar
Indian, meaning 'consoler of others'.

Jabez
Hebrew, meaning 'borne in pain'.

Jabin
Hebrew, meaning 'built by God'.

Jabir
Arabic, meaning 'comforter'.

Jabon
(alt. Jabin, Jabyn Jaban)
American, meaning 'fiesty'.

Jabulani
(alt. Jabulanie, Jabulany, Jabulaney)
African, meaning 'happy one'.

Jacan
Hebrew, meaning 'trouble'.

Jace
(alt. Jaece, Jase, Jayce)
Hebrew, meaning 'healer'.

Jacek
African, meaning 'hyacinth'.

Jachai
Hebrew, meaning 'supplanter'.

Jacinto
African, meaning 'hyacinth'.

Jack
(alt. Jacky, Jackie)
From the Hebrew John, meaning 'God is gracious'.

Jackson
English, meaning 'son of Jack'.

Jaco
From the Hebrew Jacob, meaning 'he who supplants'.

Jacob
(alt. Jacobo, Jago)
Hebrew, meaning 'he who supplants'.

Jacques
French form of Jack, meaning 'God is gracious'.

Jaden
(alt. Jaden, Jayden, Jaydin)
Hebrew, meaning 'Jehovah has heard'.

Jadal
(alt. Jadall, Jadel, Jadell)
American, meaning 'punctual'.

Jaegar
(alt. Jager, Jaecer, Jaeger)
German, meaning 'mighty hunter'.

Jael
(alt. Yael)
Hebrew, meaning 'a mountain goat'.

Jafar
Arabic, meaning 'stream'.

Jagan
(alt. Jagen, Jagin, Jagyn)
English, meaning 'self-confident'.

Jagger
Old English, meaning 'one who cuts'.

Jago
Spanish alternative of Jacob, meaning 'he who supplants'.

Jahan
Sanskrit, meaning 'the world'.

Jahi
(alt. Jahie, Jahey, Jahy)
African, meaning 'dignified'.

Jaheem
(alt. Jaheim)
Hebrew, meaning 'raised up'.

Jahir
Hindi, meaning 'jewel'.

Jai
Indian, meaning 'victory'.

Names of poets
Alfred (Lord Tennyson)
Dylan (Thomas)
Geoffrey (Chaucer)
John (Keats, Milton, Donne)
Percy (Bysshe Shelley)
Robert (Burns)
Seamus (Heaney)
Simon (Armitage)
Ted (Hughes)
William (Blake, Wordsworth)

Jaichand
(alt. Jachand, Jaychand, Jaychande)
Indian, meaning 'the moon is victorious'.

Jaidev
(alt. Jadev, Jaidev, Jaydev)
Indian, meaning 'victory of God'.

Jaime
Variant of James, meaning 'he who supplants'. J'aime is French for 'I love'.

Jaimin
(alt. Jaimyn, Jamin, Jamyn)
French, meaning 'loved'.

Jair
(alt. Jairo)
Hebrew, meaning 'God enlightens'.

Jairdan
(alt. Jardan, Jairden, Jayrden)
American, meaning 'enlightened'.

Jairo
Spanish, meaning 'shines'.

Jairus
(alt. Jair, Jaire, Jairo)
Hebrew, meaning 'enlightened by God'.

Jaiwant
(alt. Jaewant, Jawant, Jaywant)
Indian, meaning 'victorious'.

Jaja
African, meaning 'a gift from God'.

Jake
Shortened form of Jacob, meaning 'he who supplants'.

Jalen
Greek, meaning 'healer' or 'tranquil'.

Jali
Swahili, meaning 'musician'.

Jalon
Greek, meaning 'healer' or 'tranquil'.

Jamaal
(alt. Jamal)
Arabic, meaning 'handsome'.

Jamaine
(alt. Jamain, Jamayn, Jamayne)
Arabic, meaning 'attractive'.

Jamar
(alt. Jamarcus, Jamari, Jamir)
Modern variant of Jamal, meaning 'handsome'.

Jamel
Arabic, meaning 'handsome'.

James
English, meaning 'he who supplants'.

Jameson
(alt. Jamison)
English, meaning 'son of James'.

Jamie
(alt. Jamey, Jammie)
Nickname for James, meaning 'he who supplants'.

Jamil
Arabic, meaning 'handsome'.

Jamin
Hebrew, meaning 'son of the right hand'.

Jan
(alt. Janko, János)
Slavic, from John meaning 'the Lord is gracious'.

Janesh
Hindi, meaning 'leader of people'.

Names from ancient Rome

Brutus
Julius
Maximus
Nero
Remus
Romulus
Rufus
Tacitus
Titus
Virgil

Jani
(alt. Janie, Jannes, Janes)
Finnish alternative of John,
meaning 'God is gracious'.

Janus
Latin, meaning 'gateway'. Roman
god of doors, beginnings and
endings.

Japa
Indian, meaning 'chants'.

Japhet
(alt. Japheth)
Hebrew, meaning 'comely'.

Jaquez
French origin, form of Jacques,
meaning 'God is gracious'.

Jared
(alt. Jarem, Jaren, Jarod)
Hebrew, meaning 'descending'.

Jarlath
Gaelic, from Iarlaith, from Saint
Iarfhlaith.

Jarom
Greek, meaning 'to raise and
exalt'.

Jarrell
Variant of Gerald, meaning 'spear
ruler'.

Jarrett
Old English, meaning 'spear-
brave'.

Jarvis
Old German, meaning 'with
honour'.

Jason
Greek, meaning 'healer'.

Jasper
Greek, meaning 'treasure holder'.

Javen
Arabic, meaning 'youth'.

Javier
Spanish, meaning 'bright'.

Jaxon
From Jackson, meaning 'son of
Jack'.

Jay
Latin, meaning 'jaybird'.

Jaylan
Greek, meaning 'healer'.

Jeevan
Indian, meaning 'life'.

Jefferey
(alt. Jeff)
Old German, meaning 'peace'.

Jefferson
English, meaning 'son of Jeffrey'.

Jennings
(alt. Jenning, Jennyng, Jennyngs)
English, meaning 'descendent of
John'.

Jensen
Scandinavian, meaning 'son of
Jan'.

Jeremiah
(alt. Jeremia, Jeremias, Jeremiya)
Hebrew, meaning 'the Lord
exalts'.

Jeremy
(alt. Jem)
Hebrew alternative of Jeremiah,
meaning 'the Lord exalts'.

Jeriah
Hebrew, meaning 'Jehovah has seen'.

Jericho
Arabic, meaning 'city of the moon'.

Jermaine
Latin, meaning 'brotherly'.

Jerome
Greek, meaning 'sacred name'.

Jerry
English, from Gerald, meaning 'spear ruler'.

Jesse
Hebrew, meaning 'the Lord exists'.

Jesus
Hebrew, meaning 'the Lord is Salvation' and the Son of God.

Jethro
Hebrew, meaning 'eminent'.

Ji
Chinese, meaning 'organised one'.

Jibril
(alt. Jibryl, Jibri, Jibry)
Arabic, referring to the archangel Gabriel.

Jie
Chinese, meaning 'purity'.

Jignesh
(alt. Jigneshe, Jygnesh, Jygneshe)
Indian, meaning 'curious'.

Jiles
American, meaning 'shield bearer'.

Jim
(alt. Jimmy)
From James, meaning 'he who supplants'.

Jing
(alt. Jyng)
Chinese, meaning 'flawless'.

Jiri
(alt. Jiro)
Greek, meaning 'farmer'.

Joachim
Hebrew, meaning 'established by God'.

Joah
(alt. João)
Hebrew, meaning 'God is gracious' .

Joao
Portugese alternative of Joah, meaning 'God is gracious'.

Joaquin
Hebrew, meaning 'established by God'.

Joe
(alt. Joey, Johan, Johannes)
From Joseph, meaning 'Jehovah increases'.

Joel
Hebrew, meaning 'Jehovah is the Lord'.

Joey
English, meaning 'God will increase'.

Johar
(alt. Joharr, Jahar, Jahara)
Hindi, meaning 'precious like a jewel'.

John
Hebrew, meaning 'the Lord is gracious'.

Johnny
(alt. Jon, Jonny)
From Jonathan, meaning 'gift of God'.

Joji
(alt. Jojie, Jojey, Jojy)
Japanese alternative of George, meaning 'farmer'.

Jokull
Scandianvian, meaning 'ice glacier'.

Jolyon
From Julian, meaning 'young'.

Jon
English alternative of John, meaning 'gift from God'.

Jonah
Hebrew, meaning 'dove'.

Jonas
Hebrew, meaning 'dove'.

Jonathan
(alt. Johnathan, Johnathon, Jonathon)
Hebrew, meaning 'gift from God'.

Jordan
(alt. Jory, Judd)
Hebrew, meaning 'down-flowing'.

Jorge
From George, meaning 'farmer'.

José
Spanish variant of Joseph, meaning 'Jehovah increases'.

Joseph
(alt. Joss)
Hebrew, meaning 'Jehovah increases'.

Joshua
Hebrew, meaning 'Jehovah is salvation'.

Josh
Shortened form of Joshua, meaning 'Jehovah is salvation'.

Josiah
Hebrew, meaning 'Jehovah helps'.

Josué
Spanish variant of Joshua, meaning 'Jehovah is salvation'.

Jovan
Latin, meaning 'the supreme God'.

Joweese
Native American, meaning 'chirping bird'.

Joyce
Latin, meaning 'joy'.

Juan
Spanish variant of John, meaning 'the Lord is gracious'.

Jubal
Hebrew, meaning 'ram's horn'.

Judah
(alt. Juda, Jude, Judas)
Hebrew, meaning 'praises God'.

J

Jude
Hebrew, meaning 'praise' or 'thanks'.

Judson
Variant of Jude, meaning 'praise' or 'thanks'.

Jules
From Julian, meaning 'Jove's child'.

Julian
Greek, meaning 'Jove's child'.

Julien
French variant of Julian, meaning 'Jove's child'.

Julio
Italian variant of Julian, meaning 'Jove's child'.

Julius
Latin, meaning 'youthful'.

Jumoke
African, meaning 'beloved child'.

Jun
Chinese, meaning 'handsome'.

Jung
Korean, meaning 'righteous man'.

Junior
Latin, meaning 'the younger one'.

Junius
Latin, meaning 'young'.

Jupiter
Latin, meaning 'the supreme God'. Jupiter was king of the Roman gods and the god of thunder. Jupiter is also the largest planet in the solar system.

Juraj
Hebrew, meaning 'God is my judge'.

Jurgen
Greek, meaning 'farmer'.

Justice
English, from the word 'justice'.

Justin
(alt. Justus)
Latin, meaning 'just and upright'.

Juwan
Hebrew, meaning 'the Lord is gracious'.

Juvenal
(alt. Juvinal, Juvinel, Juventino)
Latin, meaning 'young boy'.

Names from ancient Greece

Aesop
Archimedes
Erasmus
Homer
Jason
Lysandos
Nikolaos
Odysseus
Paris
Pyrrhus

Boys' names

Kaamil
Arabic, meaning 'perfect'.

Kaaria
(alt. Karia, Karya)
African, meaning 'wise'.

Kabelo
African, meaning 'gift'.

Kabili
(alt. Kabilie, Kabilee, Kabily)
African, meaning 'possession'.

Kabir
(alt. Kabeer, Kabier, kabyr)
Indian, meaning 'spiritual leader'.

Kacey
(alt. Kaci, Kacie, Kasey)
Irish, meaning 'vigilent man'.

Kade
Scottish, meaning 'from the wetlands'.

Kadeem
Arabic, meaning 'one who serves'.

Kaden
(alt. Kadin, Kaedin, Kaiden)
Arabic, meaning 'companion'.

Kadir
Arabic, meaning 'capable and competent'.

Kaelan
Gaelic, meaning 'mighty warrior'.

Kaemon
Japanese, meaning 'one full of joy'.

Kafi
(alt. Kafie, Kafy)
African, meaning 'quiet and well-behaved'.

Kafka
Czech, meaning 'bird-like'. Often associated with the author of *The Metamorphosis*.

Kagen
Irish, meaning 'a thinker'.

Kahale
(alt. Kahail, Kahaile, Kahayl)
Hawaiian, meaning 'homebody'.

Kahlil
Arabic, meaning 'friend'.

Kai
Greek, meaning 'keeper of the keys'.

Kairos
Greek, meaning 'the right moment'.

Kaito
Japanese, meaning 'ocean and sake dipper'.

Kalani
Hawaiian, meaning 'sky'.

Kale
German, meaning 'free man'.

Kaleb
Hebrew, meaning 'dog' or 'aggressive'.

Kalen
Gaelic, meaning 'uncertain'.

Kaleo
Hawaiian, meaning 'the voice'.

Kalil
Arabic, meaning 'friend'.

Kalvin
French, meaning 'bald'.

Kamari
Indian, meaning 'the enemy of desire'.

Kamden
English, meaning 'winding valley'.

Kameron
Scottish, meaning 'crooked nose'.

Kamil
Arabic, meaning 'perfection'.

Kane
Gaelic, meaning 'little battler'.

Kanga
Native American, meaning 'raven'.

Kani
Hawaiian, meaning 'sound'.

Kano
(alt. Kanoe, Kanoh)
Japanese, meaning 'powerful'.

Kanye
African town. Made popular by rapper Kanye West.

Kareem
(alt. Karim)
Arabic, meaning 'generous'.

Karl
(alt. Karson)
Old German, meaning 'free man'.

Kasey
Irish, meaning 'alert'.

Kaspar
Persian, meaning 'treasurer'.

Kateb
Arabic, meaning 'writer'.

Kaushal
Sanskrit, meaning 'clever'.

Kavon
Gaelic, meaning 'handsome'.

Kayden
Arabic, meaning 'companion'.

Kaysar
Persian, meaning 'king'.

Kazimierz
Polish, meaning 'declares peace'.

Kazuki
Japanese, meaning 'radiant hope'.

Kazuo
Japanese, meaning 'harmonious man'.

Keagan
(alt. Keegan, Kegan)
Gaelic, meaning 'small flame'.

Keane
Gaelic, meaning 'fighter'.

Keanu
Hawaiian, meaning 'breeze'.

Keary
Gaelic, meaning 'black-haired'.

Keaton
English, meaning 'place of hawks'.

Keefe
(alt. Keef, Kief, Kiefe)
Gaelic, meaning 'beloved man'.

Keeler
Gaelic, meaning 'beautiful and graceful'.

Keenan
(alt. Kenan)
Gaelic, meaning 'little ancient one'.

Keiji
Japanese, meaning 'govern with discretion'.

Keir
Gaelic, meaning 'dark-haired' or 'dark-skinned'.

Keiran
Irish, meaning 'dark'.

Keitaro
Japanese, meaning 'blessed'.

Keith
Gaelic, meaning 'woodland'.

Kekoa
Hawaiian, meaning 'brave one' or 'soldier'.

Kelby
Old English, meaning 'farmhouse near the stream'.

Kell
(alt. Kellan, Kellen, Kiel)
Norse, meaning 'spring'.

Kelsey
Old English, meaning 'victorious ship'.

Kelton
Old English, meaning 'town of the keels'.

Kelvin
Old English, meaning 'friend of ships'.

Keme
Native American, meaning 'secretive'.

Kemenes
Hungarian, meaning 'maker of furnaces'.

Ken
Shortened form of Kenneth, meaning 'born of fire'.

Kendal
Old English, meaning 'the Kent river valley'.

K

Kendon
Old English, meaning 'brave guard'.

Kendrick
Gaelic, meaning 'royal ruler'.

Kenelm
Old English, meaning 'bold'.

Kenji
Japanese, meaning 'intelligent second son'.

Kennard
English, meaning 'brave' or 'royal'.

Kennedy
Gaelic, meaning 'helmet head'.

Kenneth
(alt. Kenney)
Gaelic, meaning 'born of fire'.

Kennison
English, meaning 'son of Kenneth'.

Kent
From the English county.

Kentaro
Japanese, meaning 'sharp' or 'big'.

Kenton
English, meaning 'town of Ken'.

Kenya
From the country in Africa.

Kenyatta
From Kenya.

Kenyon
From Kenya.

Kenzie
Scottish, meaning 'descendant of a handsome man'.

Kenzo
Japanese, meaning 'wise'.

Keola
Hawaiian, meaning 'life'.

Keon
(alt. Keoni)
Hawaiian, meaning 'gracious'.

Kepler
German, meaning 'hat maker'.

Keran
Armenian, meaning 'wooden post'.

Kermit
(alt. Kerwin)
Gaelic, meaning 'without envy'. Associated with Kermit the Frog, the *Muppets* character.

Kerr
English, meaning 'wetland'.

Keshav
Indian, meaning 'beautiful-haired'.

Kesler
Armenian, meaning 'independent and energetic man'.

Keto
Swahili, meaning 'depth'.

Kevin
Gaelic, meaning 'handsome beloved'.

Khalid
(alt. Khalif, Khalil)
Arabic, meaning 'immortal'.

Khalil
Arabic, meaning 'friend'.

Kian
(alt. Keyon, Kyan)
Irish, meaning 'ancient'.

Kiefer
German, meaning 'barrel maker'.

Kieran
(alt. Kyron)
Gaelic, meaning 'black'.

Kiet
(alt. Kyet, Kiete, Kyete)
Thai, meaning 'honoured one'.

Kiho
(alt. Kihoe, Kyho, Kyhoe)
African, meaning 'from the fog'.

Kijana
African, meaning 'youth'.

Kilby
From the English Cilebi, a place in Leicestershire.

Kilian
Irish, meaning 'bright headed'.

Kimani
African, meaning 'beautiful and sweet'.

Kimo
Hawaiian alternative of James, meaning 'he who supplants'.

Kin
Japanese, meaning 'golden one'.

Kinfe
African, meaning 'with wings'.

King
English, from the word 'king'.

Kingsley
English, meaning 'the king's meadow'.

Kioshi
(alt. Kioshe, Kioshie, Kioshy)
Japanese, meaning 'quiet one'.

Kiran
Sanskrit, meaning 'ray of light'.

Kirby
German, meaning 'settlement by a church'.

Kirk
Old German, meaning 'church'.

Kit
(alt. Kitt)
English alternative of Christopher, meaning 'bearing Christ inside'.

Kitchi
(alt. Kitchie, Kitchey, Kitchy)
Native American, meaning 'brave young man'.

Klaus
German, meaning 'victorious'.

Kleng
Norse, meaning 'with claws'.

Knightley
(alt. Knightly)
English, meaning 'of the knight's meadows'.

K

Knoton
Native American, meaning 'of the wind'.

Knut
Old Norse, meaning 'knot'.

Kobe
(alt. Koda, Kody)
Japanese, meaning 'a Japanese city'.

Kofi
Ghanaian, meaning 'born on Friday'.

Kohana
Japanese, meaning 'little flower'.

Kojo
Ghanaian, meaning 'Monday'.

Kolby
Norse, meaning 'settlement'.

Korbin
Gaelic, meaning 'a steep hill'.

Kovit
Scandinavian, meaning 'an expert'.

Kramer
German, meaning 'shopkeeper'.

Kris
(alt. Krish)
From Christopher, meaning 'bearing Christ inside'.

Krispin
(alt. Krispen, Krispyn, Kryspyn)
English, meaning 'curly haired'.

Kueng
Chinese, meaning 'universe'.

Kumar
Indian, meaning 'a prince'.

Kurt
German, meaning 'courageous advice'.

Kurtis
French, meaning 'courtier'.

Kwame
Ghanaian, meaning 'born on Saturday'.

Kwan
Korean, meaning 'one with a bold character'.

Kwatoko
Native American, meaning 'large beaked bird'.

Kyden
English, meaning 'narrow little fire'.

Kylan
(alt. Kyle, Kyleb, Kyler)
Gaelic, meaning 'narrow and straight'.

Kyllion
Irish, meaning 'war'.

Kyran
Persian, meaning 'lord'.

Kyree
From Cree, a Canadian tribe.

Kyros
Greek, meaning 'legitimate power'.

L Boys' names

Laban
Hebrew, meaning 'white'.

Label
(alt. Labal, Laball, Label)
Hebrew, meaning 'like a lion'.

Labhras
Irish alternative of Lawrence,
meaning 'man from Laurentum'.

Labib
Arabic, meaning 'sensible one'.

Laborc
Hungarian, meaning 'brave as a
panther'.

Lacey
French, meaning 'originally from
Normandy'.

Lachie
Scottish, meaning 'from the lake'.

Lachlan
Gaelic, meaning 'from the land
of lakes'.

Lachtna
Irish, meaning 'one who ages
gracefully'.

Lacrosse
French, meaning 'the cross'.

Lacy
Old French place name.

Ladan
Hebrew, meaning 'alert'.

Ladd
English, meaning 'servant'.

Ladden
American, meaning 'athletic'.

Ladomér
Hungarian, meaning 'trapper of
animals'.

Lae
(alt. Lai, Lay)
Laos, meaning 'dark'.

Laertes
English, meaning 'adventurous'.
Ophelia's brother in
Shakespeare's play Hamlet.

Lafayette
French, meaning 'man of faith'.
Famous French Revolutionary
general.

Laith
Arabic, meaning 'like a lion'.

Lajos
Hungarian, meaning 'holy man'.

L

Popular song names

Alexander (*Alexander's Ragtime Band*, Irving Berlin)
Daniel (*Daniel*, Elton John)
Frankie (*Frankie*, Sister Sledge)
Jack (*Jumpin' Jack Flash*, The Rolling Stones)
James (*James Dean*, The Eagles)
Johnny (*Johnny B. Goode*, Chuck Berry)
Kenneth (*What's the Frequency, Kenneth?*, REM)
Leroy (*Bad, Bad Leroy Brown*, Jim Croce)
Mack (*Mack The Knife*, Bobby Darin)
Oliver (*Oliver's Army*, Elvis Costello)

Laken
American, meaning 'of the lake'.

Lakota
Native American, meaning
'beloved friend'.

Lalam
Indian, meaning 'the best'.

Lalit
Hindi, meaning 'beautiful'.

Lamar
Old German, meaning 'water'.

Lambert
Scandinavian, meaning 'land
brilliant'.

Lambros
Greek, meaning 'brilliant and
radiant'.

Lameh
Arabic, meaning 'shining man'.

Lamont
Old Norse, meaning 'law man'.

Lance
French, meaning 'land'.

Lancelot
Variant of Lance, meaning 'land'.
The name of one of the Knights of
the Round Table.

Landen
(alt. Lando, Landon, Langdon)
English, meaning 'long hill'.

Lander
(alt. Land, Landers, Landry)
English, meaning 'territory'.

Lando
Portugese alternative of Orlando,
meaning 'old land'.

Landyn
Welsh variant of Landen,
meaning 'long hill'.

Lane
(alt. Layne)
English, from the word 'lanel.

Lannie
(alt. Lanny)
German, meaning 'precious'.

Lang
Norse, meaning 'tall man'.

Langley
English, meaning 'long meadow'.

Langundo
Native American, meaning 'peaceful man'.

Lanh
Vietnamese, meaning 'quick-witted'.

Lann
Celtic, meaning 'man of the sword'.

Larkin
Gaelic, meaning 'rough' or 'fierce'.

Laron
French, meaning 'thief'.

Larry
French, meaning 'man from Laurentum'.

Lars
Scandinavian variant of Lawrence, meaning 'man from Laurentum'.

Lasse
Finnish, meaning 'girl'. (Still, ironically, a boy's name).

Laszlo
Hungarian, meaning 'glorious rule'.

Lathyn
Latin, meaning 'fighter'.

Latif
Arabic, meaning 'gentle'.

Laurel
Latin, meaning 'bay'.

Laurent
French, from Lawrence, meaning 'man from Laurentum'.

Lawrence
Latin, meaning 'man from Laurentum'.

Lazarus
Hebrew, meaning 'God is my help'.

Leavitt
English, meaning 'a baker'.

Leandro
Latin, meaning 'lion man'.

Lear
German, meaning 'of the meadow'.

Lee
(alt. Leigh)
Old English, meaning 'meadow' or 'valley'.

Lei
Chinese, meaning 'thunder'.

Leib
German, meaning 'love'.

Leif
Scandinavian, meaning 'heir'.

Leighton
English, meaning 'a meadow near a town'.

Leith
From the name of a place in Scotland.

Leland
English, meaning 'meadow land'.

Lema
African, meaning 'cultivated one'.

Lemuel
Hebrew, meaning 'belongs to God'.

Len
Native American, meaning 'flute player'.

Lennon
English, meaning 'son of love'.

Lennox
(alt. Lenny)
Gaelic, meaning 'with many Elm trees'.

Lenton
American, meaning 'pious'.

Leo
Latin, meaning 'lion'.

Leolin
(alt. Leolyn)
Polynesian, meaning 'alert' or 'watchful'.

Leon
Latin, meaning 'lion'.

Leonard
Old German, meaning 'lion strength'.

Leopold
German, meaning 'brave people'.

Leroux
French, meaning 'red haired man'.

Leroy
French, meaning 'king'.

Lesharo
Native American, meaning 'chief'.

Lesley
(alt. Les)
Scottish, meaning 'holly garden'.

Lester
English, meaning 'from Leicester'.

Levant
French, meaning 'he who rises above'.

Lewis
French, meaning 'renowned fighter'.

Lex
English alternative of Alexander, meaning 'defending men'.

Leyati
Native American, meaning 'smooth' or 'round'.

Li
Chinese, meaning 'possessing great strength'.

Liam
German, meaning 'helmet'.

Lincoln
English, meaning 'lake colony'.

Lindsay
Scottish, meaning 'linden tree'.

Linus
Latin, meaning 'lion'.

Lionel
English, meaning 'lion'.

Llewellyn
Welsh, meaning 'like a lion'.

Lloyd
Welsh, meaning 'grey-haired and sacred'.

Lochart
English, meaning 'like a forest deer'.

Logan
Gaelic, meaning 'hollow'.

Lonnie
English, meaning 'lion strength'.

Lorcan
Gaelic, meaning 'little fierce one'.

Louis
(alt. Lou, Louie, Luigi. Luis)
German, meaning 'famous warrior'.

Lowman
English, meaning 'a man who is dearly loved'.

Lucas
(alt. Lukas)
English, meaning 'man from Lucania'.

Lucian
(alt. Lucio)
Latin, meaning 'light'.

Ludwig
German, meaning 'famous fighter'.

Ludlow
English, meaning 'ruler of the hill'.

Luke
(alt. Luc, Luka)
Latin, meaning 'from Lucanus' (in Southern Italy).

Luong
Vietnamese, meaning 'of the bamboo land'.

Lupe
Latin, meaning 'wolf'.

Luther
German, meaning 'soldier of the people'.

Ly
Vietnamese, meaning 'resonable man'.

Lyle
French, meaning 'the island'.

Lyn
(alt. Lyndon)
Spanish, meaning 'pretty'.

Lysander
Greek, meaning 'liberator'.
A character in Shakespeare's play *A Midsummer Night's Dream*.

M Boys' names

Maahes
Egyptian, meaning 'lion'.

Mabon
(alt. Maban, Maben, Mabin)
Welsh, meaning 'our son'.

Mac
(alt. Mack, Mackie)
Scottish, meaning 'son of'.

Macallister
(alt. MacAdam, McAdam,
MacAdhamh)
Gaelic, meaning 'Alistair's son'.

Macario
(alt. Macareo, Makario, Makareo)
Spanish, meaning 'filled with
happiness'.

Macaulay
Scottish, meaning 'son of the
phantom'.

Macbeth
(alt. Macbethe, McBeth, McBethe)
Gaelic, meaning 'son of
Beth'. Often associated with
Shakespeare's play of the same
name.

Maccabee
Hebrew, meaning 'hammer'.

Mace
English, meaning 'heavy staff' or
'club'.

Machar
(alt. Machair, Machaire)
Scottish, meaning 'plain'.

Machau
Hebrew, meaning 'gift from God'.

Machk
Native American, meaning 'like
a bear'.

Mackay
Gaelic, meaning 'son of fire'.

Mackenzie
Scottish, meaning 'the fair one'.

Mackland
Scottish, meaning 'land of Mac'.

Macon
French origin, name of towns in
France and Georgia.

Macsen
Scottish, meaning 'son of Mac'.

Madan
Indian, meaning 'god of love'.

Madden
Irish, meaning 'descendant of the
hound'.

Maddox
English, meaning 'good' or 'generous'.

Madigan
Irish, meaning 'little dog'.

Madison
(alt. Madsen)
Irish, meaning 'son of Madden'.

Madoc
(alt. Maddoc, Maddock)
Welsh alternative of Maddox, meaning 'good' or 'generous'.

Mads
Shortened form of Madden, meaning 'descendant of the hound'.

Magnar
(alt. Magnarr, Magnor, Magnorr)
Polish, meaning 'strong warrior'.

Magnus
(alt. Manus)
Latin, meaning 'great'.

Maguire
Gaelic, meaning 'son of the beige one'.

Mahabala
Indian, meaning 'great strength'.

Mahan
(alt. Mahen, Maehan, Mayhan)
American, meaning 'cowboy'.

Mahesh
Hindi, meaning 'great ruler'.

Mahir
Arabic, meaning 'skilful'.

Mahlon
Hebrew, meaning 'sickness'.

Mahmoud
Arabic, meaning 'praiseworthy'.

Mahoney
Irish, meaning 'bear'.

Maik
English, meaning 'like God'.

Maimun
Arabic, meaning 'lucky'.

Maj
Scandinavian, meaning 'sea of bitterness'.

Majid
Arabic, meaning 'illustrious'.

Major
English, from the word 'major'.

Makal
From Michael, meaning 'close to God'.

Makani
Hawaiian, meaning 'wind'.

Makis
Hebrew, meaning 'gift from God'.

Mako
Hebrew, meaning 'God is with us'.

Malachi
(alt. Malachy)
Irish, meaning 'messenger of God'.

Malcolm
English, meaning 'Columba's servant'.

Mali
Arabic, meaning 'full and rich'.

Mandla
African, meaning 'strength'.

Menelin
Persian, meaning 'the prince of princes'.

Manfred
Old German, meaning 'man of peace'.

Manish
English, meaning 'manly'.

Manley
English, meaning 'manly and brave'.

Mannix
Gaelic, meaning 'little monk'.

Manoi
(alt. Manos)
Japanese, meaning 'love springing from intellect'.

Manuel
Hebrew, meaning 'God is with us'.

Manzi
Italian, meaning 'steer'.

Marc
(alt. Marco, Marcos, Marcus)
French, meaning 'from the god Mars'.

Marcel
(alt. Marcelino, Marcello)
French, meaning 'little warrior'.

Marek
Polish variant of Mark, meaning 'from the god Mars'.

Mariano
Latin, meaning 'from the god Mars'.

Marin
Latin, meaning 'of the sea'.

Mario
(alt. Marius)
Latin, meaning 'manly'.

Mark
English, meaning 'from the god Mars'.

Markku
Scandinavian, meaning 'rebellious'.

Marley
(alt. Marlin)
Old English, meaning 'meadow near the lake'.

Marlon
English, meaning 'like a little hawk'. Famous as the forename of Marlon Brando.

Marlow
(alt. Marlo, Marloe, Marlowe)
English, meaning 'driftwood'.

Marnin
Hebrew, meaning 'causing joy'.

Maro
Japanese, meaning 'myself'.

Marshall
Old French, meaning 'caretaker of horses'.

Martin
Latin, meaning 'dedicated to Mars'.

Marty
Shortened form of Martin, meaning 'dedicated to Mars'.

Marvel
English, from the word 'marvel'.

Marvin
Welsh, meaning 'sea friend'.

Marwan
Arabic, meaning 'flint stone'.

Masih
Persian, meaning 'blessed one'.

Maso
Italian, meaning 'twin'.

Mason
English, from the word mason.

Massika
Native American, meaning 'turtle'.

Massimo
Italian, meaning 'greatest'.

Mathias
(alt. Matthias)
Hebrew, meaning 'gift of God'.

Mathieu
French form of Matthew, meaning 'gift of God'.

Matthew
Hebrew, meaning 'gift of the Lord'.

Maurice
(alt. Mauricio)
Latin, meaning 'dark skinned' or 'Moorish'.

Maverick
American origin, meaning 'non-conformist leader'.

Max
(alt. Maxie, Maxim)
Latin, meaning 'greatest'.

Maximillian
Latin, meaning 'greatest'.

Maximino
Latin, meaning 'little Max'.

Maxwell
Latin, meaning 'Maccus' stream'.

Maynard
Old German, meaning 'brave'.

McArthur
Scottish, meaning 'son of Arthur'.

McCoy
Scottish, meaning 'son of Coy'.

Mearl
English, meaning 'my earl'.

Mederic
French, meaning 'doctor'.

Mekhi
African, meaning 'who is God?'.

Mel
Gaelic, meaning 'smooth brow'.

Melbourne
From the city in Australia.

Melchior
Persian, meaning 'king of the city'.

Melton
English, meaning 'town of Mel'.

Melva
Hawaiian, meaning 'plumeria'.

Melville
Scottish, meaning 'town of Mel'.

Melvin
(alt. Melvyn)
English, meaning 'smooth brow'.

Memphis
Greek, meaning 'established and beautiful'. Also the name of a city in the USA.

Menawa
Native American, meaning 'great warrior'.

Mendel
German, meaning 'little man'.

Mercer
English, from the word 'mercer'.

Merl
French, meaning 'blackbird'.

Merlin
Welsh, meaning 'sea fortress'.

Merrick
Welsh, meaning 'Moorish'.

Merrill
Gaelic, meaning 'shining sea'.

Merritt
English, from the word 'merit'.

Merton
Old English, meaning 'town by the lake'.

Methuselah
Hebrew, meaning 'he was sent'. The longest living man in the Bible.

Meyer
Hebrew, meaning 'bright farmer'.

Mhina
African, meaning 'delightful'.

Miach
Gaelic, meaning 'medic'.

Michael
Hebrew, meaning 'resembles God'. One of the Archangels.

Michalis
Greek form of Michael, meaning 'resembles God'.

Michel
French form of Michael, meaning 'resembles God'.

Michelangelo
Italian, meaning 'Michael's angel'. Name of the famous painter.

Michele
Italian form of Michael, meaning 'resembles God'.

Michio
Japanese, meaning 'a man with the strength of three thousand men'.

Mickey
Variant of Michael meaning 'resembles God'.

Mieko
Japanese, meaning 'bright man'.

Miguel
Spanish form of Michael meaning 'resembles God'.

Mihir
Indian, meaning 'of the sun'.

Mikasi
Native American, meaning 'like a coyote'.

Mike
Shortened form of Michael meaning 'resembles God'.

Miklos
Greek form of Michael meaning 'resembles God'.

Milan
From the name of the Italian city.

Miles
(alt. Milo, Milos, Myles)
English, from the word 'miles'.

Milton
English, meaning 'Miller's town'. Also the name of the poet.

Miner
(alt. minar, Minir, Minor)
Latin, meaning 'one who works in a mine'.

Minh
Vietnamese, meaning 'intelligent man'.

Mirek
(alt. Mirec, Mireck, Myrek)
Czech, meaning 'peaceful ruler'.

Miro
Slavic, meaning 'peace'.

Misha
Russian, meaning 'who is like God'.

Mitch
Shortened form of Mitchell, meaning 'who is like God'.

Mitchell
English, meaning 'who is like God'.

Modesto
Italian, meaning 'modest'.

Modig
Anglo-Saxon, meaning 'courageous'.

Moe
Hebrew, meaning 'God's helmet'.

Mohamed
(alt. Mohammad, Mohammed, Mohamet)
Arabic, meaning 'praiseworthy'.

Monroe
Gaelic, meaning 'mouth of the river Rotha'.

Monserrate
Latin, meaning 'jagged mountain'.

Montague
French, meaning 'pointed hill'.

Montana
Latin, meaning 'mountain'. Also a state in the USA.

Monte
Italian, meaning 'mountain'.

Montgomery
Variant of Montague, meaning 'pointed hill'.

Monty
Shortened form of Montague, meaning 'pointed hill'.

Moody
English, from the word 'moody'.

Moran
(alt. Morane, Moraine, Morayn)
Irish, meaning 'great man'.

Mordecai
Hebrew, meaning 'little man'.

Morgan
Welsh, meaning 'circling sea'.

Moriarty
(alt. Moriarti, Moriartey, Moriatie)
Irish, meaning 'a sea warrior'.

Moritz
Latin, meaning 'dark skinned and Moorish'.

Morpheus
Greek, meaning 'shape'.

Morris
Welsh, meaning 'dark skinned and Moorish'.

Morrison
English, meaning 'son of Morris'.

Mortimer
French, meaning 'dead sea'.

Morton
Old English, meaning 'moor town'.

Moses
(alt. Moshe, Moshon)
Hebrew, meaning 'saviour'. In the Bible Moses receives the Ten Commandments from God.

Moss
English, from the word 'moss'.

Moyo
African, meaning 'heart'.

Muir
Gaelic, meaning 'of the moor'.

Mungo
Gaelic, meaning 'most dear'.

Murdock
Scottish, meaning 'one who comes from the sea'.

Murfain
American, meaning 'one with warrior spirit'.

Murl
From French, meaning 'blackbird'.

Murphy
Irish, meaning 'sea warrior'.

Murray
Gaelic, meaning 'Lord and master'.

Mustafa
Arabic, meaning 'chosen'.

Mwinyi
(alt. Mwinyie, Mwinyey, Mwinyee)
African, meaning 'lord' or 'master'.

Mwita
African, meaning 'he who calls'.

Myron
Greek, meaning 'myrrh'.

Myrzon
American, meaning 'humorous one'.

N Boys' names

Naal
Gaelic, meaning 'notable birth'.

Naalnish
(alt. nalnish, Naalnysh, Nalnysh)
Native American, meaning
'hardworker'.

Naaman
Hebrew, meaning 'pleasant man'.

Naaz
Indian, meaning 'proud'.

Nabha
Indian, meaning 'from the sky'.

Nabil
Arabic, meaning 'highborn'.

Nachshon
Hebrew, meaning 'adventurous'.

Nada
Arabic, meaning 'covered with
dew'.

Nagel
German, meaning 'maker of
nails'.

Nahele
Native American, meaning 'from
the forest'.

Naif
Arabic, meaning 'excess'.

Nairn
Scottish, meaning 'alder-tree
river'.

Najee
Arabic, meaning 'dear
companion'.

Nakia
Arabic, meaning 'pure'.

Nakos
American, meaning 'sage'.

Nakul
Indian, meaning 'mongoose'.

Nalin
Indian, meaning 'lotus flower'.

Nalo
African, meaning 'lovable'.

Nam
Vietnamese, meaning 'south' or
'manly'.

Namid
(alt. Nameed, Namied, Nasmeid)
Native American, meaning star
dancer'.

Nanne
Scandinavian, meaning 'grace'.

Nantai
Native American, meaning
'chief'.

Naoko
Japanese, meaning 'honest'.

Naor
Hebrew, meaning 'enlightened'.

Naphtali
Hebrew, meaning 'wrestling'.

Napier
Spanish, meaning 'from the new city'.

Napoleon
Italian origin, meaning 'man from Naples'. Name of the French general who became Emperor of France.

Narciso
Latin, from the myth of Narcissus, famous for falling in love with his own reflection.

Nash
English, meaning 'at the ash tree'.

Nasir
Arabic, meaning 'helper'.

Nate
Hebrew, meaning 'God has given'.

Nathan
(alt. Nathaniel)
Hebrew, meaning 'God has given'.

Naval
Indian, meaning 'wonder'.

Naveen
Indian, meaning 'new'.

Nazih
(alt. Nazeeh, Nazeem, Nazeer)
Arabic, meaning 'pure'.

Neal
Irish, meaning 'champion'.

Ned
Nickname for Edward, meaning 'wealthy guard'.

Neel
Hindi, meaning 'sapphire'.

Neftali
Hebrew, meaning 'struggling'.

Nehemiah
Hebrew, meaning 'comforter'.

Neil
(alt. Niall)
Irish, meaning 'champion'.

Nelson
Variant of Neil, meaning 'champion'.

Neilson
Irish, meaning 'son of Neil'.

Nemo
Latin, meaning 'nobody'.

Nen
Egyptian, meaning 'ancient water'.

Neo
Latin, meaning 'new'.

Nephi
Greek, meaning 'cloud'.

Nerian
(alt. Nerien, Neriun)
Anglo-Saxon, meaning 'protector'.

Neron
Spanish, meaning 'strong' or 'firm'.

Nesbit
English, meaning 'dweller near where the road bends'.

Nessim
Arabic, meaning 'breeze'.

Nestor
Greek, meaning 'traveller'.

Neville
Old French, meaning 'new village'.

Newland
(alt. Newlande, Neuland, Neulande)
English, meaning 'from new land'.

Newton
English, meaning 'new town'.

Niall
(alt. Nial)
Irish, meaning 'champion'.

Nibal
Arabic, meaning 'arrows'.

Nicholas
(alt. Niklas)
Greek, meaning 'victorious'.

Nick
(alt. Niko, Nikos)
Shortened form of Nicholas, meaning 'victorious'.

Nico
Variant of Nicholas, meaning 'victorious'.

Nicomedes
Greek, meaning 'to contemplate victory'.

Nida
Native American, meaning 'giant'.

Nigel
Gaelic, meaning 'champion'.

Nikhil
Hindi, meaning 'whole' or 'entire'.

Nikita
Greek, meaning 'unconquered'.

Nikolai
Russian variant of Nicholas, meaning 'victorious'.

Nimrod
Hebrew, meaning 'we will rebel'.

Ninian
Gaelic, associated with the 5th-century saint of the same name.

Nissim
Hebrew, meaning 'wonderful things'.

Noah
Hebrew, meaning 'peaceful'.

Noda
Hebrew, meaning 'renowned'.

Noel
French, meaning 'Christmas'.

Nolan
Gaelic, meaning 'champion'.

Noor
Arabic, meaning 'light'.

Norbert
Old German, meaning 'Northern brightness'.

Nori
Japanese, meaning 'belief'.

Norman
Old German, meaning 'Northerner'.

Normand
French, meaning 'from Normandy'.

Norris
Old French, meaning 'Northerner'.

Norton
English, meaning 'Northern town'.

Norval
French, meaning 'Northern town'.

Norwood
English, meaning 'Northern forest'.

Notin
Native American, meaning 'wind'.

Nova
Latin, meaning 'new'.

Novak
German, meaning 'newcomer'.

Nowles
English, meaning 'from the forest cove'.

Nripesh
Indian, meaning 'king of all kings'.

Nuha
Arabic, meaning 'brave man'.

Nuncio
Spanish, meaning 'messenger'.

Nuno
Latin, meaning 'ninth'.

Nunzio
Italian, meaning 'messenger'.

Nuru
Swahili, meaning 'light'.

Nyack
African, meaning 'one who won't give up'.

Nye
Welsh, meaning 'golden'.

Nyoka
African, meaning 'like a snake'.

Footballers

David (Beckham)
Frank (Lampard)
Gary (Lineker)
Geoff (Hurst)
Gordon (Banks)
Kenny (Dalglish)
Kevin (Keegan)
Ryan (Giggs)
Tony (Adams)
Wayne (Rooney)

O

Boys' names

Oakley
English, meaning 'from the oak meadow'.

Oba
African, meaning 'king'.

Obadiah
Biblical, meaning 'God's worker'.

Obama
African, meaning 'crooked'. Made famous by the American President Barack Obama.

Obed
Hebrew, meaning 'servant of God'.

Oberon
Old German, meaning 'royal bear'.

Obert
French, meaning 'noble'.

Obi
Nigerian, meaning 'one with a big heart'.

Obiajulu
African, meaning 'one who has been consoled'.

Obie
Shortened form of Oberon, meaning 'royal bear'.

Occhave
Indian, meaning 'festive occasion'.

Ocheckka
Native American, meaning 'four legs'.

Octave
(alt. Octavian, Octavio)
Latin, meaning 'eight'.

Octavian
Latin, meaning 'eighth'.

Oda
(alt. Odell, Odie, Odis)
Hebrew, meaning 'praise God'.

Odakota
Native American, meaning 'friendly one'.

Ode
Greek, meaning 'a lyrical poem'.

Oded
Hebrew, meaning 'to encourage'.

Odell
English, meaning 'of the wood hill'.

O

Odo
English, meaning 'wealthy'.

Oengu
Irish, meaning 'vigorous one'.

Offa
Anglo-Saxon, meaning 'king'.

Ofir
(alt. Ofeer, Ofyr, ofier)
Hebrew, meaning 'golden son'.

Og
Aramaic, meaning 'king'.

Ogano
Japanese, meaning 'wise'.

Ogden
Old English, meaning 'oak valley'.

Ogen
Hebrew, meaning 'anchor'.

Oghe
Irish, meaning 'rider of horses'.

Ogun
Japanese, meaning 'undaunted'.

Ohanko
Native American, meaning 'reckless'.

Ohanzee
Native American, meaning 'shadow'.

Oidhche
(alt. Oidhche, Oidhchi, Oidhchi)
Scottish, meaning 'born at night'.

Oisin
(alt. Ossian, Osheen)
From the Irish poet meaning 'young deer'.

Oistin
Irish, meaning 'venerable'.

Ojas
Sanskrit, meaning 'strong'.

Oke
Hawaiian, meaning 'one who loves deer'.

Ola
Norse, meaning 'precious'.

Olaf
(alt. Olan)
Old Norse, meaning 'ancestor'.

Olamida
African, meaning 'our son is our prosperity'.

Oldrich
Czech, meaning 'strong and healthy leader'.

Oleander
Hawaiian, meaning 'joyous'.

Oleg
(alt. Olen)
Russian, meaning 'holy'.

Olin
Russian, meaning 'rock'.

Olis
German, meaning 'powerful'.

Oliver
Latin, meaning 'olive tree'.

Olivier
French form of Oliver, meaning 'olive tree'.

Ollie
Shortened form of Oliver, meaning 'olive tree'.

Olney
English, meaning 'of the loner's field'.

Omar
(alt. Omari, Omarion)
Arabic, meaning 'speaker'.

Omri
(alt. Omrey, Omry)
Hebrew, meaning 'Jehovah's servant'.

Onan
Turkish, meaning 'wealthy man'.

Ondrej
Czech, meaning 'manly'.

Ora
Latin, meaning 'hour'.

Oran
(alt. Oren, Orrin)
Gaelic, meaning 'light and pale'.

Orange
English, from the word 'orange'.

Orel
Latin, meaning 'golden one'.

Orev
Hebrew, meaning 'raven'.

Orion
From the Greek hunter.

Orlando
(alt. Orlo)
Old German, meaning 'old land'.
Name of a city in the USA.

Orpheus
Greek, meaning 'beautiful voice'.

Orrick
English, meaning 'sword ruler'.

Orson
Latin, meaning 'bear'.

Orth
English, meaning 'honest one'.

Orville
Old French, meaning 'gold town'.

Osaka
From the Japanese city.

Osbert
English, meaning 'brilliantly divine'.

Osborne
Norse, meaning 'bear god'.

Oscar
Old English, meaning 'spear of the Gods'.

Oscard
Greek, meaning 'warrior'.

Oshea
Hebrew, meaning 'kind spirit'.

Osher
Hebrew, meaning 'happiness'.

Osias
Hebrew, meaning 'salvation'.

O

Famous male guitarists

Brian (May)
Chuck (Berry)
Eddie (Van Halen)
Eric (Clapton)
Frank (Zappa)
George (Harrison)
Matt (Bellamy)
Jeff (Beck)
Jimi /Jimmy (Hendrix/Page)
Keith (Richards)

Osman
Arabic, meaning 'tender youth'.

Osten
Latin, meaning 'maginificent one'.

Oswald
German, meaning 'God's power'.

Oswin
English, meaning 'friend of God'.

Otha
(alt. Otho)
German, meaning 'wealth'.

Othello
From the Shakespearean character.

Otieno
African, meaning 'born during the night'.

Otis
German, meaning 'wealth'.

Otten
English, meaning 'otter-like'.

Otto
Italian, meaning 'eight'.

Otu
Native American, meaning 'industrious man'.

Ouray
Native American, meaning 'arrow'.

Oved
Hebrew, meaning 'worker'.

Ovid
Latin, meaning 'sheep'.

Owain
Welsh, meaning 'youth'.

Owen
Welsh, meaning 'well born and noble'.

Oxton
English, meaning 'from the ox town'.

Oysten
Norse, meaning 'full of happiness'.

Oz
Hebrew, meaning 'strength'.

P

Boys' names

Pablo
Spanish, meaning 'little'.

Paciano
Spanish, meaning 'peaceful'.

Packard
(alt. Packer, Packert)
English, meaning 'bundle'.

Paco
Native American, meaning 'eagle' and also a Spanish alternative of Francisco.

Paden
English, meaning 'path on a hill'.

Padma
Indian, meaning 'lotus'.

Padraig
Irish, meaning 'noble'.

Pagan
English, meaning 'heathen'.

Pagiel
Hebrew, meaning 'God allots'.

Paine
(alt. Pain, Payne)
Latin, meaning 'villager'.

Paladin
(alt. Paladine, Palatin, Palladin)
French, meaning 'from the palace'. A title given to Charlemagne's 12 best knights.

Paladio
(alt. Palladius)
Spanish, meaning 'follower of Pallas'.

Palani
Hawaiian, alternative of Frank meaning 'free landowner'.

Palash
Hindi, meaning 'flowery tree'.

Palben
Basque, meaning 'blond'.

Palmer
(alt. Pallmer, Palmar, Parlmerston)
English, meaning 'pilgrim'.

Palomo
Spanish, meaning 'dove'.

Palti
(alt. Paltiel, Platya, Platyahu)
Hebrew, meaning 'God frees'.

Pan
Greek, meaning 'all' and Hindi, meaning 'feather'.

Panas
Russian, meaning 'immortal'.

Panos
Greek, meaning 'all holy'.

Paolo
Italian, meaning 'little'.

Paramesh
Hindi, meaning 'the greatest'.
Another name for the god Shiva.

Paresh
Indian, meaning 'supreme
standard'.

Paris
(alt. Paras, Parris, Parys)
From the city in France. Also
the Trojan prince in Homer's
Iliad and Juliet's suitor in
Shakespeare's *Romeo and Juliet*.

Parker
(alt. Park, Parke, Parkes)
English, meaning 'park-keeper'.

Parkin
(alt. Parken)
English, meaning 'little Peter'.

Parr
English, meaning 'enclosure'.

Parry
Welsh, meaning 'son of Harry'.

Parton
English, meaning 'pear orchard'.

Parvaiz
(alt. Parvez, Parviz, Parwiz)
Persian, meaning 'lucky'.

Pascal
Latin, meaning 'Easter child'.

Pasha
Russian, alternative of Pavel
meaning 'small'.

Pat
Shortened form of Patrick,
meaning 'noble'.

Patrice
Variant of Patrick, meaning
'noble'.

Patrick
Irish, meaning 'noble'.

Patrin
(alt. Pattin)
Gypsy, meaning 'leaf trail'.

Patten
English, meaning 'noble'.

Patterson
(alt. Paterson, Patteson, Pattison)
English, meaning 'Petter's son'.

Patton
(alt. Paden, Paten, Patten)
English, meaning 'fighters town'.

Paul
Biblical, meaning 'small'.

Pavel
Latin, meaning 'small'.

Pax
Latin, meaning 'peace'.

Paxton
English, meaning 'town of peace'.

Payne
Latin, meaning 'peasant'.

Payton
Latin, meaning 'peasant's town'.

Paz
(alt. Pazen)
Hebrew, meaning 'golden'.

Pearce
(alt. Pierce, Piers)
English, meaning 'Piers' son'.

Pedro
Spanish form of Peter, meaning 'rock'.

Pelagios
(alt. Pelagius, Pelayo)
Greek, meaning 'from the sea'.

Pelle
Scandinavian, alternative of Peter.

Pello
(alt. Peru, Piarres)
Greek, meaning 'stone'.

Penn
English, meaning 'hill'.

Penrod
(alt. Pennrod, Rod)
German, meaning 'famed commander'.

Percival
French, meaning 'pierce the valley'.

Percy
Shortened form of Percival, meaning 'pierce the valley'.

Perez
Hebrew, meaning 'breach'.

Pericles
Greek, meaning 'far-famed'.

Perrin
Greek, meaning 'rock'.

Perry
English, meaning 'rock'.

Perseus
Greek, a famous hero and the son of Zeus in mythology.

Pervis
English, meaning 'purveyor'.

Pesah
(alt. Pesach, Pessach)
Hebrew, meaning 'spared'.

Pete
Shortened form of Peter, meaning 'rock'.

Peter
English, meaning 'rock'.

Petros
Spanish form of Peter, meaning 'rock'.

Peyton
Old English, meaning 'fighting man's estate'.

Phelan
(alt. Felan, Felin, Palin)
Irish, meaning 'wolf'.

Phelps
English, meaning 'Philip's son'.

Phil
Shortened form of Phillip, meaning 'lover of horses'.

Philemon
Greek, meaning 'affectionate'.

Phillip
Greek, meaning 'lover of horses'.

Philo
Greek, meaning 'love'.

Phineas
(alt. Pinchas)
Hebrew, meaning 'oracle'.

P

Phoebus
(alt. Phoibos)
Greek, meaning 'shining'.
Another name for the Greek sun
god Apollo.

Phoenix
Greek, meaning 'dark red'.

Pierce
(alt. Pearce, Pears, Pearson)
English, meaning 'Piers' son'.
Made famous by the actor Pierce
Brosnan.

Pierre
French form of Peter, meaning
'stone'.

Piers
Greek form of Peter, meaning
'rock'.

Pierson
Variant of Peirce, meaning 'son
of Piers'.

Pili
African, meaning 'second born'.

Pinchas
(alt. Phineas, Pincus, Pinkus)
Hebrew, meaning 'oracle'.

Pip
Greek, meaning 'lover of horses'.

Piran
(alt. Peran, Pieran)
Irish, meaning 'prayer'.

Placido
Latin, meaning 'placid'.

Plato
Greek, meaning 'broad-shouldered'.
Borne by one of the most famous
philosophers of the western world.

Po
Italian, river name.

Pochanaw
Native American, meaning 'buffalo
hump'.

Poe
English, meaning 'peacock'.

Pollux
(alt. Pollock)
Greek, meaning 'crown'.

Pomeroy
(alt. Pommeray, Pommeroy)
French, meaning 'orchard of
apples'.

Pons
(alt. Pontius, Ponthos, Ponthus)
Latin, meaning 'bridge'.

Porfirio
(alt. Porphirios, Prophyrios)
Greek, meaning 'purple' and English,
meaning 'porphyry'.

Porter
English, meaning 'gatekeeper' and
French, meaning 'to carry'.

Porthos
French, from the character name
in *The Three Musketeers* by
Alexandre Dumas.

Pouria
Persian, meaning 'hero'.

Powa
Native American, meaning 'wealthy'.

Powhatan
Native American, meaning 'powwow hill'. Also the name of Pocahontas' father, a powerful chieftain.

Pradeep
Hindi, meaning 'light'.

Pranav
Hindi, meaning 'spiritual leader'.

Pranet
Indian, meaning 'leader'.

Pravar
Indian, meaning 'chief'.

Pravat
Thai, meaning 'history'.

Prem
Indian, meaning 'love'.

Presley
Old English, meaning 'priest's meadow'.

Prescott
(alt. Prescot, Prestcot, Prestcott)
Old English, meaning 'the cottage of the priest'.

Preston
Old English, meaning 'priest's town'.

Prewitt
(alt. Prewett, Prewitt, Pruitt)
French, meaning 'little brave one'.

Priel
Hebrew, meaning 'fruit of God'.

Price
(alt. Brice, Bryce, Pryce)
French, meaning 'prize'.

Primo
Italian, meaning 'first'.

Primus
Latin, meaning 'first'.

Prince
English, from the word 'prince'.

Procopio
(alt. Procopius, Prokopios)
Greek, meaning 'progressive'.

Proctor
(alt. Prockter, Procter)
Latin, meaning 'steward'.

Prospero
Latin, meaning 'prosperous'.

Prokhor
Russian, meaning 'one who leads the singers'.

Prudencio
(alt. Prudentius)
Latin, meaning 'caution'.

Pryor
English, meaning 'first'.

Ptolemy
Greek, meaning 'aggressive' or 'warlike'.

Puma
Latin, meaning 'mountain lion'.

Purvis
(alt. Purves, Purviss)
French, meaning 'purveyor'.

Pytor
Russian, meaning 'rock'.

Q Boys' names

Qadar
(alt. Kadar)
Arabic, meaning 'destination'.

Qadim
Arabic, meaning 'ancient'.

Qadir
Arabic, meaning 'powerful'.

Qaiser
(alt. Qeyser)
Arabic, meaning 'king'.

Qaletaqa
Native American, meaning
'guardian'.

Qamar
(alt. Qamarr, Quamar, Quamarr)
Arabic, meaning 'born under the
moon'.

Qasim
(alt. Qasym, Qaseem, Qasiem)
Arabic, meaning 'charitable'.

Qays
(alt. Qais, Qayse, Qaise)
Arabic, meaning 'firm'.

Qiao
Chinese, meaning 'handsome'.

Qimat
(alt. Qymat)
Hindi, meaning 'highly valued'.

Qing
(alt. Qyng)
Chinese, meaning 'deep water'.

Qochata
(alt. Qochatah, Qochatta, Qochattah)
Native American, meaning
'white-skinned man'.

Qssim
Arabic, meaning 'divides'.

Quaashie
(alt. Quashie, Quashi, Quashy)
American, meaning 'ambitious'.

Quabil
Arabic, meaning 'able'.

Quacey
(alt. Quacy, Quaci, Quacie)
Scottish, meaning 'moonlight'.

Quaddus
African-American, meaning
'bright'.

Quade
Gaelic, from a Scottish clan
name, McQuade.

Quadim
Arabic, meaning 'able'.

Quadir
Arabic, meaning 'powerful'.

Names of gods

Anubis (Death: Egyptian)
Apollo (Sun: Roman)
Brahma (Creation: Indian)
Eros (Love: Greek)
Hypnos (Sleep: Greek)
Mars (War: Roman)
Neptune (Sea: Roman)
Ra (Sun: Egyptian)
Shiva (Destruction: Indian)
Vishnu (Preservation: Indian)

Quahawn
(alt. Kwashan, Kwashaun, Kwashawn)
African-American, meaning
'tenacious'.

Quaid
Irish, meaning 'fourth'.

Quain
French, meaning 'intelligent'.

Quan
Vietnamese, meaning 'soldier'.

Quanah
(alt. Quana, Quanna, Quannah)
Native American, meaning
'pleasant scent'.

Quang
Vietnamese, meaning 'clear-
headed'.

Quannell
(alt. Kwan, Kwanell, Kwanelle)
African-American, meaning
'strong-minded'.

Quant
(alt. Quante, Quantai, Quantay)
Latin, meaning 'son's worth'.

Quaronne
(alt. Quarone, Quaron, Quaronn)
American, meaning 'haughty'.

Quarrie
(alt. Quarri, Quarry, Quarrey)
Scottish, meaning 'proud'.

Quaronne
(alt. Kwarohn, Kwaronne, Quaronn)
African-American, meaning
'haughty'.

Quashawn
(alt. Quashaun, Quasean, Quashon)
American, meaning 'tenacious'.

Quanhtli
Aztec, meaning 'like an eagle'.

Quay
(alt. Quaye, Que)
French, meaning 'wharf'.

Qubilah
(alt. Qubila, Qubeelah, Qubeela)
Arabic, meaning 'agreeable'.

Qudamah
(alt. Qudama)
Arabic, meaning 'corageous'.

Qued
Native American, meaning
'wearer of a decorated robe'.

Quelatikan
(alt. Quelatykan, Quelatican,
Quelatycan)
Native American, meaning
'possessor of a blue horn'.

Quemby
Norse, meaning 'from the
woman's estate'.

Q

Spelling options

F vs PH (Josef or Joseph)
I vs Y (Henri or Henry)
J vs G (Jorge or George)
N vs HN (Jon or John)
QUE vs CK (Frederique or
Frederick)
T vs TH (Antony or Anthony)

Quenby
English, meaning 'giving man'.

Quennel
(alt. Quennell)
French, meaning 'little oak'.

Queran
(alt. Queron, Queren, Querin)
Irish, meaning 'a man who is dark
and handsome'.

Quentin
(alt. Quinten, Quintin, Quinton)
Latin, meaning 'fifth'.

Quico
(alt. Quiko, Quicko, Quyco)
Spanish, meaning 'beloved
friend'.

Quiessencia
(alt. Quiess)
Spanish, meaning 'essential'.

Quigley
(alt. Quiglee, Quiggly, Quiggy)
Irish, meaning 'loving'.

Quillan
Gaelic, meaning 'sword'.

Quiller
(alt. Quillar, Quillor, Quillir)
English, meaning 'scriber'.

Quilliam
(alt. Quilhelm, Quilhelmus, Quilliams)
Gaelic, alternative of William,
meaning 'strong protector' or
'strong willed warrior'.

Quillon
Gaelic, meaning 'club'.

Quimby
Norse, meaning 'from the lady's
domain'.

Quince
Latin, the name of a fruit that is
similar to an apple.

Quincy
Old French, meaning 'estate of
the fifth son'.

Quinlan
Gaelic, meaning 'fit, shapely and
strong'.

Quinn
Gaelic, meaning 'counsel'.

Quintas
Spanish, meaning 'small domain'.

Quintavius
(alt. Quint)
African-American, meaning 'fifth
child'.

Quinto
(alt. Kito)
Spanish, meaning 'lively'.

Quinton
(alt. Quinntan, Quinnten, Quinntin)
English, meaning 'queen's
community'.

Quintrell
(alt. Quintrel, Quintrelle, Quyntrell)
English, meaning 'dashing man'.

Quitrel
(alt. Kwotrel, Quoitrelle)
African-American, meaning
'equalizer'.

Quiqui
(alt. Kaka, Keke)
Spanish, meaning 'friend'.

Quirin
(alt. Quiryn, Quiran, Quiren)
American, meaning 'magical'.

Quirinal
(alt. Quirino)
Roman, mythological son of Mars.

Quirinus
(alt. Quirinos, Quirynus, Quirynos)
Latin, meaning 'spear wielder'.

Quinto
(alt. Quyto, Quitos, Quytos)
Spanish, meaning 'lively'.

Quintrell
(alt. Quantrell, Quentrell)
English, meaning 'dashing' or
'elegant'.

Foreign alternatives

David – Dafydd, Davin
John – Jean, Jose, Juan
Michael – Miguel, Mikhail
Peter – Pedro, Pierre, Pieter
Richard – Ricardo
William – Guillaume

No-nickname names

Alex
Jude
Keith
Otto
Owen
Toby

Quixley
(alt. Quix)
English, meaning 'clearing'.

Quixote
Spanish, literary name from Don
Quixote.

Qunnoune
(alt. Qunnoun, Qunnoone, Qunnoon)
Native American, meaning 'tall'.

Quoc
(alt. Quok, Quock)
Vietnamese, meaning 'patriot'.

Quoitrel
(alt. Quoytrel, Quoitrell, Quoytrell)
American, meaning 'mediator'.

Quon
Chinese, meaning 'light'.

Qusay
(alt. Qusaye, Qusai, Qusae)
Arabic, meaning 'distant'.

Qutaybuh
(alt. Qutayba, Qutaibah, Qutaibea)
Arabic, meaning 'impatient'.

Qutub
Indian, meaning 'tall'.

R Boys' names

Rabi
(alt. Rabie, Rabee, Raby)
Arabic, meaning 'gentle wind'.

Racham
(alt. Rachim, Raham, Rahim)
Hebrew, meaning 'sympathetic'.

Radames
Slavic, meaning 'famous joy'.

Radcliff
(alt. Radcliffe, Ratcliff, Ratcliffe)
English, meaning 'red hill'. The name is also associated with a women's college at Harvard.

Radley
(alt. Radlee, Radleigh, Radly)
English, meaning 'field of reeds'.

Raekwon
Hebrew, meaning 'God has healed'.

Rafael
(alt. Rafael, Raphael)
Hebrew, meaning 'God has healed'. One of the Archangels.

Rafferty
(alt. Raferty, Raffarty, Raffertey)
Irish and Gaelic, meaning 'prosperous'.

Ragnar
Old Norse, meaning 'judgement warrior'.

Raheem
Arabic, meaning 'merciful and kind'.

Rahm
Hebrew, meaning 'pleasing'.

Rahul
(alt. Raoul, Raul)
Indian, meaning 'efficient'.

Rai
Japanese, meaning 'trustworthy'.

Raiden
(alt. Rainen)
From the Japanese god of thunder.

Raimi
Arabic, meaning 'fond'.

Rainer
Alternative of Raynor.

Raj
Indian, meaning 'king'.

Rajesh
(alt. Ramesh)
Indian, meaning 'ruler of kings'.

Powerful names

Aubrey
Derek
Hercules
Oswald
Michio
Oz
Roderick
Thor

Rakesh
Hindi, meaning 'king'.

Raleigh
Old English, meaning 'deer's meadow'.

Ralph
Old English, meaning 'wolf'.

Ram
English, from the word 'ram'.

Ramiro
Germanic, meaning 'powerful in battle'.

Ramone
(alt. Ramond, Raymond, Romon)
Spanish, meaning 'wise supporter' or 'romantic'.

Ramsey
(alt. Ramsay)
Old English, meaning 'wild garlic island'.

Rance
(alt. Rancye, Rans, Ranse)
American, meaning 'rebel'.

Randall
(alt. Randolph)
Old German, meaning 'wolf shield'.

Randy
Variant of Randall, meaning 'wolf shield'. In modern English, randy can also mean amorous.

Ranger
(alt. Rainge, Range, Rangur)
French, meaning 'attentive'.

Raniel
English, meaning 'God is my happiness'.

Ranjit
Indian, meaning 'influenced by charm'.

Rankin
Celtic, meaning 'little shield'.

Rannoch
Gaelic, meaning 'fern'.

Ransford
Old English, meaning 'raven ford'.

Ransley
Old English, meaning 'raven meadow'.

Ransom
Old English, meaning 'son of the shield'.

Raoul
French alternative of Ralph, meaning 'wolf'.

Rashad
Arabic, meaning 'good judgment'.

Spring names

Alvern
Atherton
Jarek
Kell
Kirkwell
Marcus
Tamiko

Rasheed
(alt. Rashid)
Indian, meaning 'rightly guided'.

Rasmus
Greek, meaning 'beloved'.
Alternative of Erasmus.

Raven
English, from the word 'raven'.

Ravi
French, meaning 'delighted'.

Rawlins
French alternative of Roland,
meaning 'renowned land'.

Ray
English, from the word 'ray'.

Raymond
(alt. Rayner)
English, meaning 'advisor'.

Raynor
(alt. Raynar, Rayne, Raynell)
German, meaning 'decisive
fighter'.

Raz
Israeli, meaning 'secret' or
'mystery'.

Reagan
Irish, meaning 'little king'.

Redman
Anglo-Saxon, meaning
'counsellor'.

Reece
(alt. Rees, Reese, Reice)
Welsh, meaning 'great enthusiasm
for life' and Welsh, meaning
'ardent' or 'fiery'.

Reed
(alt. Reade, Reid, Reide)
English, meaning 'red-haired'.

Reggie
Latin, meaning 'queen'.

Reginald
Latin, meaning 'regal'.

Regis
Shortened form of Reginald,
meaning 'regal'.

Reid
Old English, meaning 'by the
reeds'.

Reidar
Scandinavian, meaning 'home
army'.

Reilly
English, meaning courageous.

Remington
English, meaning 'ridge town'.

Remus
Latin, meaning 'swift'.

Rémy
French, meaning 'from Rheims'.

Ren
Shortened form of Reginald, meaning 'regal'.

Renato
Latin, meaning 'rebirth'.

Rene
French, meaning 'rebirth'.

Reno
Latin, meaning 'renewed'.

Reth
African, meaning 'king'.

Reuben
Spanish, meaning 'a son'.

Reuel
Hebrew, meaning 'friend of God'.

Rex
Latin, meaning 'king'.

Rey
Spanish, meaning 'king'.

Reynold
Latin, meaning 'king's advisor'.

Rhett
English, meaning 'a stream' or 'counsel' and Welsh, as an alternative of Rhys. Rhett Butler is the hero of Margaret Mitchell's *Gone with the Wind*.

Rhodes
German, meaning 'where the roses grow'. Also the name of the Greek town.

Rhodri
Welsh, meaning 'ruler of the circle'.

Rhory
American, meaning 'red king'.

Rhys
Welsh, meaning 'enthusiasm'.

Ricardo
(alt. Riccardo)
Spanish, alternative of Richard.

Richard
Old German, meaning 'powerful leader'.

Richie
Shortened form of Richard, meaning 'powerful leader'.

Richmond
Anglo-Saxon, meaning 'strong protector'.

Rick
Shortened form of Richard, meaning 'powerful leader'.

Ricki
Shortened form of Richard, meaning 'powerful leader'.

Summer names

Augustus
Balder
Dylan
Leo
Sky
Somers

R

Rickward
English, meaning 'strong protector'.

Ricky
Shortened form of Richard, meaning 'powerful leader'.

Riddock
Gaelic, meaning 'smooth pasture'.

Rider
(alt. Ridder, Ryder)
English, meaning 'horseman'.

Ridley
English, meaning 'cleared wood'.

Rigby
From the English place in Lancashire.

Ringo
English, meaning 'ring'. Ringo Starr brought the name into the spotlight.

Rio
Spanish, meaning 'river'.

Riordan
Gaelic, meaning 'bard'.

Rishi
Variant of Richard, meaning 'powerful leader'.

Ritchie
Shortened form of Richard, meaning 'powerful leader'.

Ritter
German, meaning 'knight'.

Autumn names

Aki
Akiko
Bruno
Cormac
Demitrius
George
Goren
Octavius
Rowan

Riyad
Arabic, meaning 'gardens'.

Roald
Scandinavian, meaning 'ruler'. Made famous by the British writer, Roald Dahl.

Rochester
Anglo-Saxon, meaning 'fortress'.

Rob
Shortened form of Robert, meaning 'bright fame'.

Robbie
Shortened form of Robert, meaning 'bright fame'.

Robert
Old German, meaning 'bright fame'.

Roberto
Variant of Robert, meaning 'bright fame'.

Robin
English, from the word 'robin'.

Robinson
English, meaning 'son of Robin'.

Rocco
(alt. Rocky)
Italian, meaning 'rest'.

Rockwell
English, meaning 'of the rock well'.

Rod
Short for both Rhodri and Rodney.

Roderick
(alt. Broderick, Rick, Rod)
German, meaning 'famous power'.

Rodney
Old German, meaning 'island near the clearing'.

Rodrigo
Spanish form of Roderick, meaning 'famous power'.

Roger
Old German, meaning 'spear man'.

Rohan
Indian, meaning 'ascending'.

Roland
Old German, meaning 'renowned land'.

Rolf
Old German, meaning 'wolf'.

Rollie
(alt. Rollo)
Old German, meaning 'renowned land'.

Roman
Latin, meaning 'from Rome'.

Romeo
Latin, meaning 'pilgrim to Rome'. Made famous by Shakespeare's play *Romeo and Juliet*.

Romulus
(alt. Romolo)
Latin, meaning 'Roman'. Romulus and his twin Remus were the founders of Rome.

Ron
(alt. Ronnie)
Shortened form of Ronald, meaning 'mountain of strength'.

Ronald
Norse, meaning 'mountain of strength'.

Ronan
Gaelic, meaning 'little seal'.

Rooney
(alt. Roone, Rowan, Rowen)
Gaelic, meaning 'red hair'. Made famous by Mickey Rooney, the actor, and Wayne Rooney, the English footballer.

Rory
English, meaning 'red king'.

Roscoe
English, meaning 'deer forest'.

Winter names
Aquilo
Caldwell
Jack
Mistral
Rain

Ross
(alt. Russ)
Scottish, meaning 'cape'.

Rowan
(alt. Roan)
Gaelic, meaning 'little red one'.
Also a reference to the Rowan
tree.

Roy
Gaelic, meaning 'red'.

Royden
(alt. Roydan, Roydon)
English, meaning 'hill of rye'.

Ruben
Hebrew, meaning 'son'.

Rudolph
Old German, meaning 'famous
wolf'.

Rudy
Shortened form of Rudolph,
meaning 'famous wolf'.

Rudyard
English, meaning 'red enclosure'.
Associated with Rudyard Kipling,
the author of *The Jungle Book*.

Rufus
Latin, meaning 'red-haired'.

Ruhan
Arabic, meaning 'spiritual'.

Rui
Spanish, meaning 'famous ruler'.

Rune
Norse, meaning 'secret'.

Rupert
Variant of Robert, meaning 'bright
fame'.

Ruslan
Russian, meaning 'like a lion'.

Russell
Old French, meaning 'little red
one'.

Rusty
English, meaning 'ruddy'.

Ryan
Gaelic, meaning 'little king'.

Ryder
English, meaning 'horseman'.

Rye
English, from the word 'rye'.

Ryker
From Richard, meaning 'powerful
leader'.

Rylan
English, meaning 'land where rye
is grown'.

Ryley
Old English, meaning 'rye
clearing'.

Ryu
Japanese, meaning 'dragon'.

S Boys' names

Saad
Aramaic, meaning 'offers help'.

Saar
Hebrew, meaning 'tempest'.

Saarik
Hindi, meaning 'like a small songbird'.

Sabah
Arabic, meaning 'born in the morning'.

Saber
French, meaning 'sword'.

Sabino
Latin, meaning 'one from the Sabine tribe'.

Sabir
Arabic, meaning 'sleek'.

Sacha
Russian alternative of Alexander, meaning 'defending men'.

Sachar
Hebrew, meaning 'rewarded one'.

Sachiel
Hebrew, meaning 'archangel'.

Sadaka
African, meaning 'an offering'.

Sadler
English, meaning 'maker of harnesses'.

Sae
American, meaning 'talkative'.

Sagar
African, meaning 'ruler of the water'.

Sage
English, meaning 'wise'.

Sahaj
Indian, meaning 'natural'.

Sahir
Arabic, meaning 'watchful one'.

Saith
English, meaning 'well spoken'.

Sajal
Indian, meaning 'like a cloud'.

Sakari
Native American, meaning 'sweet'.

Salil
Indian, meaning 'from the water'.

Christmas names

Balthazar
Casper
Christian
Emmanuel
Gabriel
Joseph
Nicholas
Noel
Robin
Rudolf

Salim
Arabic, meaning 'secure'.

Salvador
Spanish, meaning 'saviour'.

Salvatore
Italian, meaning 'saviour'.

Sam
(alt. Sama, Sammie, Sammy)
Hebrew, meaning 'God is heard'.

Samir
Arabic, meaning 'pleasant companion'.

Samson
Hebrew, meaning 'son of Sam'.

Samuel
Hebrew, meaning 'God is heard'.

Sandeep
Indian, meaning 'lighting the way'.

Sanderson
English, meaning 'son of Alexander'.

Sanditon
English, meaning 'sandy town'.

Sandro
Shortened form of Alessandro, meaning 'defending men'.

Sandy
Shortened form of Alexander, meaning 'defending men'.

Sang
Vietnamese, meaning 'intelligent'.

Sanjay
Indian, meaning 'victory'.

Santana
Spanish, meaning 'saintly man'.

Santiago
Spanish, meaning 'Saint James'.

Santino
Spanish, meaning 'little Saint James'.

Santo
(alt. Santos)
Latin, meaning 'Saint'.

Sarat
Indian, meaning 'wise'.

Sascha
Shortened Russian form of Alexander, meaning 'defending men'.

Scott
(alt. Scottie)
English, meaning 'from Scotland'.

Scout
American, meaning 'explorer'.

Seabrook
English, meaning 'stream from the sea'.

Seamus
Irish variant of James, meaning 'he who supplants'.

Sean
(alt. Shaun)
Variant of John, meaning 'God is gracious'.

Seaton
English, meaning 'a seaside town'.

Sebastian
Greek, meaning 'revered'.

Sébastien
French form of Sebastian, meaning 'revered'.

Sebes
Hungarian, meaning 'swift one'.

Seeley
French, meaning 'blessed one'.

Selby
English, meaning 'manor of the farm'.

Seldon
English, meaning 'valley of willows'.

Septimus
Latin, meaning 'the seventh sun'.

Sergio
Latin, meaning 'servant'.

Seth
Hebrew, meaning 'appointed'.

Severus
Latin, meaning 'severe'.

Seymour
From the place name in Northern France.

Shaan
Hebrew, meaning 'peaceful one'.

Shai
Hebrew, meaning 'gift from God'.

Shaka
Arabic, meaning 'tribal leader'.

Shane
Variant of Sean, meaning 'God is gracious'.

Sharif
Arabic, meaning 'honoured'.

Shea
Gaelic, meaning 'admirable'.

Shelby
Norse, meaning 'willow'.

Sherlock
English, meaning 'fair haired'. Made famous by Sherlock Holmes.

Food-inspired names

Ale
Basil
Berry
Cane
Rye
Shad
Tamir

S

Sherman
Old English, meaning 'shear man'.

Shmuel
Hebrew, meaning 'his name is God'.

Shola
Arabic, meaning 'energetic'.

Sid
Shortened form of Sidney, meaning 'wide meadow'.

Sidney
English, meaning 'wide meadow'.

Sidor
Russian, meaning 'talented one'.

Sigmund
Old German, meaning 'victorious hand'.

Silvanus
(alt. Silvio)
Latin, meaning 'woods'.

Sim
Shortened form of Simba, meaning 'lion'.

Simba
Arabic, meaning 'lion'.

Simon
(alt. Simeon)
Hebrew, meaning 'to hear'.

Sinbad
Literary merchant adventurer.

Sindri
Norse meaning 'dwarf'.

Sipho
African, meaning 'the unknown one'.

Sire
English, from the word 'sire'.

Sirius
Hebrew, meaning 'brightest star'. The name of Harry Potter's godfather.

Skipper
English, meaning 'ship captain'.

Skyler
English, meaning 'scholar'.

Sloan
Gaelic, meaning 'accomplished warrior'.

Smith
English, meaning 'blacksmith'.

Socrates
Greek philosopher.

Solomon
Hebrew, meaning 'peace'.

Sonny
American English, meaning 'son'.

Soren
Scandinavian variant of Severus, meaning 'brightest star'.

Spencer
English, meaning 'dispenser'.

Spike
English, from the word 'spike'.

Staffors
English, meaning 'landing ford'.

S

Stamos
Greek, meaning 'reasonable'.

Stan
Shortened form of Stanley, meaning 'stony meadow'.

Stanford
English, meaning 'stone ford'.

Stanley
English, meaning 'stony meadow'.

Stavros
Greek, meaning 'crowned'.

Stellan
Latin, meaning 'starred'.

Steno
German, meaning 'stone'.

Stephen
(alt. Stefan, Stefano, Steffan)
English, meaning 'crowned'.

Sterne
English, meaning 'serious-minded'.

Steven
(alt. Steve, Stevie)
English, meaning 'crowned'.

Stewart
English, meaning 'steward'.

Stoney
English, meaning 'stone like'.

Storm
English, from the word 'storm'.

Stuart
English, meaning 'steward'.

Subhash
Indian, meaning 'well-spoken'.

Sule
African, meaning 'adventurous'.

Sully
English, meaning 'one from the southern meadow'.

Sven
Norse, meaning 'boy'.

Swanton
English, meaning 'swan town'.

Sweeney
Gaelic, meaning 'little hero'.

Swinton
English, meaning 'swine town'.

Sydney
English, meaning 'wide meadow'.

Syed
Arabic, meaning 'lucky'.

Sylvester
Latin, meaning 'wooded'.

Syon
Indian, meaning 'followed by good'.

Bird names

Condor
Drake
Jay
Phoenix
Robin

T Boys' names

Taban
Arabic, meaning 'shining'.

Taber
Hungarian, meaning 'camp'.

Tabib
Turkish, meaning 'doctor' or 'healer'.

Tacari
African, meaning 'strength of a warrior'.

Tacitus
From the Roman historian.

Tad
English, from the word 'tadpole'.

Tadeo
Spanish alternative of Thaddeus, meaning 'having heart'.

Tadi
Native American, meaning 'wind'.

Taggart
Gaelic, meaning 'priest's son'.

Tahir
Arabic, meaning 'chaste'.

Tahoe
Native American, meaning 'big water'.

Tai
Vietnamese, meaning 'talented'.

Taine
Gaelic, meaning 'river'.

Taj
Indian, meaning 'crown'.

Takashi
Japanese, meaning 'praiseworthy'.

Takoda
Sioux, meaning 'friend to everyone'.

Talbot
(alt. Tal)
Aristocratic English name.

Tamir
Arabic, meaning 'tall and wealthy'.

Tan
Vietnamese, meaning 'new'.

Tanav
Sanskrit, meaning 'flute'.

Tanix
Spanish, meaning 'glorious'.

Tanner
(alt. Tannar)
German, meaning 'leather worker'.

Tao
Chinese, meaning 'peace'.

Tappen
Welsh, meaning 'hanging rock'.

Taras
(alt. Tarez)
Scottish, meaning 'crag'.

Taregan
Native American, meaning 'crane'.

Tarek
Arabic, meaning 'evening caller'.

Tarian
Welsh, meaning 'silver'.

Tarin
American, meaning 'of earth'.

Tariq
Arabic, meaning 'morning star'.

Taro
Japanese, meaning 'first born'.

Tarquin
From the Roman clan name.

Taru
Sanskrit, meaning 'small plant'.

Tarun
Hindi, meaning 'young'.

Tasso
Italian, meaning 'cup'.

Tatanka
Hebrew, meaning 'bull'.

Tate
(alt. Tayte)
English, meaning 'cheerful'.

Taurean
English, meaning 'bull like'.

Tavares
English, meaning 'descendant of the hermit'.

Tave
(alt. Tavian, Tavis, Tavish)
From Octave, meaning 'eight'.

Tavor
Hebrew, meaning 'misfortune'.

Tay
English, meaning 'tailor'.

Taylor
English, meaning 'tailor'.

Teagan
Irish, meaning 'little poet'.

Teague
Irish, meaning 'poet'.

Ted
(alt. Teddy)
English, from Edward, meaning 'wealthy'.

Terence
(alt. Terrill, Terry)
English, meaning 'tender'.

Tex
English, meaning 'Texan'.

Thabiti
African, meaning 'real man'.

Thabo
African, meaning 'filled with happiness'.

T

Thackary
English, meaning 'God
remembers'.

Thad
Greek, meaning 'praise'.

Thaddeus
Aramaic, meaning 'having heart'.

Than
Vietnamese, meaning 'brilliant'.

Thane
(alt. Thayer)
Scottish, meaning 'landholder'.

Thelonius
Latin, meaning 'ruler of the
people'.

Theo
Shortened form of Theodore,
meaning 'God's gift'.

Theodore
Greek, meaning 'God's gift'.

Theophile
Latin, meaning 'God's love'.

Theron
Greek, meaning 'hunter'.

Thierry
French variant of Terence,
meaning 'tender'.

Tho
Vietnamese, meaning 'long life'.

Thomas
Aramaic, meaning 'twin'.

Thomsen
English, meaning 'son of Thomas'.

Thor
Norse, meaning 'thunder'.

Tiago
From Santiago, meaning 'Saint
James'.

Tiberius
English, meaning 'from the river
Tiber'.

Tibor
Latin, from the river Tiber.

Tien
Vietnamese, meaning 'first'.

Tiernan
Gaelic, meaning 'Lord'.

Tilden
(alt. Till)
English, meaning 'fertile valley'.

Tim
(alt. Timmie, Timon)
Shortened form of Timothy, meaning
'God's honour'.

Timon
Greek, meaning 'repsected'.

Timothy
Greek, meaning 'God's honour'.

Tiru
Hindi, meaning 'pious man'.

Tito
(alt. Titus, Tizian)
Latin, meaning 'defender'.

Tivon
Hebrew, meaning 'nature lover'.

Toa
Polynesian, meaning 'brave-hearted'.

Tobias
(alt. Toby)
Hebrew, meaning 'God is good'.

Tod
(alt. Todd)
English, meaning 'fox'.

Tolan
Anglo-Saxon, meaning 'of the taxed land'.

Toltecatl
Aztec, meaning 'artist'.

Tom
(alt. Tomlin, Tommy)
Hebrew, meaning 'twin'.

Tonneau
French, meaning 'barrel'.

Tong
Vietnamese, meaning 'sweet-smelling'.

Tony
Shortened form of Anthony, from the old Roman family name.

Torey
Norse, meaning 'Thor'.

Torin
Gaelic, meaning 'chief'.

Torquil
Gaelic, meaning 'helmet'.

Toshi
Japanese, meaning 'reflection'.

Trevelian
Welsh, meaning 'of the house of Elian'.

Trevet
Gaelic, meaning 'three hills'.

Travis
French, meaning 'crossover'.

Trevor
Welsh origin, meaning 'great settlement'.

Trey
(alt. Tyree)
From French, meaning 'very'.

Tristan
(alt. Tristram)
From the Celtic hero.

Troy
Gaelic, meaning 'descended from the soldier'.

Tudor
Variant of Theodore, 'God's gift'.

Twain
English, meaning 'divided in two'.

Tyler
English, meaning 'tile maker'.

Tyne
English, meaning 'river'.

Tyrell
French, meaning 'puller'.

Tyrone
Gaelic, meaning 'Owen's county'.

Tyson
English, meaning 'son of Tyrone'.

Tzion
Hebrew, meaning 'mountain'.

U

Boys' names

U
Korean, meaning 'gentle'.

Uaide
(alt. Uaide, Uayd, Uade)
Irish, alternative of Walter
meaning 'ruler of the army'.

Uaithe
(alt. Uaithn, Uaythne, Uaythn)
Gaelic, meaning 'innocent'.

Ualan
(alt. Ualane, Ualayn, Ualayne)
Scottish, alternative of Valentine.

Ualtar
(alt. Ualtarr, Ualter, Ualterr)
Irish, meaning 'strong warrior'.

Uani
Basque, meaning 'shepherd'.

Uba
(alt. Ubah, Ubba, Ubbah)
African, meaning 'lord of the
manor'.

Ubaid
(alt. Ubaide, Ubade, Ubayde)
Arabic, meaning 'faithful'.

Ubel
(alt. Ubell, Ubele, Ubull)
German, meaning 'evil'.

Ubert
Germany, meaning 'intelligent'.

Uberto
(alt. Umberto)
From the Italian royal name.

Uchdryd
(alt. Uchdrid, Uchdred, Uchdried)
Welsh, meaning 'Erim's son'.

Uchenna
African, meaning 'God's
thoughts'.

Udadhi
(alt. Udadhie, Udadhy, Udadhey)
Indian, meaning 'of the sea'.

Udank
(alt. Udanke)
Indian, a mythological sage.

Udar
(alt. Udarr, Udarre, Udari)
Indian, meaning 'generous'.

Udath
(alt. Udathe)
Indian, meaning 'noble'.

Uday
Arabic, meaning 'fast runner'.

Udayan
(alt. Udayen)
Indian, meaning 'thriving'.

Uddam
Indian, meaning 'exceptional'.

Uddhar
(alt. Uddharr, Udhar, Udharr)
Indian, meaning 'free man'.

Uddhav
(alt. Uddhaav, Udhav, Udhaav)
Hindi, Krishna's friend in mythology.

Udeh
(alt. Ude)
Hebrew, meaning 'man who praises God'.

Udell
English, meaning 'yew valley'.

Udi
(alt. Udie, Udy, Udey)
Hebrew, meaning 'torch bearer'.

Udo
German, meaning 'power of the wolf'.

Udolf
(alt. Udolfo, Udolph)
English, meaning 'having the wealth of a wolf'.

Udup
(alt. Udupp, Uddup, Uddupp)
Indian, meaning 'born beneath the moon'.

Ueli
(alt. Uelie, Uely, Ueley)
Swedish, alternative of Ulrich meaning 'noble ruler'.

Ufa
Egyptian, meaning 'flour'.

Uftzi
Spanish, meaning 'sky'.

Ufuk
Turkish, meaning 'horizon'.

Uggi
Icelandic, meaning 'fear'.

Ugo
Italian form of Hugo, meaning 'mind and heart'.

Uigbiorn
(alt. Ugbjorn, Ugbiorn, Ugbyorn)
Norse, meaning 'soldier bear'.

Uilleag
(alt. Uileag, Uilleage, Uileage)
Irish, meaning 'with a playful heart'.

Uilleam
Gaelic, meaning 'helmeted'.

Uilliam
Irish, alternative of William meaning 'strong protector' or 'strong willed warrior'.

Uisdean
Gaelic, meaning 'intelligent'.

Uiseann
Latin-American, meaning 'vanquisher'.

Names from nature

Ash
Cliff
Flint
River
Tiger

U

Movie inspirations

Alfie (*Alfie*)
Anakin (*Star Wars*)
Austin (*Austin Powers*)
Ben (*Ben Hur*)
Conan (*Conan the Barbarian*)
Marty (*Back to the Future*)
Renton (*Trainspotting*)
Rick (*Casablanca*)
Virgil (*The Great Escape*)
Wayne (*Wayne's World*)

Uja
Indian, meaning 'grow'.

Ujwal
(*alt. Ujjal, Ujal, Ujual*)
Indian, meaning 'bright'.

Ukel
(*alt. Ukal, Uke, Ukil*)
American, meaning 'player'.

Ukiah
(*alt. Ukia, Ukyah, Ukya*)
Native American, meaning 'deep valley'.

Ukko
(*alt. Uko, Ucco, Ucko*)
Finnish, the god of sky and thunder in mythology.

Ulan
(*alt. Ullan, ulann, Ullann*)
Indian, meaning 'the first of twins'.

Uland
German, meaning 'noble land'.

Ulani
(*alt. Ulanie, Ulany, Ulaney*)
Hawaiian, meaning 'cheerful one'.

Ulbrecht
(*alt. Ulbrekt, Ulbreckt, Ulbrech*)
German, meaning 'clever wolf'.

Ulderico
(*alt. Uldericco, Uldericko, Ulderiko*)
Italian, meaning 'compassionate leader'.

Ulf
German, meaning 'wolf'.

Ulfred
Anglo-Saxon, meaning 'wolf's peace'.

Ulger
Anglo-Saxon, meaning 'spearman'.

Ulick
Irish, meaning 'little William'.

Ull
Norse, meaning 'glory'.

Ulmar
English, meaning 'famous wolf'.

Ulrich
German, meaning 'noble ruler'.

Ultan
Irish, meaning 'from Ulster'.

Ultma
Indian, meaning 'godlike'.

Ulysses
Greek, meaning 'wrathful'. Made famous by the mythological voyager.

Umair
Arabic, meaning 'clever'.

Umar
Arabic, meaning 'flourishing'.

Umberto
(alt. Uberto)
Italian, alternative of Humbert meaning 'famous giant'.

Umblai
Egyptian, meaning 'great'.

Umed
Indian, meaning 'hope'.

Umi
African, meaning 'servant'.

Umran
African, meaning 'posperous'.

Umut
Turkish, meaning 'hope'.

Unai
Spanish, meaning 'shepherd'.

Uner
Turkish, meaning 'famous'.

Uni
Norwegian, meaning 'dane'.

Unni
Norwegian, meaning 'modest'.

Unwyn
(alt. Unwin, Unwine)
English, meaning 'unfriendly'.

Uorsin
Romantsch, meaning 'bear'.

Upendo
African, meaning 'love'.

Upendra
Indian, meaning 'element'.

Upton
English, meaning 'high town'.

Urbano
Spanish, meaning 'someone who lives in a city'.

Urho
Finnish, meaning 'brave'.

Uri
(alt. Uriah, Urias)
Hebrew, meaning 'my light'.

Uriah
(alt. Uriel, Urijah)
Hebrew, meaning 'God is my Light'.

Urian
Welsh, meaning 'born in a city'.

Uriel
Hebrew, meaning 'angel of light'. One of the Archangels.

Urines
Scottish, meaning 'king'.

Biblical names

David
John
Joseph
Luke
Mark
Matthew
Michael
Paul
Peter
Simon

U

Saints' names

Anselm
Bartholomew
Francis
Gabriel
Gregory
Jerome
Nicholas
Philip
Stephen
Thomas

Urquhart
Scottish, meaning 'fountain on the hill'.

Uruj
African, meaning 'rise mount'.

Usagi
Japanese, meaning 'bunny'.

Usama
African, meaning 'lion'.

Usbeorn
English, meaning 'divine soldier'.

Usher
English, from the word 'usher'. Made famous by the American R&B star.

Usi
Egyptian, meaning 'smoke'.

Uso
Italian, meaning 'bright'.

Utcha
Indian, meaning 'high point'.

Uther
(alt. Uthar, Uthir, Uthyr)
Old English, father of Arthur in Arthurian legend.

Utt
(alt. Utte)
Arabic, meaning 'kind and wise'.

Uttam
Inidan, meaning 'best'.

Uzi
Hebrew, meaning 'my strength'.

Uzima
(alt. Uzimah, Uzimma, Uzimmah)
African, meaning 'full of life'.

Uzoma
(alt. Uzomah, Uzomma, Uzommah)
African, meaning 'born during a journey'.

Uzumati
(alt. Uzumatie, Uzumatee, Uzumaty)
Native American, meaning 'like a grizzly bear'.

Uzzi
(alt. Uzziah)
Hebrew, meaning 'my power'.

Uzziah
(alt. Uzzia, Uziah, Uzia)
Hebrew, meaning 'God is my strength'.

Boys' names

Vachel
French, meaning 'cowherd'.

Vachlan
English, meaning 'lives by the river'.

Vaclav
Czech, meaning 'receives glory'.

Vada
Hebrew, meaning 'like a rose'.

Vadar
Dutch, meaning 'fatherly'.

Vaddon
Welsh, meaning 'man from Bath'.

Vadhir
Spanish, meaning 'like a rose'.

Vadim
Russian, meaning 'scandal maker'.

Vadin
Hindi, meaning 'known speaker'.

Vagas
Spanish, meaning 'of the meadow'.

Vahan
Armenian, meaning 'shielder of others'.

Vahe
Armenian, meaning 'strong'.

Vahid
Persian, meaning 'only one'.

Vahu
Persian, meaning 'well-behaved'.

Vai
Teutonic, meaning 'mighty ruler'.

Vail
English, meaning 'a valley'.

Valdemar
German, meaning 'renowned leader'.

Valdis
Teutonic, meaning 'spirited warrior'.

Valdemar
Scandinavian, meaning 'famous rule'.

Valente
Latin, meaning 'valiant'.

Valentin
(alt. Val)
French, meaning 'valentine'.

Valentine
English, from the word 'valentine'.

Valentino
Italian, meaning 'valentine'.

151

Valerio
Italian, meaning 'valiant'.

Valeriy
Russian, meaning 'healthy'.

Valiant
English, meaning 'brave'.

Valin
Indian, meaning 'king of the monkeys'.

Valko
Bulgarian, meaning 'wolf'.

Van
Dutch, meaning 'son of'.

Vance
English, meaning 'marshland'.

Vangelis
Greek, meaning 'good news'.

Vanhi
Indian, meaning 'fire'.

Varden
English, meaning 'from Verdun'.

Varen
Indian, meaning 'gifts'.

Varick
German, meaning 'defender'.

Varro
Latin, meaning 'durable'.

Vartan
Armenian, meaning 'rose'.

Varun
Hindi, meaning 'water god'.

Vashon
Armenian, meaning 'merciful'.

Vasilis
Greek, meaning 'kingly'.

Vasiliy
Russian, meaning 'regal'.

Vassar
English, meaning 'vassal'.

Vasska
Slavic, meaning 'royal'.

Vaughan
Welsh, meaning 'little'.

Vayu
Indian, meaning 'the God of the wind and the air'.

Veda
Indian, meaning 'eternal knowledge'.

Vernell
French, meaning 'green and flourishing'.

Verner
German, meaning 'army defender'.

Vernon
(alt. Vernie)
French, meaning 'alder grove'.

Versilius
Latin, meaning 'flier'.

Vester
Latin, meaning 'wooded'.

Vibol
Cambodian, meaning 'man of plenty'.

Victor
Latin, meaning 'champion'.

Vidal
(alt. Vidar)
Spanish, meaning 'life giving'.

Vidur
Indian, meaning 'with great wisdom'.

Vieno
Finnish, meaning 'gentle'.

Viet
Vietnamese, meaning 'a descendant of the Vietnamese'.

Viho
Native American, meaning 'chief'.

Vijay
Hindi, meaning 'conquering'.

Vikram
Hindi, meaning 'sun'.

Viktor
Latin, meaning 'victory'.

Ville
French, meaning 'town'.

Vimal
Indian, meaning 'clean one'.

Vincent
(alt. Vince)
English, meaning 'victorious'.

Vineet
Indian, meaning 'modest one'.

Viorel
Romanian, meaning 'like the bluebell'.

Vipin
Indian, meaning 'from the forest'.

Viraj
Hungarian, meaning 'flowerlike'.

Virgil
From the Roman poet.

Virote
Thai, meaning 'power'.

Vitalis
Latin, meaning 'alive'.

Vito
Spanish, meaning 'life'.

Vittorio
Italian, meaning 'victory'.

Vitus
Latin, meaning 'life'.

Vivek
Indian, meaning 'wisdom'.

Vivian
Latin, meaning 'lively'.

Vladimir
Slavic, meaning 'prince'.

Volker
German, meaning 'defender of the people'.

Von
Norse, meaning 'hope'.

Vox
Latin, meaning 'voice'.

Vulcan
Latin, mythological god of fire.

Vulmaro
Spanish, meaning 'warrior'.

Vyacheslav
Russian, meaning 'famous'.

W

Boys' names

Waail
Arabic, meaning 'goes back to God'.

Wade
English, meaning 'to move forward' or 'to go'.

Wainwright
(alt. Wain, Wainright, Wayne)
English, meaning 'a maker of wagons'.

Waite
(alt. Wait, Waites, Waight)
English, meaning 'guard'.

Wafiq
Arabic, meaning 'successful'.

Wakapa
Native American, meaning 'one who excels'.

Wakaun
Native American, meaning 'serpent'.

Waldemar
German, meaning 'renowned ruler'.

Walker
English, meaning 'a fuller'.

Waldemar
German, meaning 'famous ruler'.

Walden
English, meaning 'valley of the Britons'.

Waldo
Old German, meaning 'rule'.

Waldron
German, meaning 'mighty raven'.

Walker
English, meaning 'treads the cloth'.

Wallace
English, meaning 'foreigner' or 'stranger'.

Wally
German, meaning 'ruler of the army'.

Walsh
Anglo-Saxon, alternative of Wallace, meaning 'foreigner' or 'stranger'.

Wasim
Arabic, meaning 'attractive' or 'full of grace'.

Walter
(alt. Walt)
German, meaning 'ruler of the army'.

Names with positive meanings

Auden – Friend
Basim – Smile
Dustin – Brave
Ervin – Beautiful
Gene - Noble
Jamal – Handsome
Jay – Happy
Pradeep – Light
Tate – Cheerful
Tova – Good

Walvia
Native American, meaning 'medicine root'.

Wanbli
Native American, meaning 'eagle'.

Wapi
Native American, meaning 'lucky'.

Waqar
Arabic, meaning 'majesty'.

Ward
English, meaning 'guardian'.

Wardell
Old English, meaning 'watchman's hill'.

Warley
English, meaning 'the meadow near the weir'.

Warner
German, meaning 'army guard'.

Warra
Aboriginal, meaning 'man of the water'.

Warrain
Aboriginal, meaning 'man of the sea'.

Warren
German, meaning 'guard' or 'the game park'.

Warrun
Aboriginal, meaning 'from the sky'.

Warwick
English, meaning 'farm near the weir'.

Washi
Japanese, meaning 'like an eagle'.

Washington
English, meaning 'clever' or 'clever man's settlement'. Also the surname of the first president of the United States.

Wasi
Arabic, meaning 'open-minded man'.

Wasim
Arabic, meaning 'handsome man'.

Wassily
Greek, meaning 'royal' or 'kingly'.

Watson
English, meaning 'son' or 'son of walter'.

Waverley
(alt. Waverly)
English, meaning 'quaking aspen'.

W

Waylon
English, meaning 'Land by the road'.

Wayne
English, meaning 'a cartwright'.

Webster
English, meaning 'weaver'.

Wei
Chinese, meaning 'brilliant'.

Welby
English, meaning 'from the farm near a spring'.

Weldon
English, meaning 'from the hill of well' or 'hill with a well'.

Wellington
Anglo-Saxon, meaning 'of a prosperous estate'. Borne by the Duke of Wellington, as well as associations with boots and a way to cook beef.

Wendell
(alt. Wendel)
German, meaning 'a wend'.

Girls' names for boys

Darcy
Jean
Kay
Kelly
Kelsey
Madison
Nat
Paris
Sandy
Sasha

Wentworth
English, meaning 'of the white man's manor'.

Werner
German, meaning 'army guard'.

Werther
German, meaning 'a soldier in the army'.

Wesley
(alt. Wes, Westleigh, Westley)
English, meaning 'of the western meadow'. The name Westley is borne by the male protagonist in *The Princess Bride* by William Goldman.

Weston
English, meaning 'from the west town'.

Wetherby
English, meaning 'ram farm'.

Wharton
English, meaning 'the settlement near the weir'.

Wheeler
English, meaning 'wheel maker'.

Whitaker
English, meaning 'of the white acre'.

Whitford
English, meaning 'of the white ford'.

Whitley
English, meaning 'white wood'.

Whitman
Old English, meaning 'white man'. Associated with the American poet Walt Whitman.

Whitney
Old English, meaning 'white island'.

Wichado
Native American, meaning 'willing'.

Wickham
(alt. Wickam, Wykeham)
Anglo-Saxon, meaning 'village pasture'.

Wilber
(alt. Wilbur)
Old German, meaning 'bright will'.

Wilder
(alt. Wild, Wilde)
German, meaning 'wild' or 'hunter'.

Wildon
English, meaning 'wooded hill'.

Wiley
Old English, meaning 'beguiling' or 'enchanting'.

Wilford
Old English, meaning 'The Ford by the Willows'.

Wilfredo
(alt. Wilfred, Wilfrid)
English, meaning 'to will peace'.

Wilhelm
German, meaning 'strong-willed warrior'.

Wilkes
(alt. Wilkie)
Old English, meaning 'strong-willed protector' or 'strong and resolute protector'. Borne by the British novelist Wilkie Collins, famous for *The Woman in White* and other novels.

Willard
German, meaning 'brave'.

William
(alt. Will, Willie)
English (Teutonic), meaning 'strong protector' or 'strong-willed warrior'.

Willis
English, meaning 'server of Will'.

Wilmer
English (Teutonic), meaning 'famously resolute'.

Wilmot
English, meaning 'resolute mind'.

Wilney
Native American, meaning 'flying eagles singing'.

Wilson
English, meaning 'son of William'.

Wilton
Old Norse and English, meaning 'from the farm by the brook' or 'from the farm by the streams'.

Willoughby
Old Norse and Old English, meaning 'from the farm by the trees'.

W

Wilmer
German, meaning 'strong-willed'.

Wilson
German, meaning 'son of William'.

Wincent
Polish variation of Vincent, meaning 'victorious'.

Windell
German, meaning 'wanderer' or 'seeker'.

Windsor
Old English, meaning 'river bank' or 'landing place'.

Winfield
English, meaning 'from the field of Wina'.

Winslow
Old English, meaning 'victory on the hill'.

Winston
English, meaning 'enclosed pastureland'.

Winter
Old English, meaning 'to be born in the winter'.

Winthrop
Old English, meaning 'village of friends'.

Winton
Old English, meaning 'a friends farm'.

Wirrin
Aboriginal, meaning 'a tea tree'.

Wirt
Anglo-Saxon, meaning 'worthy'.

Wistan
Old English, meaning 'battle stone' or 'mark of the battle'.

Wittan
Old English, meaning 'farm in the woods' or 'farm by the woods'.

Wolcott
(alt. Woolcott, Woollcott)
English, meaning 'cottage by a stream'.

Wolf
(alt. Wolfe)
English, meaning 'strong as a wolf'.

Wolfgang
Teutonic, meaning 'the path of wolves'.

Wolfric
German, meaning 'wolf ruler'.

Wolfrom
Teutonic, meaning 'raven wolf'.

Wolter
Dutch, a form of Walter meaning 'ruler of the army'.

Woodburn
Old English, meaning 'a stream in the woods'.

Woodrow
English, meaning 'from the row of houses by the wood'.

Woodward
English, meaning 'guardian of the forest'.

Woody
American, meaning 'path in the woods'.

Worcester
Old English, meaning 'from a Roman site'.

Worth
American, meaning 'worth much' or 'wealthy place' or 'wealth and riches'.

Wren
Old English, meaning 'tiny bird'.

Wright
Old English, meaning 'to be a craftsman' or 'from a carpenter'.

Wu
Chinese, meaning 'army' or 'sorcerer'.

Wyatt
Teutonic, meaning 'from wood' or 'from the wide water'.

Wyclef
(alt. Wycleff, Wycliff, Wycliffe)
English, meaning 'inhabitant of the white cliff'.

Wyndom
(alt. Windham, Wynndham)
English, meaning 'windy village'.

Wynn
(alt. Wyn)
Welsh, meaning 'very blessed' or 'the fair blessed one'.

Wystan
(alt. Wystann)
English, meaning 'war stone'.
Name of the poet Wystan Hughes Auden.

Wythe
English, meaning 'willow tree'.

Place names

Aidrian
Ainsley
Ashton
Bradley
Bruce
Emlyn
Glen
Tay
Wade
Wesley

Boys' names

Xabat
Basque, meaning 'saviour'.

Xacinto
Greek, meaning 'hyacinth flower'.

Xacobo
Hawaiian, meaning 'second son'.

Xadrian
American, a combination of X and Adrian, meaning 'from Hadria'.

Xakery
American alternative of Zachary, meaning 'God has remembered'.

Xalvador
Spanish, meaning 'saviour'.

Xan
Hebrew, meaning 'well-fed'.

Xander
Greek, meaning 'defender of the people'.

Xannon
American, meaning 'descendent of an ancient family'.

Xanthus
Greek, meaning 'golden-haired'.

Xanti
Basque, meaning 'honouring St James'.

Xanto
Greek, meaning 'blonde'.

Xarles
French alternative of Charles, meaning 'free man'.

Xavier
Latin, meaning 'to the new house'.

Xenocrates
Greek, meaning 'foreign ruler'.

Xenon
Greek, meaning 'the Guest'.

Xenophon
Greek, meaning 'foreign voice'.

Xerxes
Persian, meaning 'ruler of the people' or 'respected King'.

Xenxo
Greek, meaning 'family protector'.

Xerano
Latin, meaning 'porter'.

Xeven
Slavic, meaning 'lively'.

Long names

Alexander
Bartholomew
Christopher
Demetrius
Giovanni
Maximillian
Montgomery
Nathaniel
Sebastian
Zachariah

Xiang
Chinese, meaning 'soars above others'.

Xiao
Latin, meaning 'from the Lulia family'.

Xiao Chen
Chinese, meaning 'early morning'.

Xiaoping
Chinese, meaning 'little bottle'.

Xildas
German, meaning 'taxes'.

Xing
Chinese, meaning 'star'.

Xing-Fu
Chinese, meaning 'happiness'.

Xiomar
Spanish, meaning 'famous in battle'.

Xipil
Aztec, meaning 'of fire'.

Xiuhcoatl
Aztec, meaning 'weapon of destruction'.

Xi-wang
Chinese, meaning 'filled with hope'.

Xoan
Hebrew, meaning 'God is good'.

Xola
African, meaning 'stay in peace'.

Xorxe
Greek, meaning 'tiller of soil'.

Xun
Chinese, meaning 'fast'.

Xuan
Vietnamese, meaning 'born in the spring'.

Xue
Chinese, meaning 'studious'.

Xun
Chinese, meaning 'swift one'.

Xylander
Greek, meaning 'man of the forest'.

Xylon
Greek, meaning 'forest dweller'.

Boys' names

Yaakov
Hebrew, meaning 'supplanter'.

Yaal
Hebrew, meaning 'ascending' or
'one to ascend'.

Yada
Hebrew, meaning 'he knew'.

Yadid
Hebrew, meaning 'the beloved
one'.

Yadon
Hebrew, meaning 'against
judgment'.

Yael
Israeli, meaning 'God is strength'.

Yaeger
German, meaning 'hunter'.

Yafeu
African, meaning 'bold one'.

Yagil
Hebrew, meaning 'one who
celebrates'.

Yahir
Spanish, meaning 'handsome
one'.

Yaholo
Native American, meaning 'yells'.

Yahto
Native American, meaning 'blue'.

Yakar
Hebrew, meaning 'precious'.

Yakiya
Hebrew, meaning 'pure' or
'bright'.

Yair
Hebrew, meaning 'the
enlightening one' or
'illuminating'.

Yale
Welsh, meaning 'upland'.

Yama
Japanese, meaning 'mountain'.

Yamal
Indian, meaning 'a twin'.

Yarmir
Indian, meaning 'moon'.

Yanai
Aramaic, meaning 'the Lord will
answer'.

Yanis
(alt. Yannis)
Greek, a form of John meaning
'gift of God'.

Yanisin
Native American, meaning 'ashamed'.

Yantse
Native American, meaning 'yellow willow'.

Yaotl
Aztec, meaning 'great warrior'.

Yaphet
Hebrew, meaning 'handsome'.

Yarden
Hebrew, meaning 'to flow downward'.

Yardley
English, meaning 'the forest where the spars were'.

Yaro
African, meaning 'son'.

Yaroslav
Russian, meaning 'famous'.

Yarran
Aboriginal, meaning 'acais tree'.

Yas
Native American, meaning 'child of snow'.

Yasin
Arabic, meaning 'wealthy'.

Yaser
Arabic, meaning 'smooth'.

Yasu
Japanese, meaning 'tranquil'.

Yates
English, meaning 'gate keeper'.

Yavor
Bulgarian, meaning 'maple tree'.

Yaw
African, meaning 'born on a Thursday'.

Yaxha
Spanish, meaning 'green water'.

Yazid
Arabic, meaning 'increase'.

Ye
Chinese, meaning 'bright one' or 'light'.

Yedidiah
Hebrew, meaning 'beloved by God'.

Yehuda
Hebrew, meaning 'to praise and exalt'.

Yenge
African, meaning 'hardworking'.

Yered
Hebrew, a form of Jared, meaning 'descending'.

Yeriel
Hebrew, meaning 'founded by God'.

Yerik
Russian, meaning 'God appointed one'.

Short names

Al
Ben
Ed
Dai
Jay
Jon
Max
Rio
Sam
Ty

Yerodin
African, meaning 'studious'.

Yervant
Armenian, meaning 'King of people'.

Yestin
Welsh, meaning 'just'.

Yi Min
Chinese, meaning 'intelligent'.

Yigil
Hebrew, meaning 'He shall be redeemed'.

Yiska
Native American, meaning 'night is over'.

Yitro
Hebrew, meaning 'plenty'.

Yitzak
(alt. Yitzaak)
Hebrew, meaning 'laughter' or 'one who laughs'.

Ymir
Norse, mythological giant.

Yngve
Scandinavian, meaning 'first man'.

Ynyr
Welsh, meaning 'to honour'.

Yo
Cambodian, meaning 'honest'.

Yoad
Hebrew, meaning 'God is my witness'.

Yobachi
African, meaning 'one who prays to God' or 'prayed to God'.

Yogi
Japanese, meaning 'one who practices Yoga' or 'from Yoga'.

Yohance
African, meaning 'God's gift'.

Yolotli
Aztec, meaning 'heart'.

Yona
Native Amercian, meaning 'bear'.

Yona
Hebrew, meaning 'dove'.

Yoomee
Native American, meaning 'star'.

Yori
Japanese, meaning 'dependent'.

Yorick
English alternative of George, meaning 'farmer'. Forever associated with the famous skull in Shakespeare's *Hamlet*: 'Alas! Poor Yorick!'

York
Celtic, meaning 'yew tree' or
'from the farm of the yew tree'.

Yosef
Hebrew, meaning 'added by
God' or 'God shall add'.

Yoshi
Japanese, meaning 'free man'.

Yu
Chinese, meaning 'born during
the rainfall'.

Yuda
Indonesian, meaning 'war'.

Yue
Chinese, meaning 'born under
the moon'.

Yuichi
Japanese, meaning 'kind one'.

Yuki
Japanese, meaning 'snow' or
'lucky'.

Yule
English, meaning 'Christmas
time'.

Yukta
Indian, meaning 'attentive one'.

Yuma
Native American, meaning 'son of
the chief'.

Yunus
Turkish, meaning 'dolphin like'.

Yurem
Arabic, meaning 'exalted by
God'.

Yuri
Aboriginal, meaning 'to hear'.

Yuri
Russian, a form of George
meaning 'farmer'.

Yuuki
Japanese, meaning 'gentle hope'.

Yuuta
Japanese, meaning 'excellent'.

Yves
French, meaning 'miniature
archer' or 'small archer'.

Z Boys' names

Zabian
(alt. Zaabian, Zabien, Zabion)
Arabic, meaning 'worshipper of godly bodies'.

Zabulon
(alt. Zabulun, Zabulen)
Hebrew, meaning 'exalted'.

Zachariah
(alt. Zac, Zach, Zachary)
Hebrew, meaning 'remembered by the Lord' or 'God has remembered'.

Zad
Persian, meaning 'my son'.

Zadeer
(alt. Zadier, Zadir, Zadyr)
Arabic, meaning 'new son'.

Zaden
(alt. Zadan, Zadin, Zadun)
Dutch, meaning 'a man who sowed seeds.'

Zadok
Hebrew, meaning 'righteous one'.

Zador
Hungarian, meaning 'violent demeanor'.

Zafar
Arabic, meaning 'triumphant'.

Zahi
(alt. Zaheed, Zaheede, Zaheid)
Arabic, meaning 'brilliant'.

Zahid
(alt. Zaheed, Zaheede, Zahei)
Arabic, meaning 'pious'.

Zahir
(alt. Zaheer, Zaheere, Zaheir)
Arabic, meaning 'radiant'.

Zahur
(alt. Zaahur, Zahure, Zhahur)
Arabic, meaning 'like a flower'.

Zaid
African, meaning 'increase the growth' or 'growth'.

Zaide
Yiddish, meaning 'the elder ones'.

Zaim
(alt. Zaam, Zaem, Zaeme)
Arabic, meaning 'intelligent chief'.

Zain
(alt. Zane)
Arabic, meaning 'the handsome son'.

Zaire
African, meaning 'river from Zaire'.

Zaman
(alt. Zamaan, Zamane, Zhaman)
Arabic, meaning 'time keeper'.

Zamir
(alt. Zameer, Zameere, Zameir)
Hebrew, meaning 'like a
songbird'.

Zamor
(alt. Zamore, Zamori, Zamorio)
Hungarian, meaning 'a worker
who tills the ground'.

Zander
Greek, meaning 'defender of my
people'.

Zani
(alt. Zanie, Zanee, Zaney)
Hebrew, meaning 'present from
God'.

Zarek
Persian, meaning 'God protect
our King'.

Zayit
Hebrew, meaning 'olive'.

Zeal
English, meaning 'passionately'.

Zebadiah
(alt. Zeb, Zebedee)
Hebrew, meaning 'endowed by
God'.

Zed
English, meaning 'God is virtue'.

Zeke
Hebrew, meaning 'God gives
strength'.

Zelig
German, meaning 'blessed'.

Zeki
(alt. Zekee, Zekey, Zekie)
Turkish, meaning 'intelligent'.

Zelen
(alt. Zelenee, Zeleney, Zeleni)
Croatian, meaning 'innocent'.

Zene
African, meaning 'beautiful'.

Zenjiro
Japanese, meaning 'second son'.

Zeno
Greek, meaning 'guest'.

Zentaro
Japanese, meaning 'first son'.

Zephaniah
Hebrew, meaning 'God is
hidden'.

Zereen
Arabic, meaning 'golden'.

Zero
English, meaning 'no value'.

Zeroun
(alt. Zeroune, Zeroon, Zeroone)
Armenian, meaning 'wise'.

Zeru
(alt. Zeroune, Zeroo, Zerooh)
Basque, meaning 'from the sky'.

Zesiro
African, meaning 'first of twins'.

Zeus
Greek, the mythological king of
the gods.

Zev
Hebrew, meaning 'wolf'.

Zhenechka
(alt. Zhenya, Zenechka)
Russian, meaning 'noble'.

Zhi
Chinese, meaning 'with good intentions'.

Ziggy
German, alternative of Sigmund.

Zilya
Russian, meaning 'like a king'.

Zitkaduta
Native American, meaning 'a crimson bird'.

Ziv
Hebrew, meaning 'brilliance'.

Ziya
Arabic, meaning 'light'.

Zoan
African, meaning 'leaving'.

Zoltan
(alt. Zoltin)
Hungarian, meaning 'life'.

Zorion
Portuguese, meaning 'happy'.

Zorro
(alt. Zorio, Zoro, Zorrio)
Slavic, a famous hero.

Zosio
Polish, meaning 'wise'.

Zubin
Hebrew, meaning 'honour'.

Zulimar
Spanish, meaning 'blue expanse of water'.

Zulu
African, meaning 'heaven'.

Zuriel
Hebrew, meaning 'God is my rock'.

Zvi
Hebrew, meaning 'deer'.

Zwi
Hebrew, meaning 'gazelle'.

'Bad boy' names

Ace
Arnie
Axel
Bruce
Buzz
Conan
Guy
Rhett
Spike
Tyson

3

Girls' Names

Girls' names

A'mari
Variation on the Swahili or Muslim name Amira, meaning 'princess'.

Aadi
(alt. Aady, Aadee)
Hindi, meaning 'of the beginning'.

Aaliyah
(alt. Alia, Alliyah)
Variation on the Arabic name Aliya, meaning 'highborn'.

Aanya
Variation on the Russian name Anya, meaning 'favour' or 'grace'. Also of Sanskrit origin, meaning 'the inexhaustible'.

Aaryanna
Derivative of the Latin name Ariadne and the Greek Ariadne, both meaning 'the very holy one'.

Abby
(alt. Abbey, Abbie)
Form of Abigail, meaning 'My father's joy' in Hebrew.

Abebe
African, meaning 'child who is looked for for'.

Abedabun
Native American, meaning 'dawn's child'.

Abelia
(alt. Abella)
Hebrew, meaning 'sigh' or 'breath'.

Aberfa
(alt. Aberphah)
Welsh, meaning 'from the start of the river'.

Abia
(alt. Abbia, Abbiah, Abiah, Abya, Abyah)
Arabic, meaning 'great'.

Abida
(alt. Abeeda, Abyda, Abeida)
Arabic, meaning 'worshipper' and Hebrew, meaning 'having knowledge'.

Abigail
(alt. Abagail)
Hebrew, meaning 'My father's joy'.

Abilene
(alt. Abilee)
Variation of Abelena. Latin and Spanish for 'hazelnut'.

Abina
(alt. Abena)
Ghanaian, meaning 'born on Tuesday'.

Abira
(alt. Abera, Abyra)
Hebrew, meaning 'a supplier of strength'.

Abra
Female variation of Abraham. Also of Sanskrit origin, meaning 'clouds'.

Abril
Spanish for the month of April. Also of Latin origin, meaning 'open'.

Acacia
A species of flowering trees and shrubs and derived from Greek for 'point' or 'thorn'.

Acadia
An offshoot of the Greek word arcadia meaning 'paradise'. Originally, a French colony in Canada.

Acantha
(alt. Akantha)
Greek, meaning 'thorny'. In mythology Acantha was a nymph connected with Apollo, the sun god.

Aceline
(alt. Asceline)
French, meaning 'highborn'.

Achaana
Navajo, meaning 'protector'.

Actia
Greek, meaning 'beam of sunlight'.

Ada
(alt. Ada, Adair)
Hebrew, meaning 'adornment'.

Adalee
German, meaning 'noble'.

Adalgisa
(alt. Adelgise)
German, meaning 'noble' or 'vow'. It is also the name of one of Bellini's priestess' in his popular Italian opera *Norma*.

Adalia
'God is my refuge' in Hebrew.

Adalwolfa
German, meaning 'dignified she-wolf'.

Adamina
Hebrew, meaning 'of the red earth'. A female form of Adam.

Adamma
Igbo, meaning 'beautiful child'.

Adara
(alt. Adar, Adare)
Arabic, meaning 'virgin' and Hebrew, meaning 'noble'.

Addie
(alt. Adi, Addy)
Abbreviated form of Addison, Adelaide, Adele and Adeline.

Addison
(alt. Addyson)
English, meaning 'Son of Adam'.

Adelaide
(alt. Adelaida)
German, popular after the rule of William IV and Queen Adelaide of England in the 19th Century.

Adele
(alt. Adell, Adelle, Adelia)
German, meaning 'noble' or
'nobility'.

Adelinda
French, meaning 'noble' and
'sweet'.

Adelpha
(alt. Adelfa, Adelfia)
Greek, meaning 'adored sister'.

Adeline
(alt. Adalyn, Adelyn)
Variant of Adelaide, meaning
'nobility'.

Aden
(alt. Addien)
Hebrew for 'decoration'.

Adeola
(alt. Adeoloh, Adeolla)
African, meaning 'wearer of a
crown of honour'.

Aderes
Hebrew, meaning 'protector'.

Aderyn
Welsh for 'bird'.

Adesina
Nigerian for 'she paves the way'.
Usually given to a first-born
daughter.

Adia
Variant of Ada, meaning
'decoration'.

Adiba
Arabic, meaning 'cultured'.

Adiella
(alt. Adielle)
Hebrew, meaning 'God's
adornment'.

Adila
(alt. Adilah, Adeala)
Arabic, meaning 'fair' or 'just'.

Adima
(alt. Adimah, Adimma)
Teutonic, meaning 'legendary'.

Adina
(alt. Adena)
Hebrew, meaning 'high hopes' or
'precious'.

Adira
Hebrew for 'noble' or 'powerful'.
Also the north Italian city.

Aditi
Hindi, meaning 'endless'. In
Hindu mythology Aditi is the sky
and fertility goddess.

Adiva
Arabic, meaning 'gentle'.

Adora
Latin, meaning 'beloved'.

Adra
Arabic, meaning 'virgin'.

Adrian
Italian, from the northern city of
Adria.

Adrianna
(alt. Adriana)
Variant of Adrienne, meaning
'rich' or 'dark'.

A

Adrina
American, meaning 'dignified'.

Adrienne
(alt. Adriane, Adrianne)
Greek, meaning 'rich', or Latin, meaning 'dark'.

Adsila
Native American, meaning 'flower'.

Ae-Cha
Korean, meaning 'adoring daughter'.

Aegina
Greek, mythologically a sea nymph, and a place in Greece.

Aegle
Greek, meaning 'brightness' or 'splendour'.

Aelwen
Welsh, meaning 'exquisite brow'.

Aerin
Variant on Erin, meaning 'peace-making'.

Aerith
American, from a character in the computer game *Final Fantasy VII*.

Aerolynn
Combined of the Greek Aero, meaning 'water', and the English Lynn, meaning 'waterfall'.

Aeron
Variant of Aero, meaning 'water'.

Afia
(alt. Afi, Affi)
Arabic, meaning 'a child born on Friday'.

Afra
(alt. Affra, Aphra)
Hebrew, meaning 'little deer'.

Afreda
(alt. Afredah, Afrida)
English, meaning 'elf counsellor'.

Africa
Celtic for 'pleasant', as well as the name of the continent.

Afsaneh
Iranian, meaning 'a fairy tale'.

Afsha
Persian, meaning 'one who sprinkles light'.

Afton
Originally a place name in Scotland.

Agape
Greek, meaning 'love'.

Agate
English, from the semi-precious stone of the same name.

Agatha
From Saint Agatha, the patron saint of bells, meaning 'good'.

Aggie
Alternative of Agatha, meaning 'good'.

Aglaia
One of the three Greek Graces, meaning 'brilliance'.

Agnes
Greek, meaning 'virginal' or 'pure'.

Agrippina
From the Latin expression, meaning 'born feet first'.

Ahana
Irish, meaning 'little ford'.

Ahava
Hebrew, meaning 'love'.

Ai
Japanese, meaning 'love'.

Aida
'Reward' or 'present' in Arabic.

Aidanne
(alt. Aidan, Aidenn)
Gaelic for 'fire'.

Ailbhe
Irish, meaning 'noble' or 'bright'.

Aife
(alt. Aoife)
Celtic, a mythological warrior woman.

Aiko
Japanese, meaning 'little beloved one'.

Ailani
(alt. Aelani, Ailana)
Hawaiian, meaning 'chief'.

Aileen
(alt. Aleen, Aline, Eileen)
A Gaelic variant of Helen, meaning 'light'.

Ailith
(alt. Ailish)
Old English, meaning 'seasoned warrior'.

Aithne
(alt. Aine, Aithnea)
Gaelic, meaning 'fire'.

Ailsa
Scottish, meaning 'pledge from God', as well as the name of a Scottish island.

Aimee
(alt. Aimie, Amie)
The French spelling of Amy, meaning 'beloved'.

Aina
Scandinavian, meaning 'forever'.

Aine
(alt. Aino)
Celtic for 'happiness'.

Ainsley
Scottish and Gaelic, meaning 'one's own meadow'.

Aisha
(alt. Aeysha)
In Arabic Aisha means 'woman'; in Swahili it means 'life'.

Aishwarya
Variant on the Arabic Aisha, meaning 'woman'.

Aislinn
(alt. Aislin, Aisling, Aislyn)
Irish Gaelic, meaning 'dream'.

Aiyanna
(alt. Aiyana)
Native American, meaning 'forever flowering'.

Aja
Hindi, meaning 'goat'.

A

Aka
(alt. Akah, Akkah)
Maori, meaning 'loving one'.

Akakia
Greek, meaning 'naïve'.

Akela
(alt. Akilah)
Hawaiian, meaning 'noble'.

Aki
(alt. Akey, Akie)
Japanese, meaning 'born in
autumn'.

Akiko
Japanese, meaning 'shining child'.

Akilah
(alt. Aikiela, Akeela, Akylah)
Arabic, meaning 'wise'.

Akilina
Greek or Russian, meaning
'eagle'.

Akiva
Hebrew, meaning 'protect and
shelter'.

Akosua
African, meaning 'born on
Sunday'.

Aksana
(alt. Aksannah)
Russian, meaning 'offers glory to
God'. Alternative of Oksana.

Akua
African, meaning 'born on
Wednesday'.

Akuti
(alt. Akutie, Akutea)
Indian, meaning 'princess'.

Alaina
(alt. Alane, Alayna)
Feminine of Alan, originating
from the French for 'rock' or
'comely'.

Alair
(alt. Allair, Alayr)
French, meaning 'one with a
happy disposition'.

Alake
African, meaning 'honoured one'.

Alamea
Hawaiian, meaning 'precious
one'.

Alana
(alt. Alanna, Alannah)
Variant of Alaina, meaning 'rock'
or 'comely'.

Alanis
(alt. Alarice)
Variant of Alaina, meaning 'rock'
or 'comely'.

Alaqua
Native American, meaning 'a
sweet gum tree'.

Alaula
Hawaiian, meaning 'dawn light'.

Alba
Latin for 'white'. Also the Gaelic
for 'Scotland'.

Alberta
(alt. Albertha)
Feminine of Albert, from the old
English for 'bright and shining'.

Albina
Latin for 'white' or 'fair'.

Alcina
(alt. Alcee, Alcie)
Greek, meaning 'strong in mind'.

Alcyone
Greek, meaning 'kingfisher'. The source of the name Halcyon for a type of kingfishers.

Alda
German, meaning 'old' or 'prosperous'.

Aldis
English, meaning 'battle-seasoned'.

Aldona
(alt. Aldone)
American, meaning 'sweet'.

Aleah
(alt. Aileah, Alleeah)
Arabic, meaning 'high'. Persian, meaning 'one of God's beings'.

Aleela
(alt. Aleelah, Alila)
Swahili, meaning 'she cries'.

Aleesha
Alternative of Alicia, meaning 'nobility'.

Aleeza
(alt. Aleezah, Aleiza, Alieza)
Hebrew, meaning 'joy'. Alternative of Alicia.

Alegria
(alt. Allegria)
Spanish, meaning 'lovely movement'.

Aleta
(alt. Aletha)
Greek for 'footloose'.

Alessandra
(alt. Aless, Alessa)
Italian, meaning 'defender of man'.

Alethea
(alt. Aletheia)
Greek, meaning 'truth'.

Alex
(alt. Alexa, Alexi)
Shortened version of Alexandra, meaning 'man's defender'.

Alexa
Alternative of Alexandra, meaning 'man's defender'.

Alexandra
(alt. Alejandra, Aleksandra, Alessandra, Alexandrea, Alexandria)
Feminine of Alexander, from the Greek interpretation of 'man's defender'.

Alexis
(alt. Alexus, Alexys)
Greek, meaning 'helper'.

Aleydis
Variant of Alice, meaning 'nobility'.

Alfreda
Old English, meaning 'elf power'.

Ali
(alt. Allie, Ally)
Shortened version of Alexandra, Aliyah or Alice.

A

Alibeth
Variant of Elizabeth, meaning 'pledged to God'.

Alice
(alt. Alize, Alyce, Alyse)
English, meaning 'noble' or 'nobility'.

Alicia
(alt. Alecia, Alessia, Alizia, Alysia)
Variant of Alice, meaning 'nobility'.

Alida
(alt. Aleida)
Latin, meaning 'small winged one'.

Alienor
(alt. Aliana)
Variant spelling of Eleanor, from the Greek for 'light'.

Aliki
(alt. Alika)
Variant of Alice, meaning 'nobility'.

Alima
Arabic, meaning 'cultured'.

Alina
(alt. Alena)
A Slavic variation of Helen, meaning 'light'.

Alisha
(alt. Alesha, Alysha)
Variant of Alice, meaning 'nobility'.

Alison
(alt. Allison, Allisyn, Alyson)
Variant of Alice, meaning 'nobility'.

Alissa
(alt. Alessa, Alise)
Greek, meaning 'pretty'.

Alita
Alternative of Alida, meaning 'small winged one'.

Alivia
Variant spelling of Olivia, meaning 'olive tree'.

Aliya
(alt. Aaliyah)
Arabic, meaning 'exalted' or 'sublime'.

Alla
Variant on Ella or Alexandra. Also a possible reference to Allah.

Allegra
Italian, meaning 'joyous'.

Allura
From the French word for entice, meaning 'the power of attraction'.

Allyn
Feminine of Alan, meaning 'peaceful'.

Alma
Three possible origins; Latin for 'giving nurture', Italian for 'soul' and Arabic for 'learned'.

Almeda
(alt. Almeta)
Latin, meaning 'ambitious'.

Almera
(alt. Almira)
Feminine of Elmer, from the Arabic for 'aristocratic'.

Alodie
(alt. Alodee)
English, meaning 'wealthy'.

Alohi
Variant on the Hawaiian greeting Aloha, meaning 'love and affection'.

Alona
Hebrew, meaning 'oak tree'.

Alora
Variant of Alona, meaning 'oak tree'.

Alouette
(alt. Allouette, Alowette)
French, meaning 'like a bird'.

Alpha
The first letter of the Greek alphabet, usually given to a first-born daughter.

Alta
Latin, meaning 'elevated'.

Altagracia
Spanish, meaning 'grace'.

Althea
(alt. Altea, Altha)
From the Greek, meaning 'healing power'.

Alva
Spanish, meaning 'blond' or 'fair skinned'.

Alvena
(alt. Alvina)
English, meaning 'noble friend'.

Alvia
(alt. Alyvia)
Variant of Olivia or Elvira.

Alyda
(alt. Aleda, Alida, Alita)
French, meaning 'soaring'.

Alyssa
(alt. Alisa, Alysa)
Greek, meaning 'rational'.

Ama
African, meaning 'born on Saturday'.

Amabel
Variant of Annabel, meaning 'grace and beauty'.

Amadea
Feminine of Amadeus, meaning 'God's beloved'.

Amalia
Variant of Emilia, meaning 'industrious'.

Amana
Hebrew, meaning 'loyal and true'.

Amanda
Latin, meaning 'much loved'.

Amandine
Variant of Amanda, meaning 'much loved'.

Amara
(alt. Amani)
Greek, meaning 'lovely forever'.

Amarantha
Contraction of Amanda and Samantha, meaning 'much loved listener'.

Amaris
(alt. Amari, Amasa)
Hebrew, meaning 'pledged by God'.

Amaryllis
Greek, meaning 'fresh'. Also a flower by the same name.

Amber
From the French word for the semi-precious stone of the same name.

Amberly
Contraction of Amber and Leigh, meaning 'stone' and 'meadow'.

Amberlynn
Contraction of Amber and Lynn, meaning 'stone' and 'waterfall'.

Amboree
(alt. Ambor, Ambree)
American, meaning 'precocious'.

Ambrosia
(alt. Ambrozia)
Greek, meaning 'eternal'.

Amelia
(alt. Aemilia)
Greek, meaning 'industrious'.

Amelie
(alt. Amalie)
French version of Amelia, meaning 'industrious'.

Amera
Arabic, meaning 'royal birth'.

America
From the country of the same name.

Ameris
Variant of amaryllis, meaning 'fresh'.

Amethyst
From the Greek word for the precious, mulberry coloured stone of the same name.

Amina
Arabic, meaning 'honest and trustworthy'.

Amira
(alt. Amiya, Amiyah)
Arabic, meaning 'a highborn girl'.

Amity
Latin, meaning 'friendship and harmony'.

Amory
Variant on the Spanish name Amor, meaning 'love'.

Amy
(alt. Amee, Amie)
Latin, meaning 'beloved'.

Amya
Variant on Amy, meaning 'beloved'.

Ana-Lisa
Contraction of Anna and Lisa, meaning 'gracious' or 'consecrated to God'.

Anafa
Hebrew, meaning 'heron'.

Ananda
Hindi, meaning 'bliss'.

Anastasia
(alt. Athanasia)
Greek, meaning 'resurrection'.

Anatolia
From the eastern Greek town of the same name.

Andelyn
Contraction of the feminine for Andrew and Lynn, meaning 'strong waterfall'.

Andrea
(alt. Andreia, Andria)
Feminine of Andrew, from the Greek term for 'a man's woman'.

Andrine
Variant of Andrea, meaning 'a man's woman'.

Andromeda
From the heroine of a Greek legend.

Anemone
Greek, meaning 'breath'.

Angela
(alt. Angelia, Angelle)
Greek, meaning 'messenger from God' or 'angel'.

Angelica
(alt. Angelina, Angeline, Angelique)
Latin, meaning 'angelic'.

Anise
(alt. Anisa)
From the licorice flavoured plant of the same name.

Anita
(alt. Anitra)
Variant of Ann, meaning 'grace'.

Ann
(alt. Anne, Annie)
Derived from Hannah, meaning 'grace'.

Anna
(alt. Ana)
Derived from Hannah, meaning 'grace'.

Annabel
(alt. Anabelle, Annabella, Annabelle)
Contraction of Anna and Belle, meaning 'grace' and 'beauty'.

Annalise
(alt. Annaliese, Annalisa)
Contraction of Anna and Lise, meaning 'grace' and 'pledged to God'.

Annemarie
(alt. Annamae, Annmarie)
Contraction of Anna and Mary, meaning 'grace' and 'bitterness or rebellious'.

Annette
(alt. Annetta)
Derived from Anna and Hannah, meaning 'grace'.

Annis
Greek, meaning 'finished or completed'.

Annora
Latin, meaning 'honour'.

Anoushka
(alt. Anousha)
A Russian variation of Ann, meaning 'grace'.

Ansley
English, meaning 'the awesome one's meadow'.

Anthea
(alt. Anthi)
Greek, meaning 'flowerlike'.

A

Antigone
In Greek mythology, Antigone was the daughter of Oedipus.

Antoinette
(alt. Antonette, Antonietta)
Both a variation of Ann and the feminine of Anthony, meaning 'invaluable grace'.

Antonia
(alt. Antonella, Antonina)
Latin, meaning 'invaluable'.

Anwen
Welsh, meaning 'very fair'.

Anya
(alt. Aniyah, Anja)
Russian, meaning 'grace'.

Aphrodite
(alt. Afrodite)
Greek, the mythological goddess of love and beauty.

Apollonia
Feminine of Apollo, the Greek god of the sun.

Apple
Name of the fruit.

April
(alt. Avril)
Latin, meaning 'opening up'. Also the name of the month.

Aquilina
(alt. Aquila)
Spanish, meaning 'like an eagle'.

Ara
Arabic, meaning 'brings rain'.

Arabella
Latin, meaning 'answered prayer'.

Araceli
(alt. Aracely)
Spanish, meaning 'altar of Heaven'.

Araminta
Contraction of Arabella and Amita, meaning 'altar of Heaven' and 'friendship'.

Araylia
(alt. Araelea)
Latin, meaning 'golden'.

Arcadia
Greek, meaning 'paradise'.

Ardelle
(alt. Ardell, Ardella)
Latin, meaning 'burning with enthusiasm'.

Arden
(alt. Ardis, Ardith)
Latin, meaning 'burning with enthusiasm'.

Arekah
Greek, meaning 'virtuous'.

Arella
(alt. Areli, Arely)
Hebrew, meaning 'angel'.

Arete
Greek, meaning 'goodness'. Queen of the Phaeacians in Homer's *Odyssey*.

Aretha
Greek, meaning 'woman of virtue'.

Aria
(alt. Ariah)
Italian, meaning 'melody'.

Ariadne
In Greek mythology, Ariadne was the daughter of King Minos.

Ariana
(alt. Ariane, Arienne)
Welsh, meaning 'silver'.

Ariel
(alt. Ariela, Ariella, Arielle)
Hebrew, meaning 'Lioness of God'.

Arista
(alt. Aristella, Aristelle)
Greek, meaning 'wonderful'.

Arlene
(alt. Arleen, Arline)
Gaelic, meaning 'pledge'.

Armida
Latin, meaning 'little armed one'.

Artemisia
(alt. Artemis)
Of both Greek and Spanish origin, meaning 'perfect'.

Artie
(alt. Arti)
Shortened form of Artemisia, meaning 'perfect'.

Ashanti
Geographical area in Africa

Ashby
English, meaning 'ash tree farm'.

Ashley
(alt. Ashlee, Ashleigh, Ashlie, Ashly)
English, meaning 'ash tree meadow'.

Ashlynn
Irish Gaelic, meaning 'dream'.

Ashton
(alt. Ashtyn)
Place name.

Asia
Name of continent.

Asma
(alt. Asmara)
Arabic, meaning 'high-standing'.

Aspasia
(alt. Aspashia)
Greek, meaning 'witty'.

Aspen
(alt. Aspynn)
Name of the tree. Also name of a city in the USA.

Assumpta
(alt. Assunta)
Italian, meaning 'raised up'.

Asta
(alt. Astor, Astoria)
Greek or Latin, meaning 'star-like'.

Astrid
Old Norse, meaning 'beautiful like a God'.

Atara
Hebrew, meaning 'diadem'.

Athena
(alt. Athenais)
The Greek goddess of wisdom.

A

Aubrey
(alt. Aubree, Aubriana, Aubrie)
French, meaning 'elf ruler'.

Audrey
(alt. Audrie, Audry,Autry)
English, meaning 'noble strength'.

Audrina
Alternative of Audrey, meaning 'noble strength'.

Augusta
(alt. August, Augustine)
Latin, meaning 'worthy of respect'.

Aura
(alt. Aurea)
Greek or Latin, meaning either 'soft breeze' or 'gold'.

Aurelia
(alt. Aurelie)
Latin, meaning 'gold'.

Aurora
(alt. Aurore)
In Roman mythology, Aurora was the goddess of the sunrise.

Austine
(alt. Austen, Austin)
Latin, meaning 'worthy of respect'.

Autra
(alt. Aut)
Latin, meaning 'gold'.

Autumn
Name of the season.

Ava
(alt. Avia, Avie)
Latin, meaning 'like a bird'.

Avalon
(alt. Avalyn, Aveline)
Celtic, meaning 'island of apples'.

Axelle
Greek, meaning 'father of peace.'

Aya
(alt. Ayah)
Hebrew, meaning 'bird'.

Ayanna
(alt. Ayana)
American, meaning 'grace'.

Ayesha
(alt. Aisha, Aysha)
Persian, meaning 'small one'.

Azalea
Latin, meaning 'dry earth'.

Azalia
Hebrew, meaning 'aided by God'.

Aziza
Hebrew, meaning 'mighty', or Arabic, meaning 'precious'.

Azure
(alt. Azaria)
French, meaning 'sky-blue'.

Olympians

Cathy (Freeman)
Kelly (Holmes)
Maria (Mutola)
Marion (Jones)
Paula (Radcliffe)
Rebecca (Romero)
Sally (Gunnell)
Yalena (Isinbayeva)

B Girls' names

Baako
(alt. Bako)
African, meaning 'firstborn'.

Baba
(alt. Babah)
African, meaning 'born on Thursday'.

Babette
French version of Barbara, from the Greek origin meaning 'foreign'.

Baca
(alt. Bacah, Bacca)
English, meaning 'of the valley of tears'.

Bachi
(alt. Bachee, Bachey)
Japanese, meaning 'happy'.

Badia
(alt. Basdiah, Badiya, Badea)
Arabic, meaning 'elegant'.

Bahar
(alt. Bahaar, Baharr)
Arabic, meaning 'spring birth'.

Bahati
(alt. Bahatie, Bahaty)
African, meaning 'fortunate'.

Bahija
(alt. Bahigah, Bahyja, Bahyga)
Arabic, meaning 'cheerful'.

Baila
(alt. Byla, Baela)
Spanish, meaning 'dancer'.

Bailey
(alt. Baeli, Bailee)
English, meaning 'law enforcer'.

Baina
(alt. Bayna, Baena)
African, meaning 'sparkling'.

Baja
Spanish, meaning 'lower'.

Baka
Indian, meaning 'like a crane'.

Balbina
Latin, meaning 'strong'.

Baldhart
(alt. Balhart, Baldhard)
German, meaning 'a bold and strong woman'.

Baligha
(alt. Baleegha, Balygha)
Arabic, meaning 'eloquent'.

Ballade
(alt. Ballad, Ballayd)
English, meaning 'poetic'.

Bambi
Shortened version of the Italian 'bambina', meaning 'child'.

Banan
Arabic, meaning 'one who had delicate fingers'.

Bandele
(alt. Bandelle)
African, meaning 'a child born away from home'.

Bano
(alt. Banow, Banoe)
Arabic, meaning 'princess'.

Banon
Welsh, meaning 'queen'.

Bansuri
(alt. Bansari, Banseri)
Indian, meaning 'a musical person'.

Bara
(alt. Barah)
Hebrew, meaning 'chosen'.

Barbara
(alt. Barbie, Barbra)
Greek, meaning 'foreign'.

Barika
(alt. Barycca)
African, meaning 'flourishing'.

Barett
(alt. Barrette)
German, meaning 'bear-like strength' or English, meaning 'argumentative'.

Basanti
Indian, meaning 'a child born during the spring'.

Basma
Arabic, meaning 'smile'.

Bashirah
(alt. Basheera, Bashyra)
Arabic, meaning 'joyful'.

Bastet
(alt. Bastette, Basteta)
Egyptian, meaning 'fiery'.

Bathild
(alt. Bathilde, Bathilda)
German, meaning 'heroine'.

Bathsheba
Hebrew, meaning 'daughter of the oath'.

Bay
(alt. Baya)
Plant or geographical name.

Bayo
Nigerian, meaning 'finder of joy'.

Beadu
English, meaning 'female warrior'.

Beata
Latin, meaning 'blessed'.

Beatrice
(alt. Beatrix, Beatriz, Bellatrix, Betrys)
Latin, meaning 'bringer of gladness'.

Bebhinn
(alt. Bevin)
Irish, meaning 'accomplished singer'.

Becca
English, shortened form of Rebecca, meaning 'noose'.

B

Becky
(alt. Beccie, Beccy, Beckie)
Shortened form of Rebecca,
meaning 'noose'.

Beda
(alt. Beddah)
German, meaning 'goddess'.

Bedelia
(alt. Bedeleah, Bedeliah)
French, meaning 'superior
strength'.

Bee
Shortened form of Beatrice,
meaning 'bringer of gladness'.

Begum
Turkish, meaning 'princess'.

Belinda
(alt. Belen, Belina)
Contraction of Belle and Linda,
meaning 'beautiful'.

Bell
Shortened form of Isabel,
meaning 'pledged to God'.

Bella
Latin, meaning 'beautiful'.

Ballachay
American, meaning 'beautiful
hawk'.

Bellatrix
Latin, meaning 'warlike'. A
literary character in *Harry Potter*,
played by Helena Bonham Carter
in the films.

Belle
French, meaning 'beautiful'.

Belva
Latin, meaning 'beautiful view'.

Bena
Hebrew, meaning 'wise'.

Bénédicta
Latin, the feminine of Benedict,
meaning 'blessed'.

Benita
(alt. Bernita)
Spanish, meaning 'blessed'.

Bennett
Latin, meaning 'blessed little
one'. Family name of Elizabeth
in *Pride and Prejudice* by Jane
Austen.

Bennie
Shortened version of Bénédicta
and Benita.

Berit
(alt. Beret)
Scandinavian, meaning 'splendid'
or 'gorgeous'.

Bernadette
French, meaning 'courageous'.

Bernadine
French, meaning 'courageous'.

Bernice
(alt. Burnice)
Greek, meaning 'she who brings
victory'.

Bertha
(alt. Berta, Berthe, Bertie)
German origin, meaning 'bright'.

Beryl
Greek, meaning 'pale, green
gemstone'.

B

Bess
(alt. Bessie)
Shortened form of Elizabeth,
meaning 'consecrated to God'.

Beth
Hebrew, meaning 'house'. Also
shortened form of Elizabeth,
meaning 'consecrated to God'.

Bethany
(alt. Bethan)
Biblical, referring to a
geographical location.

Bethari
Indonesian, meaning 'goddess'.

Bethel
Hebrew, meaning 'house of God'.

Bettina
Spanish version of Elizabeth,
meaning 'consecrated to God'.

Betty
(alt. Betsy, Bette, Bettie)
Shortened version of Elizabeth,
meaning 'consecrated to God'.

Movie inspirations

Daisy (*Driving Miss Daisy*)
Donna (*Mamma Mia*)
Ellen/Ripley (*Alien*)
Holly (*Breakfast at Tiffany's*)
Ilsa (*Casablanca*)
Kathy (*Singing in the Rain*)
Lara (*Tomb Raider*)
Maria (*The Sound of Music*)
Scarlett (*Gone with the Wind*)
Trinity (*The Matrix*)

Beulah
Hebrew, meaning 'married'.

Beverly
(alt. Beverlee, Beverley)
English, meaning 'beaver stream'.

Bevin
Celtic, meaning 'fair lady'.

Beyoncé
American, made popular by the
singer.

Bianca
(alt. Blanca)
Italian, meaning 'white'.

Bibiana
Greek, meaning 'alive'.

Bidelia
Irish, meaning 'exalted'.

Bijou
French, meaning 'precious ring'.

Billie
(alt. Billy, Billye)
Shortened version of Wilhelmina,
meaning 'determined'.

Bimala
Indian, meaning 'pure'.

Bina
Hebrew, meaning 'knowledge'.

Birgit
(alt. Birgitta)
Norwegian, meaning 'splendid'.

Blair
Scottish Gaelic, meaning 'flat,
plain area'.

B

Blake
(alt. Blakely, Blakelyn)
English, meaning either 'pale-skinned or dark'.

Blanche
(alt. Blanch)
French, meaning 'white or pale'.

Bliss
English, meaning 'intense happiness'.

Blithe
English, meaning 'joyous'.

Blodwen
Welsh, meaning 'white flower'.

Blossom
English, meaning 'flowerlike'.

Bluma
Hebrew, meaning 'a flower'

Blythe
(alt. Bly)
English, meaning 'happy and carefree'.

Bo
Chinese, meaning 'precious'.

Bobbi
(alt. Bobbie, Bobby)
Shortened version of Roberta, meaning 'famous brilliance'.

Bonamy
(alt. Bonamee)
French, meaning 'a close friend'.

Bonita
Spanish, meaning 'pretty'.

Bonnie
(alt. Bonny)
Scottish, meaning 'fair of face'.

Botan
(alt. Botanna, Botanne)
Japanese, meaning 'like a fresh blossom'.

Bracha
(alt. Brakka)
Hebrew, meaning 'blessed one'.

Brandy
(alt. Brandee, Brandi, Brandie)
Name of the liquor.

Branka
Slavic, meaning 'glory'.

Branwen
Welsh, meaning 'a white crow'.

Braulia
Spanish, meaning 'glowing'.

Brea
(alt. Bree, Bria)
Shortened form of Brianna, meaning 'strong'.

Breena
(alt. Brina, Bryna)
Irish, meaning 'of the fairy place'.

Brenda
Old Norse meaning 'sword'.

Brianna
(alt. Breana, Briana, Brianne, Bryanna)
Irish Gaelic, meaning 'strong'.

B

Bridget
(alt. Bridgett, Bridgette, Brigette,
Brigid, Brigitta, Brigitte)
Irish Gaelic, meaning 'strength
and power'.

Brier
French, meaning 'heather'.

Brimlad
(alt. Brymlad, Brymlod)
Anglo-Saxon, meaning 'from the
sea'.

Brit
(alt. Britt, Britta)
Celtic, meaning 'spotted' or
'freckled'.

Britannia
Latin, meaning 'Britain'.

Brittany
(alt. Britany, Britney, Brittani, Brittanie)
Latin, meaning 'from England'.

Bronwyn
(alt. Bronwen)
Welsh, meaning 'fair breast'.

Brooke
(alt. Brook)
English, meaning 'small stream'.

Brooklyn
(alt. Brooklynn)
Name of a New York suburb.

Buana
Indonesian, meaning 'earth'.

Buffy
American, alternative of
Elizabeth.

Brunhilda
German, meaning 'armour-
wearing fighting maid'.

Buthainah
Arabic, meaning 'beautiful'.

Bryanne
American, meaning 'noble'.

Bryn
(alt. Brynn)
Welsh, meaning 'mount'.

Bryony
(alt. Briony)
Greek, meaning 'climbing plant'.
Also the name of a European
vine.

Bysen
(alt. Bysan, Byson)
Anglo-Saxon, meaning 'a unique
girl'.

B

C Girls' names

Cabalina
Spanish, meaning 'involved with horses'.

Cabrera
Latin, meaning 'the goat's place'.

Cabriah
Spanish, meaning 'goat herder'.

Cable
American, meaning 'strength'.

Cabot
French, meaning 'youthful beauty'.

Cabrina
(alt. Cabrinna, Cabrynna)
American, alternative of Sabrina meaning 'the River Severn'.

Cabriole
(alt. Cabriol, Cabryole, Cabriola)
French, meaning 'adorable girl'.

Caca
Latin, original mythological goddess of the hearth.

Cacalia
(alt. Cacalea, Cacaleah)
Latin, meaning 'like the plant'.

Cacee
Irish, meaning 'cautious one'.

Cache
American, meaning 'storage'.

Cachele
(alt. Cachelle)
Hebrew, alternative of Rachelle meaning 'ewe'.

Cachet
(alt. Cachette)
French, meaning 'exalted woman'.

Cacia
(alt. Caciah, Cacea)
Greek, alternative of Acacia meaning 'point' or 'thorn'. Also an alternative of Casey meaning 'watchful'.

Caddy
(alt. Caddi, Caddie, Caddee)
American, meaning 'alluring'.

Cade
(alt. Caid, Cayde, Caed)
American, meaning 'talented'.

Cadeau
French, meaning 'gift'.

Caden
(alt. Cadan, Cadin)
English, meaning 'female warrior'.

Cadence
Latin, meaning 'with rhythm'.

Cadha
(alt. Cadhah)
Scottish, meaning 'steep mountain'.

C

Cadhla
(alt. Cadhlah)
Irish, meaning 'beautiful'.

Cadis
(alt. Cadisse, Cadys)
Greek, meaning 'sparkling girl'.

Cadwyn
Welsh, meaning 'strong binding'.

Cady
(alt. Cadye, Caidee, Caidy, Kady)
English, meaning 'fun-loving'.

Cael
(alt. Caele, Caelle)
Celtic, meaning 'triumphant people'.

Caenus
(alt. Caenis, Caenius)
Greek, mythological man who had once been a woman.

Caesaria
Roman, female form of Caesar meaning 'empress'.

Caffaria
Irish, meaning 'helmeted'.

Cahira
(alt. Cahyra, Cahiera)
Irish, meaning 'female warrior'.

Cai
Vietnamese, meaning 'feminine'.

Caia
(alt. Cai, Cais)
Latin, meaning 'rejoice'.

Cailin
(alt. Caelan, Caelyn, Caileen)
Gaelic, meaning 'girl'.

Cailleach
(alt. Caillic)
Scottish, meaning 'mother of all'.

Cainell
(alt. Cainele, Caynell, Caynelle)
Welsh, meaning 'beautiful girl'.

Cainwen
(alt. Cainwenne, Cainwin, Cainwynne)
Welsh, meaning 'beautiful treasure'.

Caitlin
(alt. Cadyn, Caitlyn)
Greek, meaning 'pure'.

Cala
(alt. Calah)
Arabic, meaning 'fortress'.

Calandra
Greek, meaning 'lark'.

Calantha
(alt. Calanthe)
Greek, meaning 'lovely flower'.

Calatea
(alt. Calateah, Calatia)
Greek, meaning 'flowering'.

Cale
Latin, meaning 'respected'.

Caledonia
Latin, meaning 'from Scotland'.

Calia
(alt. Calea, Caleah)
American, meaning 'renowned beauty'.

Calida
(alt. Calyda, Caleeda)
Spanish, meaning 'warm' and 'loving'.

Calise
(alt. Calyse, Calyce)
Greek, meaning 'gorgeous'.

Calista
Greek, alternative of Kallista meaning 'most beautiful'.

Calla
Greek, meaning 'beautiful'.

Callida
(alt. Callyda)
Latin, meaning 'fiery girl'.

Callie
(alt. Cali, Calleigh)
Greek, meaning 'beauty'.

Calliope
From the muse of epic poetry in Greek mythology.

Callista
(alt. Callisto)
Greek, meaning 'most beautiful'.

Calluna
(alt. Callunah)
Latin, meaning 'like heather'.

Calpurnia
Latin, meaning 'powerful woman'.

Columina
Spanish, meaning 'calm' and 'peaceful'.

Calypso
Greek, meaning 'secret keeper'. Also a nymph in mythology accused of imprisoning Odysseus for seven years.

Camas
Native American, from the root and bulb of the same name.

Cambria
Welsh, from the alternative name of the same country.

Camden
(alt. Camdyn)
English, meaning 'winding valley'.

Cameo
Italian, meaning 'skin'.

Cameron
(alt. Camryn)
Scottish Gaelic, meaning 'bent nose'.

Camilla
(alt. Camelia, Camellia)
Latin, meaning 'spiritual serving girl'.

Camille
Latin, meaning 'spiritual serving girl'.

Candace
(alt. Candice, Candis)
Latin, meaning 'brilliant white'.

Candida
Of Latin origin, meaning 'white'.

Candra
Latin, meaning 'glowing'.

Candy
(alt. Candi)
Shortened form of Candace, meaning 'brilliant white'.

Caneadea
Native American, meaning 'horizion'.

Canei
Greek, meaning 'pure'.

Canna
Latin, meaning 'reed'.

Caoimhe
Celtic, meaning 'gentleness'.

Caprice
Italian, meaning 'ruled by whim'.

Cara
Latin, meaning 'darling'.

Caren
(alt. Caron, Caryn)
Greek, meaning 'pure'.

Carey
(alt. Cari, Carrie, Cary)
Welsh, meaning 'near the castle'.

Carina
(alt. Corina)
Italian, meaning 'dearest little one'.

Carissa
(alt. Carisa)
Greek, meaning 'grace'.

Carla
(alt. Charla)
Feminine of the German Carl, meaning 'man'.

Carlin
(alt. Carleen, Carlene)
Gaelic, meaning 'little champion'.

Carlotta
(alt. Carlota)
Italian, meaning 'free man'.

Carly
(alt. Carley, Carli, Carlie)
Feminine of the German Charles, meaning 'man'.

Carmel
(alt. Carmelita, Carmella)
Hebrew, meaning 'garden'.

Carmen
(alt. Carma, Carmina)
Latin, meaning 'song'.

Carol
(alt. Carole, Carrol, Carroll)
Shortened form of Caroline, meaning 'man'.

Caroline
(alt. Carolina, Carolyn, Carolynn)
German, meaning 'man'.

Carrington
English, meaning 'Charles's town'.

Carys
(alt. Cerys)
Welsh, meaning 'love'.

Casey
Irish Gaelic, meaning 'watchful'.

Cassandra
(alt. Cassandre)
Greek, meaning 'one who prophesises doom'.

Cassia
(alt. Casia, Cassie)
Greek, meaning 'cinnamon'.

Cassidy
Irish, meaning 'clever'.

C

Cassiopeia
(alt. Cassiopia, Cassiopea)
Greek, mythological mother of
Andromeda and a constellation.

Catalina
(alt. Catarina, Caterina)
Spanish version of Catherine,
meaning 'pure'.

Catherine
(alt. Catharine, Cathryn)
Greek, meaning 'pure'.

Cathleen
Irish version of Catherine,
meaning 'pure'.

Cathy
(alt. Cathey, Cathie)
Shortened form of Catherine,
meaning 'pure'.

Catima
Greek, meaning 'innocent'.

Caty
(alt. Caddie, Caitee, Cate, Catie)
Shortened form of Catherine,
meaning 'pure'.

Cavender
(alt. Cavendar)
American, meaning 'emotional'.

Cayla
(alt. Caileigh, Caile)
Hebrew, meaning 'laurel crown
wearer' and Gaelic, meaning
'slender'.

Cayley
(alt. Cayla, Caylee, Caylen)
American, meaning 'pure'.

Cecilia
(alt. Cecelia, Cecily)
Latin, meaning 'blind one'.

Cecile
(alt. Cecilie)
Latin, meaning 'blind one'.

Celena
Greek, meaning 'goddess of the
moon'.

Celeste
(alt. Celestina, Celestine)
Latin, meaning 'Heavenly'.

Celka
(alt. Celki, Celkee, Celkea, Celkeah)
Latin, meaning 'celestial being'.

Celine
(alt. Celia, Celina)
French version of Celeste,
meaning 'Heavenly'.

Cerise
French, meaning 'cherry'.

Chanah
Hebrew, meaning 'grace'.

Chandler
(alt. Chandell)
English, meaning 'candle maker'.

Chandra
(alt. Chanda, Chandry)
Sanskrit, meaning 'like the moon'.

Chanel
(alt. Chanelle)
French, from the designer of the
same name.

Chantal
(alt. Chantel, Chantelle)
French, meaning 'stony spot'.

C

Chardonnay
French, from the wine variety of the same name.

Charis
(alt. Charissa, Charisse)
Greek, meaning 'grace'.

Charity
Latin, meaning 'brotherly love'.

Charlene
(alt. Charleen, Charline)
German, meaning 'man'.

Charlie
(alt. Charlee, Charlize, Charly)
Shortened form of Charlotte, meaning 'little and feminine'.

Charlotte
(alt. Charnette, Charolette)
French, meaning 'little and feminine'.

Charmaine
Latin, meaning 'clan'.

Charnee
(alt. Charney, Charnea, Charnie)
American, meaning 'joyful'.

Charnelle
American, meaning 'sparkles'.

Chasteria
Vietnamese, meaning 'born in the moonlight'.

Chastity
Latin, meaning 'purity'.

Chava
(alt. Chaya)
Hebrew, meaning 'beloved'.

Chelsea
(alt. Chelsee, Chelsey, Chelsie)
English, meaning 'port or landing place'.

Cher
French, meaning 'beloved'.

Cherie
(alt. Cheri, Cherise)
French, meaning 'dear'.

Cherish
(alt. Cherith)
English, meaning 'to treasure'.

Chermona
Hebrew, meaning 'sacred mountain'.

Cherry
(alt. Cherri)
French, meaning 'cherry fruit'.

Cheryl
(alt. Cheryle)
English, meaning 'little and womanly'.

Chesney
English, meaning 'place to camp'.

Cheyenne
(alt. Cheyanne)
Native American, from the tribe of the same name.

Chiara
(alt. Ceara, Ciara)
Italian, meaning 'light'.

China
From the country of the same name.

Chiquita
Spanish, meaning 'little one'.

C

Chloe
(alt. Cloe)
Greek, meaning 'pale green shoot'.

Chloris
Of Greek origin, meaning 'pale'.

Chris
(alt. Chrissy, Christa, Christie, Christy)
Shortened form of Christina, meaning 'anointed Christian'.

Christabel
Both Latin and French, meaning 'fair Christian'.

Christina
(alt. Christiana, Cristina)
Greek, meaning 'anointed Christian'.

Christine
(alt. Christeen, Christene, Christiane, Christin)
Greek, meaning 'anointed Christian'.

Chrysantha
Greek, meaning 'the people's defender'.

Chuma
Aramaic, meaning 'warmth'.

Chun
Chinese, meaning 'born in spring'.

Chyou
Chinese, meaning 'born in autumn'.

Ciara
(alt. Ceara, Ciarra, Cyara)
Irish, meaning 'dark beauty'.

Cierra
(alt. Ciera)
Irish, meaning 'black'.

Cinderella
French, meaning 'little ash-girl'.

Cindy
(alt. Cinda, Cindi, Cyndi)
Shortened form of Cynthia, meaning 'goddess'.

Cinnamon
Greek, from the spice of the same name.

Circe
(alt. Cyrce)
Greek, in mythology a sorceress capable of turning men into swine.

Citlali
(alt. Citlalli)
Aztec, meaning 'star'.

Citrine
Latin, from the gemstone of the same name.

Claire
(alt. Clare)
Latin, meaning 'bright'.

Clara
(alt. Claira)
Latin, meaning 'bright'.

Clarabelle
(alt. Claribel)
Contraction of Clara and Isobel, meaning 'bright' and 'consecrated to God'.

C

Clarissa
(alt. Clarice, Clarisse)
Variation of Claire, meaning
'bright'.

Clarity
Latin, meaning 'lucid'.

Claudette
Latin, meaning 'lame'.

Claudia
(alt. Claudie, Claudine)
Latin, meaning 'lame'.

Clematis
Greek, meaning 'vine'.

Clementine
(alt. Clemency, Clementina)
Latin, meaning 'mild and
merciful'.

Cleopatra
Greek, meaning 'her father's
renown'.

Clio
(alt. Cleo, Cliona)
Greek, from the muse of history
of the same name.

Clodagh
Irish, meaning 'river'.

Clotilda
(alt. Clothilda, Clothilde, Clotilde)
German, meaning 'renowned
battle'.

Cloud
(alt. Cloude)
American, meaning 'lighthearted'.

Clover
English, from the flower of the
same name.

Coahoma
Native American, meaning 'like a
panther'.

Coby
(alt. Cobey, Cobee, Cobea)
Hebrew, feminine alternative
of Jacob meaning 'she who
supplants'.

Coco
Spanish, meaning 'help'.

Cody
English, meaning 'pillow'.

Colby
English, meaning 'coal town
inhabitant'.

Colleen
(alt. Coleen)
Irish Gaelic, meaning 'girl'.

Collette
(alt. Colette)
Greek and French, meaning
'people of victory'.

Connie
Latin, meaning 'steadfast'.

Constance
(alt. Constanza)
Latin, meaning 'steadfast'.

Consuelo
(alt. Consuela)
Spanish, meaning 'comfort'.

Cora
Greek, meaning 'maiden'.

Coral
(alt. Coralie, Coraline, Corelia, Corene)
Latin, from the marine life of the
same name.

C

Corazon
Spanish, meaning 'heart'.

Cordelia
(alt. Cordia, Cordie)
Latin, meaning 'heart'.

Corey
(alt. Cori, Cory)
Irish Gaelic, meaning 'the hollow'.

Corin
(alt. Corine)
Latin, meaning 'spear'.

Corinne
(alt. Corinna, Corrine)
French version of Cora, meaning 'maiden'.

Corliss
English, meaning 'cheery'.

Cornelia
Latin, meaning 'like a horn'.

Cosette
French, meaning 'people of victory'.

Cosima
(alt. Cosmina)
Greek, meaning 'order'.

Courtney
(alt. Cortney)
English, meaning 'court-dweller'.

Creola
French, meaning 'American-born, English descent'.

Crescent
French, meaning 'increasing'.

Cressida
From the heroine in Greek mythology of the same name.

Crystal
(alt. Christal, Chrystal, Cristal)
Greek, meaning 'ice'.

Cushaun
American, meaning 'elegant'.

Cwen
(alt. Cwyn, Cwin)
English, meaning 'imperial woman'.

Csilla
Hungarian, meaning 'defences'.

Cybil
(alt. Cybella)
Greek, alternative of Sybil meaning 'seer'.

Cyma
(alt. Cymah)
Greek, meaning 'flourishing'.

Cynara
Greek, meaning 'thistly plant'.

Cynthia
Greek, meaning 'goddess from the mountain'.

Cyra
Persian, meaning 'sun'.

Cyrilla
Latin, meaning 'lordly'.

Czarina
(alt. Czaryna, Czareena)
Russian, meaning 'empress'.

C

D Girls' names

D'Anna
Hebrew, meaning 'special'.

Da-Xia
Chinese, meaning 'hero'.

Dabney
(alt. Dabnee)
French, meaning 'from Aubigny'.

Dabria
(alt. Dabrea, Dabrya)
Latin, meaning 'angel'.

Dacey
Irish Gaelic, meaning 'from the south'.

Dacia
Latin, meaning 'from Dacia'.

Dada
Nigerian, meaning 'curly haired'.

Dae
(alt. Day, Daye)
English, meaning 'day'.

Daelan
(alt. Daylan)
English, meaning 'aware'.

Daffodil
Dutch, meaning 'yellow flower'.

Dafnee
(alt. Dafney, Dafnie)
American, alternative of the Greek Daphne.

Dagania
(alt. Daganya, Daganyah)
Hebrew, meaning 'ceremonial grain'.

Dagmar
German, meaning 'Day's glory'.

Dagny
Nordic, meaning 'new day'.

Dahl
Scandinavian, meaning 'a valley'.

Dahlia
Scandinavian, from the flower of the same name.

Dai
Japanese, meaning 'great'.

Daina
Latvian, meaning 'song'.

Daira
(alt. Daerira, Dayeera)
Greek, meaning 'informed'.

Daisy
(alt. Dasia)
English, meaning 'eye of the day'.

Dakota
Native American, meaning 'allies'.

Dale
(alt. Dael, Dail, Dayle)
Old English, meaning 'a valley'.

Dalia
(alt. Dalila)
Hebrew, meaning 'delicate branch'.

Dalili
Swahili, meaning 'sign from the gods'.

Dallas
Scottish Gaelic, from the village of the same name. Also city in America.

Dalmace
(alt. Dalmassa, Dalmatia)
Latin, meaning 'from Dalmatia'.

Dalta
Gaelic, meaning 'favourite'.

Damali
Arabic, meaning 'beautiful vision'.

Damani
American, meaning 'tomorrow'.

Damara
(alt. Damaris, Mara, Mari)
Greek, meaning 'gentle girl'.

Damaris
Greek, meaning 'calf'.

Damia
(alt. Damya)
Greek, meaning 'tame' or 'spirit'.

Damica
(alt. Damika)
French, meaning 'friendly'.

Damita
Spanish, meaning 'little noblewoman'.

Damla
Turkish, meaning 'water droplet'.

Dana
(alt. Dania, Dayna)
English, meaning 'from Denmark'.

Danae
Greek, from the mythological heroine of the same name.

Dangela
American, meaning 'of angels'.

Dania
(alt. Danya, Danyah)
Hebrew, alternative of Danielle.

Danica
(alt. Danika)
Latin, meaning 'from Denmark'.

Danika
(alt. Danica, Danyca, Danyka)
Norse, meaning 'morning star'.

Danielle
(alt. Daniela, Danila, Danyelle)
The feminine form of the Hebrew Daniel, meaning 'God is my judge'.

Danita
English, meaning 'God will judge'.

Danu
Celtic, meaning 'goddess of fruitfulness'.

Danya
Hebrew, meaning 'God's gift'.

Dao-ming
Chinese, meaning 'like a shining path'.

Daphne
(alt. Dafne, Daphna)
Of Greek origin, meaning 'laurel tree'.

Dara
Hebrew and Persian, meaning 'wisdom'.

Daray
American, meaning 'dark'.

Darby
(alt. Darbi, Darbie)
Irish, meaning 'park with deer'.

Darcie
(alt. Darci, Darcy)
Irish Gaelic, meaning 'dark'.

Darda
Hebrew, meaning 'knowledge'.

Daria
Greek, meaning 'rich'.

Darian
(alt. Darien, Daryan, Daryen)
Anglo-Saxon, meaning 'precious'.

Darla
English, meaning 'darling'.

Darlene
(alt. Darleen, Darline)
American, meaning 'darling'.

Darren
(alt. Darin, Daryn)
Irish, meaning 'great little one'.

Darsha
(alt. Darshika, Darshna)
Hindi, meaning 'to see'.

Daru
Hindi, meaning 'pine'.

Darva
Slavic, meaning 'honeybee'.

Daryl
(alt. Darryl)
English, originally used as a surname.

Dasha
Russian, meaning 'present from God'.

Davina
Hebrew, meaning 'loved one'.

Dawn
(alt. Dawna)
English, meaning 'the dawn'.

Dayaa
Hindi, meaning 'compassion'.

Daya
Hebrew, meaning 'bird of prey'.

Dayo
Nigerian, meaning 'arrival of joy'.

Dayton
(alt. Deyton)
English, alternative of Deighton. Also a place in Florida, USA.

D

Dea
Latin, meaning 'goddess'.

Dean
(alt. Dene, Deni)
English, meaning 'church offical'.

Deanna
(alt. Dayana, Deanne)
English, meaning 'valley'.

Debbie
(alt. Debbi, Debby)
Shortened form of Deborah,
meaning 'bee'.

Deborah
(alt. Debora, Debra, Debrah)
Hebrew, meaning 'bee'.

December
Latin, meaning 'tenth month'.

Decima
(alt. Decia)
Latin, meaning 'tenth'.

Dee
Welsh, meaning 'swarthy'.

Deidre
(alt. Deidra, Deirdre)
Irish, meaning 'raging woman'.

Deja
(alt. Dejah)
French, meaning 'already'.

Delancey
(alt. Delancie)
French, meaning 'from Lancey'.

Delaney
Irish Gaelic, meaning 'offspring of
the challenger'.

Delia
Greek, meaning 'from Delos'.

Delicia
(alt. Daleesha, Dalicia, Delisa)
Latin, meaning 'delight'.

Delilah
(alt. Delina)
Hebrew, meaning 'seductive'.

Delja
Polish, meaning 'daughter of the
sea'.

Della
(alt. Dell)
Shortened form of Adele,
meaning 'nobility'.

Dellen
(alt. Dellan, Dellin, Dellon)
Cornish, meaning 'petal'.

Delores
(alt. Deloris)
Spanish, meaning 'sorrows'.

Delphine
(alt. Delpha, Delphia, Delphina)
Greek, meaning 'dolphin'.

Delta
Greek, meaning 'fourth child'.

Delyth
(alt. Delith)
Welsh, meaning 'pretty girl'.

Dembe
African, meaning 'peace'.

Demetria
(alt. Demetrice)
Greek, from the mythological
heroine of the same name.

D

Demi
French, meaning 'half'.

Dena
(alt. Deena)
English, meaning 'from the valley'.

Denise
(alt. Denice, Denisa, Denisse)
French, meaning 'follower of Dionysius'.

Deniz
Turkish, meaning 'the sea'.

Derby
English, meaning 'from the deer park'.

Derica
American, meaning 'ruler of the people'.

Derora
Hebrew, meaning 'stream'.

Desdemona
Greek, meaning 'wretchedness'.

Desiree
(alt. Desirae)
French, meaning 'much desired'.

Desma
Greek, meaning 'blinding oath'.

Despina
Greek, meaning 'lady'.

Dessa
Russian, alternative of Odessa.

Desta
African, meaning 'joy'.

Destiny
(alt. Destinee, Destiney, Destini)
French, meaning 'fate'.

Deva
Hindi, meaning 'God-like'.

Devaki
Sanskrit, meaning 'a God'.

Devan
Irish, meaning 'poet'.

Devi
Sanskrit, meaning 'power goddess'.

Devin
(alt. Devinne)
Irish Gaelic, meaning 'poet'.

Devon
English, from the county of the same name.

Dextra
American, feminine form of Dexter.

Dhavala
Indian, meaning 'white'.

Diamond
English, meaning 'brilliant'.

Diana
(alt. Diane, Dianna, Dianne)
Roman, meaning 'divine'.

Diandra
Greek, meaning 'two males'.

Diantha
(alt. Dianthe)
Greek, meaning 'heavenly flower'.

Diara
Latin, meaning 'a present'.

Dido
(alt. Dydo)
Greek, meaning 'wanderer'. The mythological queen of Carthage.

Didrika
German, meaning 'ruler of the people'.

Dilana
American, meaning 'from the light'.

Dilwyn
Welsh, meaning 'genuine'.

Dilys
Welsh, meaning 'reliable'.

Dimitra
Greek, meaning 'follower of Demeter'.

Dimona
Hebew, meaning 'south'.

Dinah
(alt. Dina)
Hebrew, meaning 'justified'.

Dionne
Greek, from the mythological heroine of the same name.

Dionysia
(alt. Dionisa, Dionis, Dionyze)
Greek, meaning 'Dionysus' gift'.

Dior
(alt. Deor, Diorre, Dyor)
French, meaning 'golden one'. Associated now with the fashion designer.

Divine
Italian, meaning 'heavenly'.

Dixie
French, meaning 'tenth'.

Dodie
Hebrew, meaning 'well-loved'.

Dolly
(alt. Dollie)
Shortened form of Dorothy, meaning 'gift of God'.

Dolores
(alt. Doloris)
Spanish, meaning 'sorrows'.

Domina
(alt. Dominah, Domyna)
Latin, meaning 'graceful lady'.

Dominique
(alt. Domenica, Dominica)
Latin, meaning 'Lord'.

Donata
Latin, meaning 'given'.

Donna
(alt. Dona, Donnie)
Italian, meaning 'lady'.

Donoma
Native American, meaning 'sight of the sun'.

Dora
Greek, meaning 'gift'.

Dorcas
Greek, meaning 'gazelle'.

Doreen
(alt. Dorene, Dorine)
Irish Gaelic, meaning 'brooding'.

D

Dori
Greek, meaning 'present'.

Doria
Greek, meaning 'of the sea'.

Doris
(alt. Dorris)
Greek, from the place of the same name.

Dorothy
(alt. Dorathy, Doretha, Dorotha, Dorothea, Dorthy)
Greek, meaning 'gift of God'.

Dorrit
(alt. Dorit)
Greek, meaning 'gift of God'.

Dory
(alt. Dori)
French, meaning 'gilded'.

Dottie
(alt. Dotty)
Shortened form of Dorothy, meaning 'gift of God'.

Dove
(alt. Dovie)
English, from the bird of the same name.

Dracen
English, meaning 'dragon'.

Drea
Greek, meaning 'courageous'.

Drew
Greek, meaning 'masculine'.

Drury
English, meaning 'love'.

Drusilla
(alt. Drucilla)
Latin, meaning 'of the Drusus clan'.

Duaa
Arabic, meaning 'prayer to God'.

Dulcie
(alt. Dulce, Dulcia)
Latin, meaning 'sweet'.

Dunne
English, meaning 'brown'.

Durriyah
Arabic, meaning 'shining'.

Duscha
Slavic, meaning 'heavenly spirit'.

Dusty
(alt. Dusti)
English, from the place of the same name. Made famous by the singer Dusty Springfield.

Duyen
Vietnamese, meaning 'grace'.

Dyan
American, meaning 'celestial'.

Dympna
Irish, meaning 'fawn'.

Dysis
Greek, meaning 'sunset'.

D

E Girls' names

Eachna
Irish, meaning 'horse'.

Eacnung
Anglo-Saxon, meaning 'fertile'.

Eada
(alt. Eadia, Eadea, Eadiah)
English, meaning 'prosperous'.

Eadaion
German, meaning 'joyous friend'.

Eadlin
(alt. Eadlyn)
Anglo-Saxon, meaning 'royalty'.

Eadrianne
(alt. Edreiann, Edrian, Edrie)
American, meaning 'standout'.

Ealasaid
Hebrew, meaning 'devotee to God'.

Ealga
(alt. Ealgia, Ealgiah, Ealgeah)
Irish, meaning 'noble born'.

Earla
English, meaning 'leader'.

Earline
English, feminine form of Earl.

Earna
(alt. Earnia, Earnea, Earneah)
English, meaning 'like an eagle'.

Eartha
English, meaning 'earth'.

Earric
(alt. Errica, Errika)
English, meaning 'powerful'.

Easter
Egyptian, from the festival of the same name.

Easton
(alt. Eastan, Easten, Eastyn)
American, meaning 'wholesome'.

Eathelin
(alt. Eathelyn, Eathelina)
English, meaning 'woman of the waterfall'.

Eavan
Irish, meaning 'beautiful'.

Ebba
English, meaning 'fortress of riches'.

Ebere
(alt. Ebera, Ebiere)
African, meaning 'merciful'.

Ebony
(alt. Eboni)
Latin, meaning 'deep, black wood'.

E

Ebrill
(alt. Ebrille, Evril)
Welsh, meaning 'born in April'.

Ecaterina
Greek, alternative of Catherine.

Ece
Turkish, meaning 'queen'.

Echo
Greek, from the mythological nymph of the same name.

Eda
(alt. Edda)
English, meaning 'wealthy and happy'.

Edalene
(alt. Edaline, Edilyne)
Gaelic, meaning 'noble'.

Edda
(alt. Eddah, Edwiga)
German, alternative of Hedwig.

Edel
(alt. Edele, Edelle)
German, meaning 'intelligent woman'.

Edelmira
Spanish, meaning 'admired for nobility'.

Eden
Hebrew, meaning 'pleasure'.

Edie
(alt. Eddie)
Shortened form of Eden, meaning 'pleasure'.

Edina
Scottish, meaning 'from Edinburgh'.

Edith
(alt. Edyth)
English, meaning 'prosperity through battle'.

Edna
Hebrew, meaning 'enjoyment'.

Edolie
English, meaning 'good'.

Edusa
(alt. Educa)
Latin, a mythological goddess who protected children.

Edrea
English, meaning ' wealthy and powerful'.

Edris
(alt. Edrisse, Edrys)
Anglo-Saxon, meaning 'prosperous ruler'.

Edwina
English, meaning ' wealthy friend'.

Efia
(alt. Efiah, Efea)
African, meaning 'born on Friday'.

Effemy
(alt. Effemie, Effemea)
Greek, meaning 'gifted songstress'.

Effie
Greek, meaning 'pleasant speech'.

E

Egeria
(alt. Egeriah, Egerea)
Latin, meaning 'wise counsellor'.
Also a mythological water nymph.

Eglantine
French, from the shrub of the
same name.

Eibhlín
Irish Gaelic, meaning 'shining and
brilliant'.

Eila
Hebrew, meaning 'oak tree'.

Eileen
Irish, meaning 'shining and
brilliant'.

Eilidh
Scottish, meaning 'the sun'.

Eir
Norse, meaning 'peacefulness'.

Eira
Welsh, meaning 'snow'.

Eireen
(alt. Erene, Irene)
Scandinavian, alternative of Irene,
meaning 'peacemaker'.

Eirian
Welsh, meaning 'silver'.

Eithne
Irish, meaning 'fire'.

Ekanta
Sanskrit, meaning 'solitude'.

Ekaterina
(alt. Ekaterini)
Slavic, meaning 'pure'.

Ekin
Turkish, meaning 'harvest'.

Ekundayo
African, meaning 'sorrow turned
to joy'.

El
Hawaiian, meaning 'black'.

Elaina
(alt. Elana, Elani)
Greek, alternative form of Helen.

Elaine
(alt. Elaina, Elayne)
French, meaning 'bright, shining
light'.

Elama
Greek, meaning 'from the
mountains'.

Elata
Latin, meaning 'happy'.

Elba
Italian, from the island of the
same name.

Elberta
English, meaning 'highborn'.

Elda
Anglo-Saxon, meaning 'princess'.

Eldora
Spanish, meaning 'covered with
gold'.

Eldoris
(alt. Eldorise, Eldorys)
Greek, meaning 'woman of the
sea'.

E

Eleacie
(alt. Eleacy, Eleacea)
American, meaning 'forthright'.

Eleanor
(alt. Elanor,Eleanora, Eleanore, Elina, Elinore)
Greek, meaning 'light'.

Electra
(alt. Elektra)
Greek, meaning 'shining'.

Eleora
Hebrew, meaning 'God is my light'.

Eleri
Welsh, the name of a river.

Elexis
English, alternative of Alexis.

Elfin
(alt. Elfyn, Elfie, Elfi)
American, meaning 'a little girl resembling an elf'.

Elfrida
(alt. Elfrieda)
English, meaning 'elf power'.

Elga
(alt. Elgiva, Ellga, Helga)
Slavic, meaning 'sacred'.

Eliane
Hebrew, meaning 'Jehovah is God'.

Elica
(alt. Elicah, Elicka, Elyca)
German, meaning 'noble one'.

Elida
(alt. Elyda, Eleeda)
English, meaning 'like a winged creature'.

Eliphal
(alt. Eliphala, Eliphall)
Hebrew, meaning 'delivered from God'.

Elisheba
(alt. Elishebah, Elishyba, Elyshyba)
Hebrew, meaning 'God's promise'.

Eliska
(alt. Elishka, Elyska, Elyshka)
Slavic, meaning 'truthful'.

Elissa
(alt. Elisa)
Of French origin, meaning 'pledged to God'.

Elita
(alt. Elitah, Elyta, Eleta)
Latin, meaning 'chosen one'.

Eliya
Hebrew, meaning 'God is my lord'.

Eliza
(alt. Elisha)
Of Hebrew origin, meaning 'pledged to God'.

Elizabeth
(alt. Elisabeth, Elisabet, Elizabella, Elizabelle, Elsbeth, Elspeth)
Hebrew, meaning 'pledged to God'.

Elkana
Hebrew, meaning 'God has acquired'.

E

Elke
Dutch, meaning 'kind'.

Elke
German, meaning 'nobility'.

Ella
German, meaning 'completely'.

Ellan
(alt. Ellane, Ellann)
American, meaning 'coy'.

Elle
(alt. Ellie)
French, meaning 'she'.

Ellema
(alt. Ellemah)
African, meaning 'dairy farmer'.

Ellen
(alt. Elin, Eline, Ellyn)
Greek, meaning 'shining'.

Ellice
(alt. Elyse)
Greek, meaning 'the Lord is God'.

Elma
(alt. Elna)
Latin, meaning 'soul'.

Elmas
(alt. Elmaz, Elmes, Elmis)
Armenian, meaning 'like a diamond'.

Elmira
Arabic, meaning 'aristocratic lady'.

Elodie
French, meaning 'marsh flower'.

Eloise
(alt. Elois, Eloisa, Elouise)
French, meaning 'renowned in battle'.

Elsa
(alt. Else, Elsie)
Hebrew, meaning 'pledged to God'.

Elva
Irish, meaning 'noble'.

Elvina
English, meaning 'noble friend'.

Elvira
(alt. Elvera)
Spanish, from the place of the same name.

Elwy
Welsh, meaning 'benefit'.

Elysia
(alt. Elicia, Elise)
Latin, meaning 'idyllic sweetness'.

Eman
Arabic, meaning 'faith'.

Emanuela
Hebrew, meaning 'God is with you'.

Embla
Scandinavian, meaning 'elm'.

Ember
(alt. Embry)
English, meaning 'spark'.

Emelda
Spanish, meaning 'a whole battle'.

E

Emele
French, meaning 'industrious'.

Emeline
German, meaning 'industrious'.

Emer
(alt. Emyr, Emir)
Irish, meaning 'swift'.

Emera
German, meaning 'diligent leader'.

Emerald
English, meaning 'green gemstone'.

Emergence
French, meaning 'worthy of recognition'.

Emery
German, meaning 'ruler of work'.

Emiko
(alt. Emyko)
Japanese, meaning 'pretty child'.

Emilia
Latin, meaning 'from the Emily clan'.

Emily
(alt. Emalee, Emelie, Emely, Emilee, Emilie, Emlyn)
Latin, from the clan of the same name.

Emlen
Latin, meaning 'charming'.

Emma
German, meaning 'embraces everything'.

Emmanuelle
Hebrew, meaning 'God is among us'.

Emmeline
(alt. Emmelina)
German, meaning 'embraces everything'.

Emmy
(alt. Emi, Emme, Emmie)
German, meaning 'embraces everything'.

Ena
Shortened form of Georgina, meaning 'farmer'.

Enakai
Hawaiian, meaning 'glowing sea'.

Encarna
Spanish, meaning 'incarnation'.

Enfys
Welsh, meaning 'rainbow'.

Engla
Scandinavian, meaning 'angel'.

Enid
(alt. Eneida)
Welsh, meaning 'life spirit'.

Enola
Native American, meaning 'solitary'.

Enya
Irish Gaelic, meaning 'fire'.

Eolande
American, meaning 'violet flower'.

E

Epona
(alt. Eponine)
Latin, a horse goddess.

Eranthe
(alt. Erantha, Eranthia, Eranthea)
Greek, meaning 'delicate like the spring'.

Erasto
Italian, meaning 'beloved'.

Ercilia
(alt. Erciliah, Ercilea, Ercilya)
American, meaning 'frank'.

Erela
(alt. Erelah)
Hebrew, meaning 'messenger'.

Erica
(alt. Ericka, Erika)
Scandinavian, meaning 'ruler forever'.

Erin
(alt. Eryn)
Irish Gaelic, meaning 'from the isle to the west'.

Eris
Greek, from the mythological heroine of the same name.

Erlinda
Hebrew, meaning 'spirited'.

Erling
Scandinavian, meaning 'descendant'.

Erma
German, meaning 'universal'.

Ermine
French, meaning 'weasel'.

Erna
English, meaning 'sincere'.

Ernestine
(alt. Ernestina)
English, meaning 'sincere'.

Ersilia
(alt. Ercilia, Ersila, Erzilia)
Greek, meaning 'delicate' and Latin, meaning 'liberator'.

Esme
French, meaning 'esteemed'.

Esmeralda
Spanish, meaning 'emerald'.

Esperanza
Spanish, meaning 'hope'.

Essien
(alt. Essienne, Esien)
African, meaning 'child of the people'.

Esta
(alt. Estah, Estia, Eastea)
Italian, meaning 'woman from the west'.

Estelle
(alt. Estela, Estell, Estella)
French, meaning 'star'.

Esther
(alt. Esta, Ester, Etha, Ethna, Ethne)
Persian, meaning 'star'.

Etana
(alt. Etanah, Etanna, Ethania)
Hebrew, meaning 'strong woman'.

E

Etenia
(alt. Eteniah, Etenea, Eteniya)
Native American, meaning 'prosperous'.

Eternity
Latin, meaning 'forever'.

Ethel
(alt. Ethyl)
English, meaning 'noble'.

Etta
(alt. Etter, Ettie)
Shortened form of Henrietta, meaning 'ruler of the house'.

Eudora
Greek, meaning 'generous gift'.

Eugenia
(alt. Eugenie)
Greek, meaning 'wellborn'.

Eulalia
(alt. Eula, Eulah, Eulalie)
Greek, meaning 'sweet-speaking'.

Eunice
Greek, meaning 'victorious'.

Euphemia
Greek, meaning ' favourable speech'.

Eva
Hebrew, meaning 'life'.

Evadne
Greek, meaning 'pleasing one'.

Evangeline
(alt. Evangelina)
Greek, meaning 'good news'.

Evanthe
Greek, meaning 'good flower'.

Eve
(alt. Evie)
Hebrew, meaning 'life'.

Evelina
(alt. Evelia)
German, meaning 'hazelnut'.

Evelyn
(alt. Evalyn, Evelin, Eveline, Evelyne)
German, meaning 'hazelnut'.

Everly
(alt. Everleigh, Everley)
English, meaning 'grazing meadow'.

Evette
French, meaning 'yew wood'.

Evonne
(alt. Evon)
French, meaning 'yew wood'.

E

F

Girls' names

Faba
(alt. Fabah, Fava)
Latin, meaning 'bean'.

Fabia
(alt. Fabiana, Fabienne, Fabriana)
Latin, meaning 'from the Fabian clan'.

Fabiola
Latin, meaning 'a good worker'.

Fabrianne
Latin, meaning 'resourceful'.

Fabrizia
Italian, meaning 'works with hands'.

Fadhiler
(alt. Fadheler, Fadila, Fahila)
Arabic, meaning 'virtuous'.

Fadia
Arabic, meaning 'protector'.

Fadila
Arabic, meaning 'excellent'.

Fadwa
(alt. Fadwah)
Arabic, meaning 'self-sacrificing'.

Fae
English, meaning 'fairy'.

Faghira
(alt. Fagirah, Faghyra)
Arabic, meaning 'like jasmine'.

Fahari
Swahili, meaning 'splendor'.

Fahima
(alt. Faheema, Fahhama, Fahimah)
Arabic, meaning 'quick-witted'.

Faida
Arabic, meaning 'abundant'.

Faiga
(alt. Faega, Fayga)
German, meaning 'birdlike'.

Faillace
(alt. Faillase, Falace)
French, meaning 'delicately beautiful'.

Faina
Russian, meaning 'shining'.

Faine
(alt. Faina, Fayne)
Old English, meaning 'joyful'.

Fainche
Irish, meaning 'independent' or 'free'.

Fairuza
Turkish, meaning 'turquoise'.

Faith
English, meaning 'loyalty'.

Faiza
Of Arabic origin, meaning 'victorious'.

Fala
Native American, meaning 'crow'.

Falak
(alt. Falac, Falack)
Arabic, meaning 'starlike'.

Falesyia
(alt. Falesyiah, Falisyia)
Spanish, meaning 'exotic'.

Faline
(alt. Fayline, Felina, Feyline)
Latin, meaning 'catlike'.

Fall
(alt. Falle)
American, meaning 'the autumn season'.

Fallon
Irish Gaelic, meaning 'descended from a ruler'.

Fama
(alt. Fammah)
Latin, meaning 'fame'.

Fana
(alt. Fannah)
African, meaning 'light'.

Fanchon
French, meaning 'free'.

Fanny
(alt. Fannie)
Latin, meaning 'from France'.

Fantine
Latin, meaning 'child'. Also a character in *Les Misérables* by Victor Hugo.

Faolitiama
(alt. Faoilitiarna)
Irish, meaning 'wolf lady'.

Farica
German, meaning 'peaceful ruler'.

Farida
(alt. Fareeda)
Arabic, meaning 'unique'.

Farrah
English, meaning 'lovely and pleasant'.

Farrell
(alt. Farrelly)
Irish, meaning 'courageous'.

Farsiris
Persian, meaning 'princess'.

Faryl
(alt. Farelle, Faril)
American, meaning 'inspiration'.

Fascienne
(alt. Fusciene, Fasciene)
Latin, meaning 'dark beauty'.

Fasiha
(alt. Fasyha, Faseeha)
Arabic, meaning 'eloquent'.

Faten
Arabic, meaning 'charming'.

Fathia
Arabic, meaning 'conquest'.

F

Fatima
Arabic, from the daughter of Mohammed with the same name.

Fauna
(alt. Faune, Fawna)
Latin, goddess of fertility and nature in Roman mythology.

Fausta
Italian, alternative of Faustine.

Faustine
Latin, meaning 'fortunate'.

Fauve
French, meaning 'wild'.

Fawn
French, meaning 'young deer'.

Fay
(alt. Fae, Faye)
French, meaning 'fairy'.

Fayina
(alt. Fayena)
Russian, meaning 'independent'.

Fayola
(alt. Fayolla, Fayollah)
African, meaning 'walks with honour'.

Febe
(alt. Febee, Febea)
Polish, meaning 'clever'.

Fedora
(alt. Feodora, Fyodora)
Greek, alternative of Theodora.

Feeidha
Arabic, meaning 'generous'.

Felicia
(alt. Felecia, Felice, Felisha)
Latin, meaning 'lucky and happy'.

Felicity
Latin, meaning 'fortunate'.

Felipa
Greek, meaning 'lover of horses'.

Felixa
(alt. Felicja, Felisha, Felixia)
Latin, meaning 'happy'.

Femi
(alt. Femmi, Femy)
African, meaning 'beloved'.

Fenella
Irish Gaelic, meaning 'white shoulder'.

Feng
Chinese, meaning 'phoenix'.

Fenia
Scandinavian, from the mythological giantess of the same name.

Fenn
(alt. Fen)
American, meaning 'intelligent'.

Feo
(alt. Feeo)
Greek, meaning 'gift from God'.

Fern
(alt. Ferne, Ferrin)
English, from the plant of the same name.

Fernanda
German, meaning 'peace and courage'.

Ffion
(alt. Fion)
Irish Gaelic, meaning 'fair and pale'.

F

Fflur
Welsh, meaning 'flower'.

Fia
Italian, meaning 'flame'.

Fiala
Czech, meaning 'purple flower'.

Fiamma
(alt. Fiammetta)
Italian, meaning 'fiery'.

Fidelia
(alt. Fidelina, Fidella)
Spanish, meaning 'faithful one'.

Fifi
Hebrew, meaning 'Jehovah increases'.

Filia
(alt., Fillia, Filiya)
Greek, meaning 'dear friend'.

Filomena
Greek, meaning 'loved one'.

Fina
Italian, alternative of Serafina.

Fini
French, alternative of Josephine.

Finlay
(alt. Finley)
Irish Gaelic, meaning 'fair-headed courageous one'.

Finola
(alt. Fionnula)
Irish Gaelic, meaning 'fair shoulder'.

Fiona
Irish Gaelic, meaning 'fair and pale'.

Fiora
Irish Gaelic, meaning 'fair and pale'.

Fiorella
Italian, meaning 'little flower'.

Firenze
Hungarian, meaning 'blossom'.

Firtha
(alt. Fertha, Fyrtha)
Scottish, meaning 'woman from the sea'.

Flamina
(alt. Flamyna)
Latin, meaning 'pious'.

Flanna
(alt. Flannery)
Irish Gaelic, meaning 'russet hair'.

Flavia
Latin, meaning 'yellow hair'.

Fleta
(alt. Fleda)
Anglo-Saxon, meaning 'swift one'.

Fleur
French, meaning 'flower'.

Fleurdelice
French, meaning 'iris'or 'lily'.

Flis
(alt. Flisse, Flys)
Polish, meaning 'well-behaved'.

Flo
(alt. Florrie, Flossie, Floy)
Shortened forms of Florence, meaning 'in bloom'.

F

Flora
Latin, meaning 'flower'.

Florence
(alt: Florencia, Florene, Florine)
Latin, meaning 'in bloom'.

Florida
Latin, meaning 'flowery'. Also a state in America.

Flutura
Albanian, meaning 'butterfly'.

Fola
African, meaning 'honour'.

Folami
African, 'desires respect'.

Fonda
Spanish, meaning 'foundation'.

Fone
Native American, meaning 'snow child'.

Fouada
Arabic, meaning 'dearest'.

Fran
(alt. Frankie, Frannie)
Shortened form of Frances, meaning 'from France'.

Frances
(alt. Francine, Francis)
Latin, meaning 'from France'.

Francesca
(alt. Franchesca, Francisca)
Latin, meaning 'from France'.

Freda
(alt. Freeda, Freida, Frida, Frieda)
German, meaning 'peaceful'.

Frederica
German, meaning 'peaceful ruler'.

Freira
Spanish, meaning 'sister'.

Freya
(alt. Freja)
Scandinavian, the mythological Norse goddess of love.

Frigg
(alt. Friga, Fryga)
Norse, a goddess of the household in mythology.

Fronia
(alt. Fronea, Froniyah)
Latin, meaning 'wise woman'.

Frula
(alt. Frulah)
German, meaning 'hardworking'.

Frythe
(alt. Frytha, Frith, Fritha)
English, meaning 'calm'.

Fuchsia
German, from the flower of the same name.

Fukayna
(alt. Fukaina, Fukana)
Egyptian, meaning 'intelligent'.

Fulgencia
(alt. Fulgenciah, Fulgencea)
Latin, meaning 'glowing'.

Fulvia
Latin, meaning 'golden girl'.

Fumiko
Japanese, meaning 'little friend'.

F

G

Girls' names

Gabbatha
Hebrew, meaning 'temple mound'.

Gabby
(alt. Gabbi)
Shortened form of Gabrielle, meaning 'heroine of God'.

Gabrielle
(alt. Gabriel, Gabriela, Gabriella)
Hebrew, meaning 'heroine of God'.

Gada
Hebrew, meaning 'lucky'.

Gadara
Armenian, meaning 'mountain's peak'.

Gael
Gaelic, meaing 'from Ireland'.

Gaelle
German, meaning 'stranger'.

Gafna
Hebrew, meaning 'from the vine'.

Gaho
Native American, meaning 'motherly'.

Gaia
(alt. Gaea)
Greek, meaning 'the earth'.

Gail
(alt. Gale, Gayla, Gayle)
Hebrew, meaning 'my father rejoices'.

Gaira
Scottish, meaning 'petite woman'.

Gala
French, meaning 'festive merrymaking'.

Galatea
(alt. Galatee, Galathea)
Greek, meaning 'white as milk'.

Galeed
Hebrew, meaning 'friendship'.

Galena
Greek feminine form of Galen, meaning 'peaceful'.

Gali
Hebrew, meaning 'fountain'.

Galiana
Arabic, the name of a Moorish princess.

Galiena
German, meaning 'high one'.

Galila
Hebrew, meaning 'one from the rolling hills'.

Galina
Russian, meaning 'shining brightly'.

Gamada
African, meaning 'pleasing one'.

Gambhira
Hindi, meaning 'noble born'.

Garaitz
Basque, meaning 'victorious'.

Garima
Indian, meaning 'woman of great importance'.

Garnet
(alt. Garnett)
English, meaning 'red gemstone'.

Gay
(alt. Gaye)
French, meaning 'glad and lighthearted'.

Gaynor
Welsh, meaning 'white and smooth'.

Gayora
Hebrew, meaning 'valley of the sun'.

Geba
Hebrew, meaning 'one from the hill'.

Geela
Hebrew, meaning 'joy'.

Gelasia
Greek, meaning 'laughing'.

Gelsey
Persian, meaning 'flower'.

Gemini
Greek, meaning 'twin'.

Gemma
Italian, meaning 'precious stone'.

Gen
Japanese, meaning 'spring'.

Gena
Alternative of Gina, meaning 'queen'.

Gene
Greek, meaning 'wellborn'.

Genesis
Greek, meaning 'beginning'.

Geneva
(alt. Genevra)
French, meaning 'juniper tree'.

Genevieve
German, meaning 'white wave'.

Genie
Shortened form of Genevieve, meaning 'white wave'.

Georgeanna
English combination of Georgia and Anna.

Georgette
French, meaning 'farmer'.

Georgia
(alt. Georgiana, Georgianna, Georgie)
Latin, meaning 'farmer'.

Georgiana
English alternative of Georgia, meaning 'farmer'.

G

Georgina
(alt. Georgene, Georgine, Giorgina)
Latin, meaning 'farmer'.

Geraldine
German, meaning 'spear ruler'.

Gerda
Nordic, meaning 'shelter'.

Geri
(alt. Gerri, Gerry)
Shortened form of Geraldine,
meaning 'spear ruler'.

Germaine
French, meaning 'from Germany'.

Gerry
English alternative of Geraldine,
meaning 'spear ruler'.

Gertie
Shortened form of Gertrude,
meaning 'strength of a spear'.

Gertrude
German, meaning 'strength of a
spear'.

Geva
Hebrew, meaning 'of the farm'.

Ghada
Arabic, meaning 'beautiful girl'.

Ghislaine
French, meaning 'pledge'.

Ghita
(alt. Ghitah, Gheeta, Ghyta)
Italian, meaning 'like a pearl'.

Gia
(alt. Ghia)
Italian, meaning 'God is gracious'.

Giada
Italian, meaning 'jade'.

Gianina
(alt. Giana)
Hebrew, meaning 'God's
graciousness'.

Gigi
(alt. Giget)
Shortened form of Georgina,
meaning 'farmer'.

Gilda
English, meaning 'gilded'.

Gilia
Hebrew, meaning 'joy of the
Lord'.

Gillian
Latin, meaning 'youthful'.

Gin
Japanese, meaning 'silver'.

Gina
(alt. Geena, Gena)
Shortened form of Regina,
meaning 'queen'.

Ginevra
Italian alternative of Guinevere,
meaning 'white and smooth'.

Ginger
Latin, from the root of the same
name.

Ginny
Shortened form of Virginia,
meaning 'virgin'.

Gioia
Italian, meaning 'bringer of joy'.

G

Giordana
Italian alternative of Jordana,
meaning 'descend'.

Giovanna
Italian, meaning 'God is gracious'.

Giselle
(alt. Gisela, Gisele, Giselle, Gisselle)
German, meaning 'pledge'.

Gita
(alt. Geeta)
Sanskrit, meaning 'song'.

Gitana
(alt. Gitane, Jeetanna)
Spanish, meaning 'gypsy'.

Giulia
(alt. Giuliana)
Italian, meaning 'youthful'.

Gladys
(alt. Gladyce)
Welsh, meaning 'lame'.

Glain
Welsh, meaning 'precious as a
jewel'.

Glenda
Welsh, meaning 'fair and good'.

Glenna
(alt. Glennie)
Irish Gaelic, meaning 'glen'.

Glenys
Welsh, meaning 'riverbank'.

Gloria
(alt. Glory)
Latin, meaning 'glory'.

Glynda
(alt. Glinda)
Welsh, meaning 'fair'. The good
witch in *The Wizard of Oz*.

Glynis
Welsh, meaning 'small glen'.

Godiva
English, meaning 'gift from God'.

Golda
(alt. Goldia, Goldie)
English, meaning 'gold'.

Gota
Swedish, meaning 'having
strength'.

Grace
(alt. Graça, Gracie, Grayce)
Latin, meaning 'grace'.

Grady
Irish, meaning 'noble'.

Grainne
(alt. Grania)
Irish Gaelic, meaning 'love'.

Gratia
(alt. Grasia)
Latin, meaning 'blessing'.

Grazia
(alt. Graziana, Graziella)
Italian, meaning 'grace'.

Greer
(alt. Grier)
Latin, meaning 'alert and
watchful'.

Gregoria
Latin, meaning 'alert'.

G

Greta
(alt. Gretel)
Greek, meaning 'pearl'.

Gretchen
German, meaning 'pearl'.

Grid
Norse, meaning 'peaceful'.

Griselda
(alt. Griselle)
German, meaning 'grey fighting maid'.

Gro
Norwegian, meaning 'works with the earth'.

Gryphon
Greek, a mythological beast that represents strength, security and vigilence.

Guadalupe
Arabic, meaning 'a river of black stones'.

Gudrun
Scandinavian, meaning 'battle'.

Guida
Italian, meaning 'a guide'.

Guinevere
Welsh, meaning 'white and smooth'. King Arthur's queen in mythology.

Gula
Arabic, meaning 'like a rose'.

Gunhilda
Norse, meaning 'battle maiden'.

Gulzar
Arabic, meaning 'of the gardens'.

Guri
Hebrew, meaning 'lioness'.

Guthrie
Scottish, meaning 'wind'.

Gwanwyn
Welsh, meaning 'born in the spring'.

Gwen
Shortened form of Gwendolyn, meaning 'fair bow'.

Gwenda
Welsh, meaning 'fair and good'.

Gwendolyn
(alt. Gwendolen, Gwenel)
Welsh, meaning 'fair bow'.

Gwynn
(alt. Gwyn)
Welsh, meaning 'fair blessed'.

Gwyneth
(alt. Gwynneth, Gwynyth)
Welsh, meaning 'happiness'.

Gypsy
English, meaning 'of the Roman tribe'.

Gythae
English, meaning 'fiery'.

G

H Girls' names

Ha
Vietnamese, meaning 'happy'.

Haarisah
Hindi, meaning 'daughter of the sun'.

Haarithah
Arabic, meaning 'divine messenger'.

Habibah
(alt. Habiba)
Arabic, meaning 'beloved'.

Hachi
Native American, meaning 'of the river'.

Hada
African, meaning 'one that comes from the salty place'.

Hadara
Hebrew, meaning 'beautiful ornament'.

Hadassah
Hebrew, meaning 'myrtle tree'.

Hadeel
Arabic, meaning 'like a dove'.

Hadenna
English, meaning 'meadow of flowers'.

Hadiya
Arabic, meaning 'righteous'.

Hadley
English, meaning 'heather meadow'.

Hadria
Latin, meaning 'from Adria'.

Hady
Greek, meaning 'soulful'.

Hafsa
Arabic, meaning 'young lioness'.

Hafwen
Welsh, meaning 'one with the beauty of summer'.

Hagen
Irish, meaning 'youthful'.

Haggith
Hebrew, meaning 'dancer'.

Haidee
Greek, meaning 'modest one'.

Haimi
Hawaiian, meaning 'pursuer of the truth'.

Haiwee
Native American, meaning 'dove'.

Hala
Arabic, meaning 'halo'.

Halene
Russian, meaning 'steadfast one'.

Haley
(alt. Haelee, Hailee, Hailey, Hailie, Haleigh)
English, meaning 'hay meadow'.

Halima
(alt. Halina)
Arabic, meaning 'gentle'.

Halla
African, meaning 'unexpected present'.

Hallie
(alt. Halle, Halley, Hallie)
German, meaning 'ruler of the home or estate'.

Haloke
Native American, meaning 'like the salmon'.

Hama
Arabic, meaning 'one from the city on the river'.

Hamilton
(alt. Hamiltyn, Hamylton, Hamyltyn)
American, meaning 'dreamer'.
Also a place in Scotland.

Hana
Japanese, meaning 'flower blossom'.

Hang
Vietnamese, meaning 'from the moon'.

Hannah
(alt. Haana, Hana, Hanna)
Hebrew, meaning 'grace'.

Hao
Vietnamese, meaning 'well behaved'.

Harika
Turkish, meaning 'superior one'.

Harla
English, meaning 'of the fields'.

Harley
(alt. Harlene)
English, meaning 'the long field'.

Harlow
English, meaning 'army hill'.

Harmony
Latin, meaning 'harmony'.

Harper
English, meaning 'minstrel'.

Harriet
(alt. Harriett, Harriette)
German, meaning 'ruler of the home or estate'.

Harsha
Hebrew, meaning 'enchantress'.

Haru
Japanese, meaning 'born during the spring'.

Hasna
Arabic, meaning 'beautiful'.

Hatita
Hebrew, meaning 'explorer'.

Hattie
Shortened form of Harriet, meaning 'ruler of the home or estate'.

Haven
English, meaning 'a place of sanctuary'.

Hayden
English, meaning 'hedged valley'.

Hayley
(alt. Haylee, Hayleigh, Haylie)
English, meaning 'hay meadow'.

Hazel
(alt. Hazle)
English, from the tree of the same name.

Hazina
African, meaning 'good'.

Heartha
Teutonic, meaning 'Mother Earth's gift'.

Heather
English, from the flower of the same name.

Heaven
English, meaning 'everlasting bliss'.

Heba
Arabic, meaning 'gift'.

Hebe
Greek, meaning 'young'.

Hecate
Greek, mythological goddess of witchcraft and fertility.

Hedasaa
Hebrew, meaning 'like a star'.

Hedda
German, meaning 'warfare'.

Hedia
Hebrew, meaning 'echo of God'.

Hedva
Hebrew, meaning 'joy'.

Hedwig
German, meaning 'warfare and strife'.

Heidi
(alt. Heidy)
German, meaning 'nobility'.

Helaine
English, meaning 'light'.

Helen
(alt. Helena, Helene, Hellen)
Greek, meaning 'light'.

Helga
German, meaning 'holy and sacred'.

Helia
Greek, meaning 'sun'.

Heloise
French, meaning 'renowned in war'.

Hemanti
Indian, meaning 'born during the winter'.

Hemera
Greek, meaning 'child born in the daylight'.

Heng
Chinese, meaning 'eternal beauty'.

H

Henrietta
(alt. Henriette)
German, meaning 'ruler of the house'.

Hephzibah
Hebrew, meaning 'my delight is in her'.

Hera
Greek, meaning 'queen'.

Hermia
(alt. Hermina, Hermine, Herminia)
Greek, meaning 'messenger'.

Hermione
Greek, meaning 'earthly'.

Hero
Greek, meaning 'brave one of the people'.

Hertha
English, meaning 'earth'.

Hesper
Greek, meaning 'evening star'.

Hester
(alt. Hestia)
Greek, meaning 'star'.

Hiawatha
Native American, meaning 'maker of rivers'.

Hibernia
Latin, meaning 'from Ireland'.

Hideko
(alt. Hide, Hideyo, Hydeko)
Japanese, meaning 'superior woman'.

Hien
Vietnamese, meaning 'gentle'.

Hilary
(alt. Hillary)
Greek, meaning 'cheerful and happy'.

Hilda
(alt. Hildur)
German, meaning 'battle woman'.

Hildegarde
(alt. Hildegard)
German, meaning 'battle stronghold'.

Hildred
German, meaning 'battle counsellor'.

Hilina
Hawaiian, meaning 'celestial body'.

Hilma
German, meaning 'will-helmet'.

Hinda
Hebrew, meaning 'doe-like'.

Hinto
Native American, meaning 'one with dark blue eyes'.

Hirkani
Indian, meaning 'like a diamond'.

Hitomi
Japanese, meaning 'beautiful eyes'.

Hoa
Vietnamese, meaning 'peaceful'.

Hodesh
Hebrew, meaning 'child born at the new moon'.

Holda
German, meaning 'secretive'.

Holden
English, meaning 'eager'.

Hollis
English, meaning 'near the holly bushes'.

Holly
(alt. Holli, Hollie)
English, from the tree of the same name.

Honesty
Armerican, meaning 'truthful'.

Honey
English, meaning 'honey'.

Honor
(alt. Honour)
Latin, meaning 'woman of honour'.

Honora
(alt. Honoria)
Latin, meaning 'woman of honour'.

Hope
English, meaning 'hope'.

Hortense
(alt. Hortencia, Hortensia)
Latin, meaning 'of the garden'.

Hosah
Hebrew, meaning 'provider of shelter'.

Hoshi
Japanese, meaning 'shining one'.

Hotaru
Japanese, meaning 'firefly'.

Hourig
Slavic, meaning 'fiery'.

Hua
Chinese, meaning 'like a flower'.

Hubab
Arabic, meaning 'focussed'.

Hudson
English, meaning 'adventurous'.

Hue
Vietnamese, meaning 'lily'.

Hulda
German, meaning 'loved one'.

Hunter
English, meaning 'great hunteress'.

Hurit
Native American, meaning 'beauty'.

Hurley
English, meaning 'healthy'.

Huyana
Native American, meaning 'daughter of the rain'.

Hyacinth
Greek, from the flower of the same name.

Hydeira
Greek, meaning 'woman from the water'.

H

Girls' names

Iamar
Arabic, meaning 'from the moon'.

Iana
Greek, meaning 'flowering'.

Ianeke
Hawaiian, meaning 'God is gracious'.

Iantha
Greek, meaning 'purple flower'.

Ibis
Latin, meaning 'long-legged bird'.

Ibetesam
Arabic, meaning 'smiling'.

Ichigo
Japanese, meaning 'strawberry'.

Ichtaca
Aztec, meaning 'secret'.

Ida
English, meaning 'prosperous'.

Idahlia
Greek, meaning 'child with a sweet disposition'.

Idalika
Arabic, meaning 'queen'.

Idarah
American, meaning 'social butterfly'.

Ide
Irish, meaning 'thirsty'.

Idell
(alt. Idella)
English, meaning 'prosperous'.

Idona
Nordic, meaning 'renewal'.

Idra
Hebrew, meaning 'fig tree'.

Ifama
African, meaning 'all is well'.

Ife
African, meaning 'art lover'.

Ignacia
Latin, meaning 'ardent'.

Iha
Sanskrit, meaning 'wish'.

Ila
French, meaning 'island'.

Ilana
Hebrew, meaning 'tree'.

Ilandere
American, meaning 'woman of the moon'.

Ilaria
Italian, meaning 'cheerful'.

Ildri
Scandinavian, meaning 'fire'.

Ilene
American, meaning 'light'.

Iliana
(alt. Ileana)
Greek, meaning 'Trojan'.

Ilissa
American, meaning 'noble kin'.

Ilka
Slavic, meaning 'hardworking'.

Ilma
German alternative of
Wilhelmina, meaning 'helmet'.

Ilona
Hungarian, meaning 'light'.

Ilsa
German, meaning 'pledged to
God'.

Ilta
Finnish, meaning 'born in the
night'.

Ilyse
German, meaning 'noble born'.

Ima
German, meaning 'embraces
everything'.

Imala
Native American, meaning
'disciplines others'.

Iman
Arabic, meaning 'faith'.

Imara
Hungarian, meaning 'great ruler'.

Imari
Japanese, meaning 'daughter of
today'.

Imelda
German, meaning 'all-consuming
fight'.

Imogen
(alt. Imogene)
Latin, meaning 'last-born'.

Ina
Latin, meaning 'to make
feminine'.

Inanna
Sumerian, meaning 'lady of the
sky'.

Inari
Finnish, meaning 'lady of the
lake'.

Inaya
Arabic, meaning 'taking care'.

Inca
Indian, meaning 'adventurer'.

India
(alt. Indie)
Hindi, from the country of the
same name.

Indiana
Latin, meaning 'from India'.

Indigo
Greek, meaning 'deep blue dye'.

Indira
(alt. Inira)
Sanskrit, meaning 'beauty'.

Indu
Hindi, meaning 'woman of the moon'.

Inez
(alt. Ines)
Spanish, meaning 'pure'.

Inga
(alt. Inge, Ingeborg, Inger)
Scandinavian, meaning 'guarded by Ing'.

Ingrid
Scandinavian, meaning 'beautiful'.

Inoke
Hawaiian, meaning 'faithful'.

Insula
Native American, meaning 'red feather'.

Intan
Indonesian, meaning 'diamond'.

Io
Greek, from the mythological heroine of the same name.

Ioanna
Greek, meaning 'grace'.

Iola
(alt. Iole)
Greek, meaning 'cloud of dawn'.

Iolana
Hawaiian, meaning 'soaring like an eagle'.

Iolani
Hawaiian, meaning 'fly like a hawkl'.

Iolanthe
Greek, meaning 'violet flower'.

Iona
Greek, from the island of the same name.

Ione
Greek, meaning 'violet'.

Iorwen
Welsh, meaning 'fair'.

Iowa
Native American, meaning 'beautiful land'.

Iphigenia
Greek, meaning 'sacrifice'.

Ira
(alt. Iva)
Hebrew, meaning 'watchful'.

Irene
(alt. Irelyn, Irena, Irina, Irini)
Greek, meaning 'peace'.

Iria
American, meaning 'rainbow'.

Irina
Russian, meaning 'peace'.

Iris
Greek, meaning 'rainbow'.

Irma
German, meaning 'universal'.

Isabel
(alt. Isabelle, Isobel, Izabella)
Spanish, meaning 'pledged to God'.

Isabella
Spanish, meaning 'pledged to God'.

Isadora
Latin, meaning 'gift of Isis'.

Isamu
Japanese, meaning 'rock'.

Ishana
Hindi, meaning 'desire'.

Isis
Egyptian, from the goddess of the same name.

Isla
(alt. Isa, Isela, Isley)
Scottish Gaelic, meaning 'river'.

Isolde
Welsh, meaning 'fair lady'.

Istas
Native American, meaning 'snow'.

Itotia
Aztec, meaning 'dance'.

Itzel
Spanish, meaning 'rainbow'.

Ivana
Slavic, meaning 'Jehovah is gracious'.

Ivette
Variation on Yvette, meaning 'yew wood'.

Ivonne
Variation on Yvonne, meaning 'yew wood'.

Ivory
Latin, meaning 'white as elephant tusks'.

Ivria
Hebrew, meaning 'a Hebrew woman'.

Ivy
English, from the plant of the same name.

Iwalani
Hawaiian, meaning 'divine seagull'.

Ixia
South African, from the flower of the same name.

Iyeshia
American, meaning 'prosperous'.

Ize
Native American, meaning 'sun'.

Izzy
Spanish alternative to Isabella, meaning 'pledged to God'.

J Girls' names

Jaala
Hebrew, meaning 'wild goat'.

Jaamini
Hindi, meaning 'evening'.

Jabmen
Arabic, meaning 'high forehead'.

Jacaranda
(alt. Jacarranda, Jakaranda)
Spanish, the name of a flower
with purple blossoms.

Jacey
(alt. Jace, Jaci, Jacie)
Greek alternative of Jacinda,
meaning 'hyacinth'.

Jachan
Hebrew, meaning 'sorrow'.

Jacinda
(alt. Jacinta)
Spanish, meaning 'hyacinth'.

Jackie
(alt. Jacque, Jacqui)
Shortened form of Jacqueline,
meaning 'he who supplants'.

Jacqueline
(alt. Jacalyn, Jacklyn, Jacquelyn, Jaqlyn)
French, meaning 'he who
supplants'.

Jada
Spanish, meaning 'jade'.

Jade
(alt. Jada, Jaida, Jayda, Jayde)
Spanish, meaning 'green stone'.

Jaden
(alt. Jadyn, Jaiden, Jaidyn, Jayden)
Contraction of Jade and Hayden,
meaning 'green hedged valley'.

Jaeda
Arabic, meaning 'goodness'.

Jael
Hebrew, meaning 'mountain
goat'.

Jaime
(alt. Jaima, Jaimie, Jami, Jamie)
Spanish, meaning 'he who
supplants'.

Jaira
Hebrew, meaning 'shining'.

Jairdan
American, meaning 'educator'.

Jakayla
Native American, meaning
'crowned with a laurel'.

Jaleh
Persian, meaning 'born of the
rain'.

Jalia
American, meaning 'noble woman'.

Jalila
Arabic, meaning 'important one'.

Jamari
French, meaning 'warrior woman'.

Jamila
Arabic, meaning 'lovely'.

Jan
(alt. Jann, Janna)
Hebrew, meaning 'the Lord is gracious'.

Jana
(alt. Jaana)
Hebrew, meaning 'the Lord is gracious'.

Janae
(alt. Janay)
American, meaning 'the Lord is gracious'.

Jane
(alt. Jayne)
Feminine form of the Hebrew John, meaning 'the Lord is gracious'.

Janelle
(alt. Janel, Janell, Jenelle)
American, meaning 'the Lord is gracious'.

Janet
(alt. Janette)
Scottish, meaning 'the Lord is gracious'.

Janice
(alt. Janis)
American, meaning 'the Lord is gracious'.

Janie
(alt. Janney, Jannie)
Shortened form of Janet, meaning 'the Lord is gracious'.

Janine
(alt. Janeen)
English, meaning 'the Lord is gracious'.

Janis
Alternative of Jane, meaning 'the Lord is gracious'.

Janoah
(alt. Janiya, Janiyah)
Hebrew, meaning 'quiet and calm'.

January
English, meaning 'the first month'.

Jarah
Hebrew, meaning 'honey'.

Jarita
Hindi-Sanskrit, meaning 'famous bird'.

Jasmine
(alt. Jasmin, Jazim, Jazmine)
Persian, meaning 'jasmine flower'.

Jay
Latin, meaning 'jaybird'.

Jayna
Sanskrit, meaning 'bringer of victory'.

J

Jean
(alt. Jeane, Jeanne)
Scottish, meaning 'the Lord is gracious'.

Jeana
(alt. Jeanna)
Latin, meaning 'queen'.

Jeanette
(alt. Jeannette, Janette)
French, meaning 'the Lord is gracious'.

Jeanie
(alt. Jeannie)
Shortened form of Jeanette, meaning 'the Lord is gracious'.

Jeanine
(alt. Jeannine)
Latin, meaning 'the Lord is gracious'.

Jehan
Arabic, meaning 'worldly woman'.

Jehosheba
Hebrew, meaning 'oath of the Lord'.

Jelena
Slavic, meaning 'bright'.

Jelissa
American, meaning 'white bee'.

Jemima
Hebrew, meaning 'dove'.

Jemina
Hebrew, meaning 'listened to'.

Jemma
Italian, meaning 'precious stone'.

Jemsa
Spanish, meaning 'gem'.

Jena
Arabic, meaning 'little bird'.

Jendayi
Egyptian, meaning 'thankful one'.

Jeneil
American, meaning 'champion'.

Jenna
Hebrew, meaning 'the Lord is gracious'.

Jennifer
(alt. Jenifer)
Welsh, meaning 'white and smooth'.

Jenny
(alt. Jennie)
Shortened form of Jennifer, meaning 'white and smooth'.

Jensine
Danish, meaning 'God is gracious'.

Jerrie
(alt. Jeri, Jerri, Jerrie, Jerry)
German, meaning 'spear ruler'.

Jersey
American, a place name.

Jerusha
Hebrew, meaning 'married'.

Jeryl
English, meaning 'spear ruler'.

Jess
Shortened form of Jessica, meaning 'He sees'.

Jessa
Shortened form of Jessica,
meaning 'He sees'.

Jessamine
French, meaning 'jasmine'.

Jessamy
(alt. Jessame, Jessamine, Jessamyn)
Persian, meaning 'jasmine
flower'.

Jessenia
Arabic, meaning 'delicate like a
flower'.

Jessica
(alt. Jesica, Jesika, Jessika)
Hebrew, meaning 'He sees'.

Jessie
(alt. Jesse, Jessi, Jessye)
Shortened form of Jessica,
meaning 'He sees'.

Jesusa
Spanish, meaning 'mother of the
Lord'.

Jethetha
Hebrew, meaning 'princess'.

Jette
(alt. Jetta, Jettie)
Danish, meaning 'black as coal'.

Jewel
(alt. Jewell)
French, meaning 'delight'.

Jezebel
(alt. Jezabel, Jezabelle)
Hebrew, meaning 'pure and
virginal'.

Jia li
Chinese, meaning 'beautiful and
kind'.

Jiera
Lithuanian, meaning 'lively'.

Jiles
American, meaning 'young goat'.

Jill
Latin, meaning 'youthful'.

Jillian
Latin, meaning 'youthful'.

Jimena
Spanish, meaning 'heard'.

Jin
Japanese, meaning 'tenderness'.

Jinx
Latin, meaning 'performs spells'.

Jivanta
Hindi, meaning 'life giver'.

Jo
Shortened form of Joanna,
meaning 'the Lord is gracious'.

Joan
Hebrew, meaning 'the Lord is
gracious'.

Joanna
(alt. Joana, Joanie, Joanne, Johanna)
Hebrew, meaning 'the Lord is
gracious'.

Jobina
(alt. Jobey, Jobyna)
Hebrew, meaning 'persecuted'.

J

Jocasta
Italian, meaning 'lighthearted'.

Jocelyn
(alt. Jauslyn, Joscelin, Joslyn)
German, meaning 'cheerful'.

Jocose
Latin, meaning 'gleeful'.

Jody
(alt. Jodee, Jodi, Jodie)
Shortened form of Judith,
meaning 'Jewish'.

Joelle
(alt. Joela)
Hebrew, meaning 'Jehovah is the
Lord'.

Joey
Alternative of Josephine or
Joanna.

Joie
French, meaning 'joy'.

Jolan
Greek, meaning 'violet flower'.

Joalnda
Italian, meaning 'purple'.

Jolene
Contraction of Joanna and
Darlene, meaning 'gracious
darling'.

Jolie
(alt. Joely)
French, meaning 'pretty'.

Jora
Hebrew, meaning 'autumn rain'.

Jorah
Hebrerw, meaning 'autumn rose'.

Jordan
(alt. Jordana, Jordin, Jordyn)
Hebew, meaning 'descend'.

Jorunn
Norse, meaning 'lover of horses'.

Josephine
(alt. Josefina, Josephina)
Hebrew, meaning 'Jehovah
increases'.

Josie
(alt. Joss, Jossie)
Shortened form of Josephine,
meaning 'Jehovah increases'.

Jovita
(alt. Jovie)
Latin, meaning 'made glad'.

Joy
Latin, meaning 'joy'.

Joyce
Latin, meaning 'joyous'.

Juanita
(alt. Juana)
Spanish, meaning 'the Lord is
gracious'.

Juba
African, meaning 'born on a
Monday'.

Jubilee
Hebrew, meaning 'horn of a ram'.

Judith
(alt. Judit)
Hebrew, meaning 'Jewish'.

Judy
(alt. Judi, Judie)
Shortened form of Judith,
meaning 'Jewish'.

Jules
French, meaning 'Jove's child'.

Julia
Latin, meaning 'youthful'.

Julianne
(alt. Juliana, Juliann, Julianne)
Latin, meaning 'youthful'.

Julie
(alt. Juli)
Shortened form of Julia, meaning 'youthful'.

Juliet
(alt. Joliet, Juliette)
Latin, meaning 'youthful'. Shakespeare protagonist in *Romeo & Juliet*.

Jumana
(alt. Jumanah, Jummanah)
Arabic, meaning 'silver pearl'.

June
(alt. Juna)
Latin, after the month of the same name.

Juniper
Dutch, from the shrub of the same name.

Juno
(alt. Juneau)
Latin, meaning 'queen of heaven'.

Justice
English, meaning 'to deliver what is just'.

Justine
(alt. Justina)
Latin, meaning 'fair and righteous'.

Juturna
Latin, mythological goddess of fountains and spings.

Jwahir
African, meaning 'golden woman'.

Jyoti
Indian, meaning 'born into the light'.

Jyotsna
Indian, meaning 'lady of the moonlight'.

Names from literature

Alice (*Alice in Wonderland*, Lewis Carroll)
Anna (*Anna Karenina*, Leo Tolstoy)
Bella (*Twilight*, Stephenie Meyer)
Clarissa (*Mrs Dalloway*, Virginia Woolf)
Elizabeth (*Pride and Prejudice*, Jane Austen)
Hermione (*Harry Potter*, J.K. Rowling)
Jane (*Jane Eyre*, Charlotte Brontë)
Rebecca (*Rebecca*, Daphne du Maurier)
Emma (*Emma*, Jane Austen)
Tess (*Tess of the D'Urbervilles*, Thomas Hardy)

J

K Girls' names

Kacela
African, meaning 'huntress'.

Kacey
American alternative to Casey, meaning 'watchful'.

Kahina
Native American, meaning 'spiritual dancer'.

Kacondra
American, meaning 'bold'.

Kadenza
(alt. Kadence)
Latin, meaning 'with rhythm'.

Kadin
Arabic, meaning 'companion'.

Kadisha
Hebrew, meaning 'religious one'.

Kaede
Japanese, meaning 'like a maple leaf'.

Kaelyn
English, meaning 'lovely girl from the meadow'.

Kafi
African, meaning 'quiet one'.

Kagami
Japanese, meaning 'true image'.

Kai
Hindi, meaning 'lady of the sea'.

Kaila
Hebrew, meaning 'crowned with a laurel'.

Kaliani
Hawaiian, meaning 'sky and sea'.

Kaimi
Polynesian, meaning 'seeker'.

Kairos
Greek, meaning 'opportunity'.

Kaitlin
(alt. Kaitlyn)
Greek, meaning 'pure'.

Kala
(alt. Kaela, Kaiala, Kaila)
Sanskrit, meaning 'black one'.

Kalani
Hawaiian, meaning 'of the heavens'.

Kali
(alt. Kailee, Kailey, Kaleigh, Kaley, Kalie, Kalli, Kally, Kaylee, Kayleigh)
Sanskrit, meaning 'black one'.

Kalika
Greek, meaning 'rosebud'.

Kalila
Arabic, meaning 'beloved'.

Kalina
Slavic, meaning 'flower'.

Kallan
Scandinavian, meaning 'stream'.

Kalliope
Greek, from the muse of the
same name.

Kallista
Greek, meaning 'most beautiful'.

Kama
Sanskrit, meaning 'love'.

Kami
Japanese, meaning 'lord'.

Kamilla
(alt. Kamilah)
Slavic, meaning 'serving girl'.

Kamari
Swahili, meaning 'moonlight'.

Kamilah
Arabic, meaning 'perfect'.

Kana
Hawaiian, from the demi-god of
the same name.

Kandace
(alt. Kandice)
Latin, meaning 'glowing white'.

Kandy
(alt. Kandi)
Shortened form of Kandace,
meaning 'glowing white'.

Kanika
Africa, meaning 'black cloth'.

Kara
Latin, meaning 'dear one'.

Karashie
African, meaning 'wisdom'.

Karcsi
French, meaning 'joyful singer'.

Karen
*(alt. Karan, Karalyn, Karin, Karina,
Karon)*
Greek, meaning 'pure'.

Kari
(alt. Karie, Karri, Karrie)
Shortened form of Karen,
meaning 'pure'.

Karimah
Arabic, meaning 'giving'.

Karina
Russian, meaning 'dear one'.

Karishma
Sanskrit, meaning 'miracle'.

Karissa
Greek, meaning 'full of grace'.

Karla
German, meaning 'man'.

Karly
(alt. Karlee, Karley, Karli)
German, meaning 'free man'.

Karlyn
German, meaning 'man'.

Karma
Hindi, meaning 'destiny'.

K

Karmiti
Native American, meaning 'of the trees'.

Karnesha
American, meaning 'fiesty'.

Karol
(*alt. Karolina, Karolyn*)
Slavic, meaning 'little and womanly'.

Karrington
English, meaning 'admired'.

Karuna
Indian, meaning 'compassionate one'.

Kasen
Scandinavian, meaning 'pure'.

Kasi
Indian, meaning 'shining'.

Kassandra
Greek, meaning 'she who entangles men'.

Kasey,
(*alt. Kacey ,Kacie, Kasie*)
Irish Gaelic, meaning 'alert and watchful'.

Kassidy
English alternative of Cassidy, meaning 'clever'.

Kasumi
Japanese, meaning 'of the mist'.

Katarina
(*alt. Katarine, Katerina, Katharina*)
Greek, meaning 'pure'.

Kate
(*alt. Kat, Katie, Kathie, Kathy, Katy*)
Shortened form of Katherine, meaning 'pure'.

Katelyn
(*alt. Katelin, Katelynn, Katlin, Katlyn*)
Greek, meaning 'pure'.

Katherine
(*alt. Katharine, Katheryn, Kathryn*)
Greek, meaning 'pure'.

Kathleen
(*alt. Kathlyn*)
Greek, meaning 'pure'.

Katima
American, meaning 'powerful'.

Katrina
(*alt. Katina*)
Greek, meaning 'pure'.

Kaveri
Indian, meaning 'sacred river'.

Kay
(alt. Kaye)
Shortened form of Katherine, meaning 'pure'.

Kayla
(alt. Kaylah)
Greek, meaning 'pure'.

Kayley
(alt. Kayley, Kayli)
American, meaning 'pure'.

Kaylin
American, meaning 'pure'.

Keahi
Hawaiian, meaning 'fiery'.

Keanu
Hawaiian, meaning 'like the cool mountain breeze'.

Keaton
English, meaning 'shed town'.

Kedma
Hebrew, meaning 'from the east'.

Keelan
Irish, meaning 'slender and beautiful'.

Keeley
(alt. Keely)
Irish, meaning 'battle maid'.

Keidra
American, meaning 'alert'.

Keiko
Japanese, meaning 'respectful child'.

Keila
Hebrew, meaning 'citadel'.

Keira
Irish Gaelic, meaning 'dark'.

Keisha
(alt. Keesha)
Arabic, meaning 'woman'.

Kelby
Gaelic, meaning 'of the waters'.

Kelilah
Hebrew, meaning 'victorious'.

Kelis
American, meaning 'beautiful'.

Keller
Irish, meaning 'daring'.

Kelly
(alt. Keli, Kelley, Kelli, Kellie)
Irish Gaelic, meaning 'battle maid'.

Kelsey
(alt. Kelcee, Kelcie, Kelsea, Kelsi, Kelsie)
English, meaning 'island'.

Kendall
(alt. Kendal)
English, meaning 'the valley of the Kent'.

Kendra
English, meaning 'knowing'.

Kenna
Irish Gaelic, meaning 'handsome'.

Kennedy
(alt. Kenadee, Kennedi)
Irish Gaelic, meaning 'helmet head'.

Kenya
African, from the country of the same name.

Kerensa
Cornish, meaning 'love'.

Keres
Greek, mythological vengeful spirits.

Kerrigan
Irish, meaning 'black haired'.

Kerry
(alt. Keri, Kerri, Kerrie)
Irish, from the county of the same name.

Keyla
English, meaning 'wise daughter'.

Khadijah
(alt. Khadejah)
Arabic, meaning 'premature baby'.

Kiana
(alt. Kia, Kiana)
American, meaning 'fibre'.

Kiara
Italian, meaning 'light'.

Kiera
Irish, meaning 'litte dark-haired child'.

Kiho
African, meaning 'out of the fog'.

Kiki
Spanish, meaning 'home ruler'.

Killian
Irish, meaning 'warrior woman'.

Kim
Shortened form of Kimberly, from the town of the same name.

Kimama
Native American, meaning 'butterfly'.

Kimberly
(alt. Kimberleigh, Kimberley)
English, from the South African town of the same name.

Kin
Japanese, meaning 'golden one'.

Kineta
Greek, meaning 'full of energy'.

Kingsley
(alt. Kinsley)
English, meaning 'king's meadow'.

Kinsey
English, meaning 'king's victory'.

Kira
Greek, meaning 'lady'.

Kiri
Maori, meaning 'tree bark'.

Kirsten
(alt. Kirstin)
Scandinavian, meaning 'Christian'.

Kirstie
Shortened form of Kirsten, meaning 'Christian'.

Kasha
Russian, meaning 'genius'.

K

Kismet
English, meaning 'fate' or 'destiny'.

Kit
American, meaning 'possessing great strength'.

Kitty
(alt. Kittie)
Shortened form of Katherine, meaning 'pure'.

Kizzy
Hebrew, meaning 'Cassia'.

Klara
Hungarian, meaning 'bright'.

Kobi
American, meaning 'from California'.

Komal
Hindi, meaning 'soft and tender'.

Kona
Hawaiian, meaning 'girly'.

Konstantina
Latin, meaning 'steadfast'.

Kora
(alt. Kori)
Greek, meaning 'maiden'.

Kosta
Latin, meaning 'steadfast one'.

Kris
(alt. Krista, Kristi, Kristie, Kristy)
Shortened form of Kristen, meaning 'Christian'.

Kristen
(alt. Kristan, Kristin, Kristine, Krysten)
Greek, meaning 'Christian'.

Krystal
(alt. Kristal, Kristel)
Greek, meaning 'ice'.

Kura
Turkish, meaning 'from the river'.

Kwanza
(alt. Kwanzaa)
African, meaning 'beginning'.

Kyla
(alt. Kya, Kylah, Kyle)
Scottish, meaning 'narrow split of land'.

Kylie
(alt. Kiley, Kylee)
Irish Gaelic, meaning 'graceful'.

Kyoko
Japanese, meaning 'girl who sees her true image'.

Kyra
Greek, meaning 'lady'.

Kyrie
Greek, meaning 'the Lord'.

Kyrielle
French, meaning 'poetess'.

Gem and precious stone names
Amber
Crystal
Emerald
Garnet
Jade
Opal
Pearl
Ruby

K

L Girls' names

Laadan
Hebrew, meaning 'distinguished one'.

Laasya
Indian, meaning 'graceful dancer'.

Labiba
Arabic, meaning 'intelligent'.

Labonita
Spanish, meaning 'beautiful'.

Lacey
(alt. Laci, Lacie, Lacy)
French, from the town of the same name.

Lachelle
American, meaning 'sweet one'.

Ladonna
Italian, meaning 'lady'.

Lady
English, meaning 'bread kneader'.

Lael
Hebrew, meaning 'belonging to God'.

Laguna
American, meaning 'from the beach'.

Laila
(alt. Laelia, Layla, Leila, Lela, Lelah, Lelia)
Arabic, meaning 'night'.

Laima
Latvian, meaning 'fortunate'.

Lainey
(alt. Laine, Laney)
French, meaning 'bright light'.

Laire
Scottish, meaning 'like a mare'.

Laidh
Hebrew, meaning 'lioness'.

Lajean
French, meaning 'soothing'.

Lajita
Indian, meaning 'truthful'.

Lake
American, meaning 'still waters'.

Lakeisha
(alt. Lakeshia)
American, meaning 'woman'.

Laksha
Indian, meaning 'beautiful as a white rose'.

Lakshmi
(alt. Laxmi)
Sanskrit, meaning 'good omen'.

Lala
Slavic, meaning 'like a tulip'.

Lalaine
American, meaning 'hardworking'.

Lalasa
Indian, meaning 'like a dove'.

Lana
Greek, meaning 'light'.

Lani
(alt. Lanie)
Hawaiian, meaning 'sky'.

Lansing
English, meaning 'filled with hope'.

Lantana
English, meaning 'like a flower'.

Lanza
Italian, meaning 'noble'.

Lara
Latin, meaning 'famous'.

Laraine
French, meaning 'from Lorraine'.

Larch
American, meaning 'full of life'.

Larina
Spanish, meaning 'queen'.

Larissa
(alt. Larisa)
Greek, meaning 'lighthearted'.

Lark
English, meaning 'playful songbird'.

Larkin
American, meaning 'pretty young woman'.

Larsen
Scandinavian, meaning 'son of Lars'.

Latanya
American, meaning 'fairy queen's daughter'.

Latifa
Arabic, meaning 'gentle and pleasant'.

Latika
Hindi, meaning 'a plant'.

Latisha
Latin, meaning 'happiness'.

Latona
(alt. Latonia)
Roman, from the mythological heroine of the same name.

Latoya
Spanish, meaning 'victorious one'.

Latrice
(alt. Latricia)
Latin, meaning 'noble'.

Laudine
English, meaning 'lady of the fountain'.

Laura
Latin, meaning 'laurel'.

L

Laurel
Latin, meaning 'laurel tree'.

Lauren
(alt. Lauran, Loren)
Latin, meaning 'laurel'.

Laurent
French, meaning 'graceful one'.

Lavada
American, meaning 'creative'.

Laveda
(alt. Lavada)
Latin, meaning 'cleansed'.

Lavender
Latin, from the plant of the same name.

Laverne
(alt. Lavern, Laverna)
Latin, from the goddess of the same name.

Lavinia
(alt. Lavina)
Latin, meaning 'woman of Rome'.

Lavita
American, meaning 'charming'.

Lavonne
(alt. Lavon)
French, meaning 'yew wood'.

Le
Chinese, meaning 'bringer of joy'.

Lea
English, meaning 'meadow'.

Leah
(alt. Lea, Leia)
Hebrew, meaning 'weary'.

Leandra
Greek, meaning 'lion man'.

Leanne
(alt. Leann, Leanna, Leeann)
Contraction of Lee and Ann, meaning 'meadow grace'.

Leba
Hebrew, meaning 'dearly loved one'.

Leda
Greek, meaning 'gladness'.

Ledell
Greek, meaning 'queenly'.

Lee
(alt. Leigh)
English, meaning 'pasture or meadow'.

Leela
Indian, meaning 'accomplished actress'.

Legia
Spanish, meaning 'bright'.

Lehava
Hebrew, meaning 'fiery'.

Lei
Haiwaiian, meaning 'a flower adornment'.

Leilani
Hawaiian, meaning 'flower from heaven'.

Leith
Scottish Gaelic, meaning 'broad river'.

Leitha
Greek, meaning 'forgetful'.

Lejoi
French, meaning 'filled with happiness'.

Lemuela
Hebrew, meaning 'devoted to God'.

Lena
(alt. Leena, Lina)
Latin, meaning 'light'.

Lenesha
American, meaning 'smiles a lot'.

Lenmana
Native American, meaning 'flute girl'.

Lenna
(alt. Lennie)
German, meaning 'lion's strength'.

Lenore
(alt. Lenora)
Greek, meaning 'light'.

Léonie
(alt. Leona, Leone)
Latin, meaning 'lion'.

Leonora
(alt. Leonor, Leonore)
Greek, meaning 'light'.

Leora
Greek, meaning 'light'.

Leotie
Native American, meaning 'wildflower'.

Lerola
Latin, meaning 'like a blackbird'.

Leslie
(alt. Leslee, Lesley, Lesli)
Scottish Gaelic, meaning 'the grey castle'.

Leta
Latin, meaning 'glad and joyful'.

Letha
Greek, meaning 'forgetfulness'.

Letitia
(alt. Leticia, Lettice, Lettie)
Latin, meaning 'joy and gladness'.

Levana
Latin, meaning 'raised up'.

Levina
Latin, meaning 'lightning bolt'.

Levitt
American, meaning 'straightforward'.

Lewa
African, meaning 'beautiful'.

Lexia
(alt. Lexi)
Greek, meaning 'defender of mankind'.

Leya
Spanish, meaning 'upholds the law'.

Lhasa
Indian, meaning 'sacred'.

Li
Chinese, meaning 'one with great strength'.

Lia
Italian, meaning 'bringer of the gospel'.

L

Liana
French, meaning 'to twine around'.

Libby
(alt. Libbie)
Shortened form of Elizabeth, meaning 'pledged to God'.

Liberty
English, meaning 'freedom'.

Licia
Latin, meaning 'woman from Lycia'.

Lida
Slavic, meaning 'loved by the people'.

Lidwina
Scandinavian, meaning 'friend to all'.

Lien
Vietnamese, meaning 'like a lotus'.

Liese
(alt. Liesel, Liesl)
German, meaning 'pledged to God'.

Lieu
Vietnamese, meaning 'willow tree'.

Ligia
Greek, meaning 'musically talented'.

Liguria
Greek, meaning 'music lover'.

Lila
(alt. Lilah)
Arabic, meaning 'night'.

Lilac
Latin, from the flower of the same name.

Lilette
Latin, meaning 'budding lily'.

Lilia
(alt. Lilias)
Scottish, meaning 'lily'.

Lilith
Arabic, meaning 'ghost'.

Lillian
(alt. Lilian, Liliana, Lillianna)
Latin, meaning 'lily'.

Lilo
Hawaiian, meaning 'generous one'.

Liluye
Native American, meaning 'soaring hawk'.

Lily
(alt. Lillie, Lilly)
Latin, from the flower of the same name.

Lina
Arabic, meaning 'palm tree'.

Linda
(alt. Lynda)
Spanish, meaning 'pretty'.

Linden
(alt. Lindie, Lindy)
European, from the tree of the same name.

L

Lindsay
(alt. Lindsey, Linsey)
English, meaning 'island of linden trees'.

Linette
Welsh, meaning 'idol'.

Linn
Scottish, meaning 'cascade of waterfall'.

Linnea
(alt. Linnae, Linny)
Scandinavian, meaning 'lime or linden tree'.

Liora
(alt. Lior)
Hebrew, meaning 'I have a light'.

Lirit
Hebrew, meaning 'musically talented'.

Lisa
(alt. Leesa, Lise, Liza)
Hebrew, meaning 'pledged to God'.

Lishan
African, meaning 'awarded a medal'.

Lissa
Greek, meaning 'bee'.

Lissandra
(alt. Lisandra)
Greek, meaning 'man's defender'.

Liv
Nordic, meaning 'defence'.

Livia
Latin, meaning 'olive'.

Liz
(alt. Lizzie, Lizzy)
Shortened form of Elizabeth, meaning 'pledged to God'.

Llesenia
Spanish alternative of Yesenia, from the female lead in a 1970s soap opera.

Lleucu
Welsh, meaning 'treasured light'.

Lo
American, meaning 'fiesty'.

Loanna
American, meaning 'gracious and loving'.

Lodema
English, meaning 'provides guidance'.

Logan
Irish Gaelic, meaning 'small hollow'.

Loicy
American, meaning 'delightful'.

Lois
Of German origin, meaning 'renowned in battle'.

Lojean
America, meaning 'bravehearted'.

Lokelani
Hawaiian, meaning 'like a small red rose'.

Lola
Spanish, meaning 'sorrows'.

Loleen
American, meaning 'joyful'.

Lolita
Spanish, meaning 'sorrows'.

Lona
Latin, meaning 'lion'.

Lora
Latin, meaning 'laurel'.

Lomasi
Native American, meaning 'beautiful flower'.

Lomita
Spanish, meaning 'good woman'.

Londa
American, meaning 'shy'.

Loranden
American, meaning 'genius'.

Lordyn
American, meaning 'enchanting'.

Lorelei
(alt. Loralai, Loralie)
German, meaning 'dangerous rock'.

Lorenza
Latin, meaning 'from Laurentium'.

Loretta
(alt. Loreto)
Latin, meaning 'laurel'.

Lori
(alt. Laurie, Lorie, Lorri)
Latin, meaning 'laurel'.

Lorna
Scottish, from the place of the same name.

Lorraine
(alt. Loraine)
French, meaning 'from Lorraine'.

Lottie
(alt. Lotta, Lotte)
French, meaning 'little and womanly'.

Lotus
Greek, meaning 'lotus flower'.

Lou
(alt. Louie, Lue)
Shortened form of Louise, meaning 'renowned in battle'.

Louise
(alt. Louisa, Luisa)
German, meaning 'renowned in battle'.

Lourdes
French, from the town of the same name.

Love
English, meaning 'love'.

Loveada
Spanish, meaning 'loving'.

Loveanna
American, meaning 'gracious and loving'.

Lovella
Native American, meaning 'soft spirit'.

Lowri
Welsh, meaning 'crowned with laurels'.

Luana
Hawaiian, meaning 'content'.

Luanne
(alt. Luann, Luanna)
German, meaning 'renowned in battle'.

Luba
Hebrew, meaning 'dearly loved'.

Lucerne
Latin, meaning 'surrounded by light'.

Lucia
(alt. Luciana)
Italian, meaning 'light'.

Lucille
(alt. Lucile, Lucilla)
French, meaning 'light'.

Lucinda
English, meaning 'light'.

Lucja
Polish, meaning 'lady of light'.

Lucretia
(alt. Lucrece)
Spanish, meaning 'light'.

Lucy
(alt. Lucie)
Latin, meaning 'light'.

Ludmilla
Slavic, meaning 'beloved of the people'.

Luella
English, meaning 'renowned in battle'.

Lulu
(alt. Lula)
German, meaning 'renowned in battle'.

Lulubell
American, meaning 'renowned beauty'.

Lumina
Latin, meaning 'surrounded by light'.

Luna
Latin, meaning 'moon'.

Lupe
Spanish, from the town of the same name.

Lur
Spanish, meaning 'earth'.

Luvina
English, meaning 'dearly loved'.

Lux
Latin, meaning 'lady of light'.

Luz
Spanish, meaning 'light'.

Lydia
(alt. Lidia)
Greek, meaning 'from Lydia'.

Lynn
(alt. Lyn, Lynne)
Spanish, meaning 'pretty'.

Lynton
English, meaning 'town of lime trees'.

Lyra
Latin, meaning 'lyre'.

Lysett
American, meaning 'pretty girl'.

L

Girls' names

Maachah
Hebrew, meaning 'one who has been oppressed'.

Maarath
Hebrew, meaning 'from desolate land'.

Maarii
German, meaning 'like a dragonfly'.

Maata
Australian, meaning 'highborn'.

Math
Hebrew, meaning 'petite one'.

Mab
Irish Gaelic, meaning 'joy'.

Mabel
(alt. Mabelle, Mable)
Latin, meaning 'loveable'.

Mabina
Celtic, meaning 'nimble'.

Mabli
Welsh, meaning 'beautiful'.

Macanta
Gaelic, meaning 'kind and gentle'.

Macaria
Spanish, meaning 'blessed'.

Macha
Irish, meaning 'goddess of war'.

Machiko
Japanese, meaning 'beautiful one'.

Macy
(alt. Macey, Maci, Macie)
French, meaning 'Matthew's estate'.

Mada
English, meaning 'from Magdala'.

Madden
(alt. Maddyn)
Irish, meaning 'little dog'.

Maddie
(alt. Maddi, Maddie, Madie)
Shortened form of Madeline, meaning 'from Magdala'.

Madeira
Spanish, meaning 'place of sweet wine'.

Madeline
(alt. Madaline, Madalyn, Madeleine)
Greek, meaning 'from Magdala'.

Madge
Greek, meaning 'pearl'.

Madhu
Indian, meaning 'sweet like honey'.

Madhuri
Hindi, meaning 'sweet girl'.

Madini
Swahili, meaning 'gemstone'.

Madison
(alt. Maddison, Madisyn, Madyson)
English, meaning 'son of the mighty warrior'.

Madonna
Latin, meaning 'my lady'.

Madora
Greek, meaning 'great ruler'.

Maeko
Japanese, meaning 'truthful'.

Maertisa
English, meaning 'well-known'.

Maeve
Irish Gaelic, meaning 'intoxicating'.

Mafalda
Spanish, meaning 'battle-mighty'.

Mafuane
Egyptian, meaning 'daughter of the earth'.

Magali
Greek, meaning 'pearl'.

Magdalene
(alt. Magdalen, Magdalena)
Greek, meaning 'from Magdala'.

Magena
Hebrew, meaning 'protected'.

Maggie
Shortened form of Margaret, meaning 'pearl'.

Magna
Latin, meaning 'having great strength'.

Magnolia
Latin, from the flower of the same name.

Maha
African, meaning 'one with beautiful eyes'.

Mahal
Native American, meaning 'tender and loving'.

Mahala
(alt. Mahalia)
Hebrew, meaning 'tender affection'.

Mahina
Hawaiian, meaning 'daughter of moonlight'.

Mahira
Arabic, meaning 'clever and adroit'.

Mahlah
Hebrew, meaning 'to be pitied'.

Mahola
Hebrew, meaning 'enjoys dancing'.

Mahsa
Persian, meaning 'like the moon'.

Maia
(alt. Maja)
Greek, meaning 'mother'.

Maida
English, meaning 'maiden'.

M

Maiki
Japanese, meaning 'like a dancing flower'.

Maimun
Arabic, meaning 'lucky'.

Maine
French, meaning 'from the mainland'.

Mairwen
Welsh, meaning 'fair'.

Maisie
(alt. Maisey, Maisy, Maizie, Masie, Mazie)
Greek, meaning 'pearl'.

Maiya
Japanese, meaning 'rice valley'.

Majda
Arabic, meaning 'glorious woman'.

Makaio
Hawaiian, meaning 'gift from God'.

Makani
Hawaiian, meaning 'like the wind'.

Makarim
Arabic, meaning 'honourable one'.

Makea
Finnish, meaning 'sweet one'.

Malka
Hebrew, meaning 'queen'.

Mallory
(alt. Malorie)
French, meaning 'unhappy'.

Malvina
Gaelic, meaning 'smooth brow'.

Mamie
(alt. Mammie)
Shortened form of Margaret, meaning 'pearl'.

Mandy
(alt. Mandi)
Shortened form of Amanda, meaning 'much loved'.

Manisha
Sanskrit, meaning 'desire'.

Mansi
Hopi, meaning 'plucked flower'.

Manuela
Spanish, meaning 'the Lord is among us'.

Mara
Hebrew, meaning 'bitter'.

Biblical names

Elizabeth
Eve
Hannah
Leah
Mary
Miriam
Rachel
Rebecca
Ruth
Sarah

Marcela
(alt. Marcella, Marceline, Marcelle)
Latin, meaning 'war-like'.

Marcia
Latin, meaning 'war-like'.

Marcy
(alt. Marci, Marcie)
Latin, meaning 'war-like'.

Margaret
(alt. Margarete, Margaretta, Margarette, Margret)
Greek, meaning 'pearl'.

Margery
(alt. Marge, Margie, Margit, Margy)
French, meaning 'pearl'.

Margo
(alt. Margot)
French, meaning 'pearl'.

Marguerite
(alt. Margarita)
French, meaning 'pearl'.

Maria
(alt. Mariah)
Latin, meaning 'bitter'.

Marian
(alt. Mariam, Mariana, Marion)
French, meaning 'bitter grace'.

Marianne
(alt. Mariana, Mariann, Maryann, Maryanne)
French, meaning 'bitter grace'.

Maribel
American, meaning 'bitterly beautiful'.

Marie
French, meaning 'bitter'.

Mariel
(alt. Mariela, Mariella)
Dutch, meaning 'bitter'.

Marietta
(alt. Marieta)
French, meaning 'bitter'.

Marigold
English, from the flower of the same name.

Marika
Dutch, meaning 'bitter'.

Marilyn
(alt. Marilee, Marilene, Marilynn)
English, meaning 'bitter'.

Marin
American, from the county of the same name.

Marina
(alt. Marine)
Latin, meaning 'from the sea'.

Mariposa
Spanish, meaning 'butterfly'.

Maris
Latin, meaning 'of the sea'.

Marisa
Latin, meaning 'of the sea'.

Marisol
Spanish, meaning 'bitter sun'.

Marissa
American, meaning 'of the sea'.

Marjolaine
French, meaning 'marjoram'.

Marjorie
(alt. Marjory)
French, meaning 'pearl'.

Marla
Shortened form of Marlene,
meaning 'bitter'.

Marlene
(alt. Marlen, Marlena)
Hebrew, meaning 'bitter'.

Marley
(alt. Marlee)
American, meaning 'bitter'.

Marlo
(alt. Marlowe)
American, meaning 'bitter'.

Marseille
French, from the city of the same
name.

Marsha
English, meaning 'war-like'.

Martha
(alt. Marta)
Aramaic, meaning 'lady'.

Martina
Latin, meaning 'war-like'.

Marvel
French, meaning 'something to
marvel at'.

Mary
Latin, meaning 'star of the sea'.

Masada
Hebrew, meaning 'foundation'.

Matilda
(alt. Mathilda, Mathilde, Matide)
German, meaning 'battle-mighty'.

Mattea
Hebrew, meaning 'gift of God'.

Maude
(alt. Maud)
German, meaning 'battle-mighty'.

Maura
Irish, meaning 'bitter'.

Maureen
(alt. Maurine)
Irish, meaning 'bitter'.

Mavis
French, meaning 'thrush'.

Maxine
(alt. Maxie)
Latin, meaning 'greatest'.

May
(alt. Mae, Maya, Maye, Mayra)
Hebrew, meaning 'gift of God'.
Also from the month.

Mckenna
(alt. Mackenna)
Irish Gaelic, meaning 'son of the
handsome one'.

Mckenzie
(alt. Mackenzie, Mckenzy, Mikenzi)
Irish Gaelic, meaning 'son of the
wise ruler'.

Meara
Gaelic, meaning 'filled with
happiness'.

Medea
(alt. Meda)
Greek, meaning 'ruling'.

Christmas names

Carol
Eve
Gloria
Holly
Ivy
Mary
Natasha
Noël
Robin

Meg
Shortened form of Margaret,
meaning 'pearl'.

Megan
(alt. Meagan, Meghan)
Welsh, meaning 'pearl'.

Mehitabel
Hebrew, meaning 'benefited by
God'.

Mehri
Persian, meaning 'kind'.

Mei
Latin, meaning 'great one'.

Meishan
Chinese, meaning 'virtuous and
beautiful'.

Meiwei
Chinese, meaning 'forever
enchanting'.

Melanie
(alt. Melania, Melany, Melonie)
Greek, meaning 'dark-skinned'.

Melba
Australian, meaning 'from
Melbourne'.

Melia
(alt. Meliah)
German, meaning 'industrious'.

Melina
Greek, meaning 'honey'.

Melinda
Latin, meaning 'honey'.

Melisande
French, meaning 'bee'.

Melissa
(alt. Melisa, Mellissa)
Greek, meaning 'bee'.

Melita
Greek, meaning 'sweet as honey'.

Melody
(alt. Melodie)
Greek, meaning 'song'.

Melva
Celtic, meaning 'chief'.

Melvina
Celtic, meaning 'chieftain'.

Menachema
Hebrew, meaning 'offers
consolation'.

Menaka
Indian, meaning 'heavenly
maiden'.

Menora
Hebrew, meaning 'candlestick'.

Mercedes
Spanish, meaning 'mercies'.

Mercy
English, meaning 'mercy'.

Meredith
(alt. Meridith)
Welsh, meaning 'great ruler'.

Merle
French, meaning 'blackbird'.

Merry
English, meaning 'lighthearted'.

Meryl
(alt. Merrill)
Irish Gaelic, meaning 'sea-bright'.

Meta
German, meaning 'pearl'.

Mia
Italian, meaning 'mine'.

Michaela
(alt. Makaela, Mikaila, Mikala, Mikayla)
Hebrew, meaning 'who is like the Lord'.

Michelle
(alt. Machelle, Michele)
French, meaning 'who is like the Lord'.

Mickey
(alt. Mickie)
Shortened form of Michelle, meaning 'who is like the Lord'.

Mide
Irish, meaning 'thirsty'.

Mieko
Japanese, meaning 'born into wealth'.

Migdalia
Greek, meaning 'from Magdala'.

Mignon
French, meaning 'cute'.

Mika
(alt. Micah)
Hebrew, meaning 'who resembles God'.

Milada
Czech, meaning 'my love'.

Milagros
Spanish, meaning 'miracles'.

Milan
Italian, from the city of the same name.

Mildred
English, meaning 'gentle strength'.

Milena
Czech, meaning 'love and warmth'.

Miley
American, meaning 'smiley'.

Millicent
German, meaning 'highborn power'.

Millie
(alt. Milly)
Shortened form of Millicent, meaning 'highborn power'.

Mimi
Italian, a variant of Mary, meaning 'star of the sea'. Famous as the protagonist of Puccini's opera *La Bohème*.

Mina
(alt. Mena)
German, meaning 'love'.

M

Popular song names

Barbara Ann (*Barbara Ann*, The Beach Boys)
Caroline (*Sweet Caroline*, Neil Diamond)
Delilah (*Delilah*, Tom Jones)
Eileen (*Come on Eileen*, Dexy's Midnight Runners)
Eleanor (*Eleanor Rigby*, The Beatles)
Julia (*Julia*, The Beatles)
Layla (*Layla*, Eric Clapton)
Lola (*Lola*, The Kinks)
Roxanne (*Roxanne*, The Police)
Sadie (*Sexy Sadie*, The Beatles)

Mindy
(alt. Mindi)
Latin, meaning 'honey'.

Minerva
Roman, from the goddess of the same name.

Ming
Chinese, meaning 'bright'.

Minnie
(alt. Minna)
German, meaning 'will-helmet'.

Mira
Latin, meaning 'admirable'.

Mirabel
(alt. Mirabella, Mirabelle)
Latin, meaning 'wonderful'.

Miranda
(alt. Meranda)
Latin, meaning 'admirable'.

Mirella
(alt. Mireille, Mirela)
Latin, meaning 'admirable'.

Miriam
Hebrew, meaning 'bitter'.

Mirta
Spanish, meaning 'crown of thorns'.

Missy
Shortened form of Melissa, meaning 'bee'.

Misty
(alt. Misti)
English, meaning 'mist'.

Mitzi
German, a variant of Mary, meaning 'star of the sea'.

Miu
Japanese, meaning 'beautiful feather'.

Moira
(alt. Maira)
English, a variant of Mary, meaning 'star of the sea'.

Molly
(alt. Mollie)
Irish, a variant of Mary, meaning 'star of the sea'.

M

Momo
Japanese, meaning 'like a peach'.

Mona
Irish Gaelic, meaning 'aristocratic'.

Monica
(alt. Monika, Monique)
Latin, meaning 'adviser'.

Montserrat
(alt. Monserrate)
Spanish, from the town of the same name.

Morag
Scottish, a variant of Mary, meaning 'star of the sea'.

Morgan
(alt. Morgann)
Welsh, meaning 'great and bright'.

Moriah
Hebrew, meaning 'the Lord is my teacher'.

Morwenna
Welsh, meaning 'maiden'.

Moselle
(alt. Mozell, Mozella, Mozelle)
Hebrew, meaning 'saviour'.

Mulan
Chinese, meaning 'wood orchid'.

Munaya
African, meaning 'rainmaker'.

Munin
Scandinavian, meaning 'good memory'.

Muriel
Irish Gaelic, meaning 'sea-bright'.

Mushana
African, meaning 'born in morning light'.

Mushira
Arabic, meaning 'wise counsellor'.

Mutia
African, meaning 'respected'.

Mya
(alt. Myah)
Greek, meaning 'mother'.

Myfanwy
Welsh, meaning 'my little lovely one'.

Myma
Irish, meaning 'greatly loved'.

Myra
Latin, meaning 'scented oil'.

Myrna
(alt. Mirna)
Irish Gaelic, meaning 'tender and beloved'.

Myrtle
Irish, from the shrub of the same name.

Mythri
Indian, meaning 'values friendship'.

N Girls' names

Naamah
Hebrew, meaning 'sweetness'.

Naara
Japanese, meaning 'deer'.

Naava
Hebrew, meaning 'beautiful'.

Nabiha
Arabic, meaning 'intelligent'.

Nabila
Arabic, meaning 'noble'.

Nachine
Spanish, meaning 'fiery'.

Nadda
Arabic, meaning 'generous'.

Nadezhda
Russian, meaning 'hope'.

Nadia
(alt. Nadya)
Russian, meaning 'hope'.

Nadine
French, meaning 'hope'.

Naeva
French, meaning 'evening'.

Nafisa
Arabic, meaning 'precious gem'.

Nahara
Aramaic, meaning 'light'.

Nahla
Arabic, meaning 'drink water'.

Nailah
Arabic, meaning 'successful'.

Naima
Arabic, meaning 'water nymph'.

Naiya
Arabic, meaning 'reed'.

Najwa
Arabic, meaning 'passionate'.

Najya
Arabic, meaning 'free'.

Nakia
Egyptian, meaning 'pure'.

Nakita
American, meaning 'victory of people'.

Nala
African, meaning 'successful'.

Nalani
Hawaiian, meaning 'serenity of the skies'.

N

Saints' names

Ada
Agatha
Catherine
Felicity
Helena
Joan
Lydia
Margaret
Mary
Teresa

Nan
(alt. Nanna, Nannie)
Hebrew, meaning 'grace'.

Nancy
(alt. Nanci, Nancie)
Hebrew, meaning 'grace'.

Nanette
(alt. Nannette)
French, meaning 'grace'.

Naoko
Japanese, meaning 'honest'.

Naomh
Irish, meaning 'holy'.

Naomi
(alt. Naoma, Noemi)
Hebrew, meaning 'pleasant'.

Narcissa
Greek, meaning 'daffodil'.

Nastasia
Greek, meaning 'resurrection'.

Natalie
(alt. Natalee, Natalia, Natalya, Nathalie)
Latin, meaning 'birth day'.

Natasha
(alt. Natasa)
Russian, meaning 'birth day'.

Natividad
Spanish, meaning 'Christmas'.

Neda
English, meaning 'wealthy'.

Nedra
English, meaning 'underground'.

Neema
Swahili, meaning 'born of prosperity'.

Neka
Native American, meaning 'goose'.

Nell
(alt. Nelda, Nella, Nell, Nellie, Nelly)
Shortened form of Eleanor, meaning 'light'.

Nemi
Italian, from the lake of the same name.

Nenetl
Aztec, meaning 'doll'.

Neoma
Greek, meaning 'new moon'.

Nereida
Spanish, meaning 'sea nymph'.

Nerissa
Of Greek origin, meaning 'sea nymph'.

Nettie
(alt. Neta)
Shortened form of Henrietta, meaning 'ruler of the house'.

Neva
Spanish, meaning 'snowy'.

Nevaeh
American, meaning 'heaven'.

Nhi
Vietnamese, meaning 'little one'.

Nhuung
Vietnamese, meaning 'velvet'.

Nia
Welsh, meaning 'bright'.

Niamh
(alt. Neve)
Irish, meaning 'brightness'.

Nicki
(alt. Nicky, Nikki)
Shortened form of Nicola,
meaning 'victory of the people'.

Nicola
Greek, meaning 'victory of the
people'.

Nicole
(alt. Nichole, Nicolette, Nikole)
Greek, meaning 'victory of the
people'.

Nidia
Spanish, meaning 'graceful'.

Nikita
Greek, meaning 'unconquered'.

Nigella
Irish Gaelic, meaning 'champion'.

Nika
Slavic, meaning 'bringer of
victory'.

Nila
Egyptian, meaning 'nile'.

Nilda
German, meaning 'battle
woman'.

Nimeesha
African, meaning 'princess'.

Nimra
Arabic, meaning 'number'.

Nina
Spanish, meaning 'girl'.

Nissa
Hebrew, meaning 'sign'.

Nita
Spanish, meaning 'gracious'.

Nitsa
Greek, meaning 'light'.

Nitza
Hebrew, meaning 'flower bud'.

Nixie
German, meaning 'water sprite'.

Njema
Swahili, meaning 'good'.

Noa
Hebrew, meaning 'movement'.

Noel
(alt. Noelle)
French, meaning 'Christmas'.

Nola
Irish Gaelic, meaning 'white
shoulder'.

Nolcha
Native American, meaning 'sun'.

N

Opera heroines

Carmen (*Carmen*, Georges Bizet)
Elektra (*Elektra*, Richard Strauss)
Ellen (*Peter Grimes*, Benjamin Britten)
Floria (*Tosca*, Puccini)
Liza (*The Queen of Spades*, Tchaikovsky)
Mimi (*La Bohème*, Puccini)
Pamina (*The Magic Flute*, Mozart)
Turandot (*Turandot*, Puccini)
Violetta (*La Traviata*, Giuseppe Verdi)
Vitellia (*La Clemenza di Tito*, Mozart)

Nomatha
African, meaning 'big surprise'.

Nomble
African, meaning 'beauty'.

Nona
Latin, meaning 'ninth'.

Nora
(*alt. Norah*)
Shortened form of Eleanor, meaning 'light'.

Noreen
(*alt. Norine*)
Irish, meaning 'light'.

Norma
Latin, meaning 'pattern'.

Normandie
(*alt. Normandy*)
French, from the province of the same name.

Novia
Latin, meaning 'new'.

Nox
Latin, meaning 'night'.

Noxolo
African, meaning 'peaceful'.

Nsombi
African, meaning 'abundant joy'.

Nu
Vietnamese, meaning 'girl'.

Nuala
Irish Gaelic, meaning 'white shoulder'.

Nyathera
African, meaning 'she survived'.

Nydia
Latin, meaning 'nest'.

Nyimbo
Swahili, meaning 'song'.

Nyofu
Swahili, meaning 'candid'.

Nysa
(*alt. Nyssa*)
Greek, meaning 'ambition'.

Nyx
Greek, meaning 'night'.

N

O Girls' names

Obelia
Greek, meaning 'needle'.

Obioma
African, meaning 'kind hearted'.

Oceana
(alt. Ocean, Océane, Ocie)
Greek, meaning 'ocean'.

Octavia
Latin, meaning 'eighth'.

Oda
(alt. Odie)
Shortened form of Odessa,
meaning 'long voyage'.

Odanda
Spanish, meaning 'the well-
known land'.

Oddfrid
Norse, meaning 'sharp like the
point of a sword'.

Ode
Greek, meaning 'a lyric poem'.

Odeda
Hebrew, meaning 'to encourage'.

Odele
(alt. Odell)
English, meaning 'woad hill'.

Odelia
Hebrew, meaning 'I will praise
the Lord'.

Odelita
Spanish, meaning 'who sings'.

Odessa
Greek, meaning 'long voyage'.

Odette
(alt. Odetta)
French, meaning 'wealthy'.
Famous as the name of the
Princess in *Swan Lake*.

Odile
(alt. Odilia)
French, meaning 'prospers in
battle'.

Odina
Feminine form of Odin, from the
Nordic god of the same name.

Odyssey
Greek, meanining 'long journey'.
Also the title of Homer's famous
epic poem, *The Odyssey*.

Ofa
Polynesian, meaning 'beloved'.

Ofira
Hebrew, meaning 'gold'.

O

Names from ancient Greece

Alexandra
Apollonia
Corinna
Irene
Lysandra
Melaina
Pelagia
Sophia
Xenia
Zenobia

Ogin
Native American, meaning 'like a wild rose'.

Ohanna
Armenian, meaning 'gift from God'.

Ohela
Hebrew, meaning 'tent'.

Oheo
Native American, meaning 'beautiful woman'.

Oighrig
Gaelic, meaning 'freckled one'.

Oihane
Spanish, meaning 'from the forest'.

Oira
Latin, meaning 'one who prays'.

Ojal
Sanskrit, meaning 'vision'.

Okalani
Hawaiian, meaning 'heaven'.

Oki
Japanese, meaning 'ocean centred'.

Oksana
Russian, meaning 'praise to God'.

Ola
(alt. Olie)
Greek, meaning 'man's defender'.

Olathe
Native American, meaning 'lovely'.

Olena
(alt. Olene)
Russian, meaning 'light'.

Olga
Russian, meaning 'holy'.

Oliana
American, meaning 'the Lord has answered'.

Olina
Scandinavian, meaning 'ancestor's heir'.

Oliva
English, meaning 'elf army'.

Olivia
(alt. Olivev, Oliviana, Olivié)
Latin, meaning 'olive'.

Ollie
Shortened form of Olivia, meaning 'olive'.

Olwen
Welsh, meaning 'white footprint'.

Olya
Slavic, meaning 'holy'.

O

Olympia
(alt. Olimpia)
Greek, meaning 'from Mount Olympus'.

Oma
(alt. Omie)
Arabic, meaning 'leader'.

Omyra
Latin, meaning 'scented oil'.

Ona
(alt. Onnie)
Shortened form of Oneida, meaning 'long awaited'.

Ondine
French, meaning 'wave of water'.

Oneida
Native American, meaning 'long awaited'.

Onella
Hungarian, meaning 'torch light'.

Oni
Native American, meaning 'born on holy ground'.

Onyx
Latin, meaning 'veined gem'.

Oona
Irish, meaning 'unity'.

Opal
Sanskrit, meaning 'gem'.

Ophelia
(alt. Ofelia, Ophélie)
Greek, meaning 'help'.

Oprah
Hebrew, meaning 'young deer'.

Ora
Latin, meaning ' prayer'.

Orabela
Latin, meaning 'prayer'.

Oraefo
African, meaning 'affectionate'.

Oralee
American, meaning 'golden'.

Oralie
(alt. Oralia)
French, meaning 'golden'.

Orane
French, meaning 'born at sunrise'.

Orbelina
American, meaning 'bringer of excitement'.

Orchid
Greek, from the flower of the same name.

Orane
French, meaning 'rising'.

Colour names

Blanche
Coral
Ebony
Fawn
Hazel
Olive
Rose
Scarlett
Sienna
Violet

O

269

Orea
Greek, meaning 'from the mountains'.

Orella
Italian, meaning 'golden'.

Orenda
Native American, meaning 'great spirit'.

Oriana
(alt. Oriane)
Latin, meaning 'dawning'.

Orinda
Hebrew, meaning 'pine trees'.

Orla
(alt. Orlaith, Orly)
Irish Gaelic, meaning 'golden lady'.

Orlaith
Irish, meaning 'gold queen'.

Orlean
French, meaning 'plum'.

Orlena
American, meaning 'golden'.

Orma
African, meaning 'free men'.

Ornella
Italian, meaning 'flowering ash tree'.

Orrtha
American, meaning 'charm'.

Orsa
(alt. Osia, Ossie)
Latin, meaning 'bear'.

Orya
Russian, meaning 'peace'.

Otthid
Greek, meaning 'prospers in battle'.

Ottilie
(alt. Ottie)
French, meaning 'prospers in battle'.

Ouida
French, meaning 'renowned in battle'.

Owena
Welsh, meaning 'desire'.

Ownah
Irish, meaning 'unity'.

Oya
African, meaning 'wind warrior goddess'.

Oyintsa
Native American, meaning 'white duck'.

Ozette
Native American, from the village of the same name.

Names of writers

Emily (Brontë)
Charlotte (Brontë)
Daphne (du Maurier)
Dorris (Lessing)
Jane (Austen)
Mary (Shelley)
Pam (Ayres)
Stephenie (Meyer)
Virginia (Woolf)
Wendy (Cope)

O

P

Girls' names

Pa
Spanish, meaning 'free'.

Pabiola
(alt. Pabiole)
Spanish, meaning 'little girl'.

Paciencia
Spanish, meaning 'patient'.

Pacifica
(alt. Pacifika)
Spanish, meaning 'peaceful'.

Padma
Hindi, meaning 'lotus'. One of
the twins in *Harry Potter*. It is also
another name for the goddess
Lakshmi.

Padmaja
Indian, meaning 'born from a
lotus'.

Padmini
Indian, meaning 'a lotus pond'.

Padraigin
Irish, meaning 'noble'.

Pagan
Old English, meaning 'country
dweller'. It is also a word used
to describe alternative religious
beliefs.

Pageant
(alt. Padgeant, Padgent, Pagent)
American, meaning 'theatrical'.

Paige
(alt. Page)
French, meaning 'serving boy'.

Paili
Hebrew, meaning 'bitter'.

Paisley
Scottish, from the town of the
same name.

Paiva
Scandinavian, meaning 'sun god'.

Pakeezah
Arabic, meaning 'pure'.

Paki
African, meaning 'witness'.

Pakuna
Native American, meaning 'a
deer jumping downhill'.

Palemon
(alt. Palem, Palemond)
Spanish, meaning 'kind'.

Palesa
African, meaning 'flower'.

Palila
Hawaiian, meaning 'bird'.

Pallas
(alt. Paladia, Palladia, Palles)
Greek, meaning 'wisdom'. It was
also another name for Athena in
Greek mythology.

Pallavi
Sanskrit, meaning 'new leaves'.

Palma
(alt. Palmira)
Latin, meaning 'palm tree'.

Paloma
Spanish, meaning 'dove'.

Pam
Shortened form of Pamela,
meaning 'all honey'.

Pamela
(alt. Pamala, Pamella, Pamla)
Greek, meaning 'all honey'.

Panchali
Sanskrit, meaning 'princess'.

Pandora
Greek, meaning 'all gifted'.

Pang
Chinese, meaning 'innovative'.

Pangiota
Greek, meaning 'all is holy'.

Paniz
Persian, meaning 'candy'.

Pansy
French, from the flower of the
same name.

Panya
Slavic, meaning 'crown'.

Paola
Italian, meaning 'troublemaker'.

Paolabella
Italian, meaning 'lovely
troublemaker'.

Papina
Native American, meaning 'ivy'.

Paquita
Spanish, meaning 'free'.

Paradisa
(alt. Paradis)
Greek, meaning 'garden orchard'.

Paris
(alt. Parisa)
Greek, from the mythological
hero of the same name. Also from
the city.

Parisa
Persian, meaning 'fairy-like'.

Parker
English, meaning 'park keeper'.

Parminder
Hindi, meaning 'beautiful'.

Parnelle
(alt. Parnel, Parnell, Parney)
French, meaning 'little stone'.

Parthenia
Greek, meaning 'virginal'.

Parthenope
Greek, from the mythological
siren of the same name.

Parvani
Sanskrit, meaning 'full moon'.

Parvati
Sanskrit, meaning 'daughter of
the mountain'. One of the twins'
names in *Harry Potter*.

Pascale
French, meaning 'Easter'.

P

Pat
(alt. Patsy, Patti, Pattie, Patty)
Shortened form of Patricia,
meaning 'noble'.

Patia
Greek, meaning 'highest'.

Patience
French, meaning 'the state of
being patient'.

Patricia
(alt. Patrice)
Latin, meaning 'noble'.

Paula
Latin, meaning 'small'.

Pauline
(alt. Paulette, Paulina)
Latin, meaning 'small'.

Paxton
Latin, meaning 'peaceful town'.

Paz
Spanish, meaning 'peace'.

Pazia
Hebrew, meaning 'golden'.

Peace
English, meaning 'peace'.

Peaches
English, from the fruit of the same
name.

Pearl
(alt. Pearle, Pearlie, Perla)
Latin, meaning 'pale gemstone'.

Pegeen
Irish, meaning 'pearl'.

Peggy
(alt. Peggie)
Greek, meaning 'pearl'.

Pelagia
Greek, meaning 'sea'.

Pelia
Hebrew, meaning 'marvel of
God'.

Penelope
Greek, meaning 'bobbin worker'.

Penka
Bulgarian, meaning 'rock'.

Penny
(alt. Penni, Pennie)
Greek, meaning 'bobbin worker'.

Peony
Greek, from the flower of the
same name.

Perdita
Latin, meaning 'lost'.

Perenna
Latin, meaning 'eternal'.

Peri
(alt. Perri)
Hebrew, meaning 'outcome'.

Perpetua
Spanish, meaning 'everlasting'.

Perry
French, meaning 'pear tree'.

Persephone
Greek, meaning 'bringer of
destruction'.

Peta
Native American, meaning
'golden eagle'.

Petra
(alt. Petrina)
Greek, meaning 'rock'.

P

Petula
Latin, meaning 'to seek'.

Petunia
Greek, from the flower of the same name.

Peyton
(alt. Payton)
English, meaning 'from Pacca's town'.

Phaedra
Greek, meaning 'bright'.

Phalin
Thai, meaning 'sapphire'.

Phalen
Latin, meaning 'peaceful'.

Phenyo
African, meaning 'victory'.

Phila
Greek, meaning 'love'.

Philippa
Greek, meaning 'horse lover'.

Philomena
(alt. Philoma)
Greek, meaning 'loved one'.

Philyra
Greek, meaning 'music lover'.

Phoebe
Greek, meaning 'shining and brilliant'.

Phoenix
Greek, meaning 'red as blood'.

Phyllida
Greek, meaning 'leafy bough'.

Phyllis
(alt. Phillia, Phylis)
Greek, meaning 'leafy bough'.

Paiv
Native American, meaning 'honeydew of the mountains'.

Pia
Latin, meaning 'pious'.

Piapot
Native American, meaning 'lightning'.

Piera
Italian, meaning 'rock'.

Pieta
Latin, meaning 'piety'.

Pilialoha
Hawaiian, meaning 'loved one'.

Pilar
Spanish, meaning 'pillar'.

Piper
English, meaning 'pipe player'.

Pippa
Shortened form of Philippa, meaning 'horse lover.'

Pixie
Irish, meaning 'fairy'.

Pizi
Native American, meaning 'bravery'.

Pleasance
French, meaning 'agreeable'.

Plum
Latin, from the fruit of the same name.

Pocahontas
Native American, meaning 'to play'.

Polly
Hebrew, meaning 'bitter'.

Pollyanna
English, combination name of Polly and Anna. The title character in Eleanor H. Porter's novel *Pollyanna*.

Pomona
Latin, meaning 'apple'.

Poppy
Latin, from the flower of the same name.

Portia
(alt. Porsha)
Latin, meaning 'from the Portia clan'.

Poseanye
Native American, meaning 'dripping dew'.

Posy
English, meaning 'small flower'.

Povitamun
Native American, meaning 'morning flower'.

Poviyemo
Native American, meaning 'falling flower'.

Precious
Latin, meaning 'of great worth'.

Prema
Indian, meaning 'love'.

Premala
Indian, meaning 'loving'.

Presencia
Spanish, meaning 'presence'.

Priela
Hebrew, meaning 'fruit of God'.

Primavera
Spanish, meaning 'springtime'.

Primrose
English, meaning 'first rose'.

Princess
English, meaning 'daughter of the monarch'.

Priscilla
(alt. Prisca, Priscila)
Latin, meaning 'ancient'.

Prita
Indian, meaning 'dear one'.

Priti
Indian, meaning 'love'.

Priya
Hindi, meaning 'loved one'.

Prudence
Latin, meaning 'caution'.

Prudie
Shortened form of Prudence, meaning 'caution'.

Prunella
Latin, meaning 'small plum'.

Psyche
Greek, meaning 'breath'.

Pules
Native American, meaning 'pigeon'.

Purity
English, meaning 'clean'.

P

Q Girls' names

Qabalah
Muslim, meaning 'responsible'.

Qabool
Muslim, meaning 'accepted'.

Qadesh
(alt. Quedesh, Qadeshia)
Syrian, a mythological goddess of love.

Qadira
Arabic, meaning 'powerful'.

Qahira
Muslim, meaning 'victorious'.

Qamra
(alt. Qamrah)
Arabic, meaning 'from the moon'.

Qaraah
Muslim, meaning 'cloud'.

Boys' names for girls

Ashley
Billie
Casey
Charlie
Elliott
Geri
Jamie
Jordan
Leigh
Toni

Qaysar
Muslim, meaning 'woman'.

Qi
Chinese, meaning 'life force'.

Qiana
(alt. Qianah, Qiania, Qyana)
American, meaning 'gracious'.

Qimat
(alt. Qimate, Qimatta)
Indian, meaning 'valuable woman'.

Qing
Chinese, meaning 'blue'.

Qismah
(alt. Quisma)
Arabic, meaning 'destiny'.

Quan
Chinese, meaning 'compassionate'.

Quana
(alt. Quannah, Quaniya, Quanea)
Native American, meaning 'one who smells sweet'.

Qanesha
(alt. Quaneisha, Quanisha)
African-American, meaning 'singing'.

Old name, new fashion?

Bella
Carolyn
Clara
Dorothy
Emmeline
Hazel
Matilda
Nora
Penelope
Rosalie

Quantina
(alt. Quantinna, Quantyna)
American, meaning 'courageous queen'.

Qubilah
Arabic, meaning 'agreeable'.

Queen
(alt. Queenie)
English, meaning 'queen'.

Quiana
American, meaning 'silky'.

Quincy
(alt. Quincey)
French, meaning 'estate of the fifth son'.

Quinn
Irish Gaelic, meaning 'counsel'.

Quenby
(alt. Quenbi, Quenbie, Quinbee)
Swedish, meaning 'feminine'.

Querida
(alt. Queridah, Queryda, Quereada)
Spanish, meaning 'beloved'.

Questa
(alt. Questah, Queste, Quyste)
Latin, meaning 'seeker'.

Queta
(alt. Keta)
Spanish, meaning 'head of the house'.

Quilla
(alt. Quila, Quillah)
English, meaning 'writer'.

Quinby
(alt. Quin, Quinbie, Quinnie)
Scandinavian, meaning 'living like royalty'.

Quinella
Latin, meaning 'very beautiful'.

Quinta
Spanish, meaning 'fifth born'.

Quintana
(alt. Quentana, Quinn)
Latin, meaning 'lovely girl'.

Quintessa
Latin, meaning 'creative'.

Quita
(alt. Keeta, Keetah)
French, meaning 'calm'.

Quisha
African, meaning 'physical and spiritual beauty' or 'lovely mind'.

Q

R Girls' names

Rabia
Arabic, meaning 'spring'.

Rachel
(alt. Rachael, Rachelle)
Hebrew, meaning 'ewe'.

Rada
Bulgarian, meaning 'joy'.

Radha
Indian, meaning 'prosperity'.

Radhika
Sanskrit, meaning 'prosperous'.

Rae
(alt. Ray)
Shortened form of Rachel,
meaning 'ewe'.

Rafferty
Irish, meaning 'abundance'.

Rafiya
Swahili, meaning 'dignified'.

Ragni
Indian, meaning 'melody'.

Rahima
Arabic, meaning 'compassionate'.

Raina
(alt. Raine, Rayne)
Latin, meaning 'queen'.

Raissa
(alt. Raisa)
Yiddish, meaning 'rose'.

Raja
Indian, meaning 'king'.

Raleigh
(alt. Rayleigh)
English, meaning 'meadow of roe
deer'.

Rama
(alt. Ramey, Ramya)
Hebrew, meaning 'exhalted'.

Ramira
Spanish, meaning 'wise'.

Ramla
Swahili, meaning 'prophet'.

Ramona
(alt. Romona)
Spanish, meaning 'wise guardian'.

Ramsey
English, meaning 'raven island'.

Ranae
American, meaning 'resurrected'.

Randa
American, meaning 'admirable'.

Randy
(alt. Randi)
Shortened form of Miranda,
meaning 'admirable'.

Rana
(alt. Rania, Rayna)
Arabic, meaning 'beautiful thing'.

Rani
Sanskrit, meaning 'queen'.

Ranjana
Indian, meaning 'entertaining'.

Ransom
English, meaning 'rescue'.

Raphaela
(alt. Rafaela, Raffaella)
Spanish, meaning 'healing God'.

Raquel
(alt. Racquel)
Hebrew, meaning 'ewe'.

Rasha
Arabic, meaning 'like a young
gazelle'.

Rashida
Turkish, meaning 'righteous'.

Ratana
Thai, meaning 'like a crystal'.

Ratri
Indian, meaning 'born during the
evening'.

Raven
(alt. Ravyn)
English, from the bird of the same
name.

Place names

Africa
Brittany
Devon
Florence
India
Paris
Persia
Sienna
Skye
Virginia

Raya
Israeli, meaning 'beloved friend'.

Rayna
Hebrew, meaning 'pure'.

Razia
Arabic, meaning 'contented'.

Reagan
(alt. Reagen, Regan)
Irish Gaelic, meaning 'descendent
of Riagán'.

Reba
Shortened form of Rebecca,
meaning 'joined'.

Rebecca
(alt. Rebekah)
Hebrew, meaning 'joined'.

Redell
English, meaning 'red meadow'.

Reed
English, meaning 'red hair lady'.

Reese
Welsh, meaning 'fiery and
zealous'.

R

Regan
Gaelic, meaning 'born into royalty'.

Regina
Latin, meaning 'queen'.

Rehan
Armenian, meaning 'like a flower'.

Reiko
Japanese, meaning 'thankful one'.

Rekha
Indian, meaning 'walks a straight line'.

Reina
(alt. Reyna, Rheyna)
Spanish, meaning 'queen'.

Remy
French, meaning 'from the town of Rheims'.

Rena
(alt. Reena)
Hebrew, meaning 'serene'.

Renata
Latin, meaning 'reborn'.

Rene
Greek, meaning 'peace'.

Renée
(alt. Renae)
French, meaning 'reborn'.

Renita
Latin, meaning 'resistant'.

Reshma
(alt. Resha)
Sanskrit, meaning 'silk'.

Reta
(alt. Retha, Retta)
Shortened form of Margaret, meaning 'pearl'.

Rexanne
Latin, meaning 'graceful queen'.

Rezeph
Hebrew, meaning 'solid as stone'.

Rhan
Welsh, meaning 'one's destiny'.

Rhea
Greek, meaning 'earth'.

Rheta
Greek, meaning 'eloquent speaker'.

Rhiamon
Welsh, meaning 'magical woman'.

Rhiannon
(alt. Rhian, Rhianna, Reanna)
Welsh, meaning 'witch'.

Rhoda
Greek, meaning 'rose'.

Tennis players

Anna (Kounikova)
Billie Jean (King)
Chris (Evert)
Margaret (Smith Court)
Maria (Sharapova)
Martina (Hingis/Navrátilová)
Monica (Seles)
Serena (Williams)
Steffi (Graf)
Venus (Williams)

R

Rhona
Nordic, meaning 'rough island'.

Rhonda
(alt. Ronda)
Welsh, meaning 'noisy'.

Ría
(alt. Rie, Riya)
Shortened form of Victoria,
meaning 'victor'.

Ricki
(alt. Rieko, Rika, Rikki)
Shortened form of Frederica,
meaning 'peaceful ruler'.

Rida
Arabic, meaning 'favoured by
God'.

Riley
Irish Gaelic, meaning
'courageous'.

Rilla
German, meaning 'small brook'.

Rima
Arabic, meaning 'antelope'.

Riona
Irish Gaelic, meaning 'like a
queen'.

Ripley
English, meaning 'shouting man's
meadow'.

Risa
Latin, meaning 'laughter'.

Rita
Shortened form of Margaret,
meaning 'pearl'.

Names of goddesses

Aphrodite (Love: Greek)
Demeter (Harvest: Greek)
Eos (Dawn: Greek)
Isis (Life: Egyptian)
Kali (Death: Indian)
Lakshmi (Wealth: Indian)
Minerva (Wisdom: Roman)
Nephthys (Death: Egyptian)
Saraswati (Arts: Indian)
Vesta (Hearth: Roman)

River
(alt. Riviera)
English, from the body of water of
the same name.

Rizpah
Greek, meaning 'full of hope'.

Robbie
(alt. Robi, Roby)
Shortened form of Roberta,
meaning 'bright flame'.

Roberta
English, meaning 'bright flame'.

Robin
(alt. Robbin, Robyn)
English, from the bird of the same
name.

Rochelle
(alt. Richelle, Rochel)
French, meaning 'little rock'.

Rogue
French, meaning 'beggar'.

Rohina
(alt. Rohini)
Sanskrit, meaning 'sandalwood'.

R

Rohini
Indian, meaning 'beautiful'.

Roja
Spanish, meaning 'red haired lady'.

Roisin
Irish Gaelic, meaning 'bright flame'.

Rolanda
German, meaning 'famous land'.

Roma
Italian, meaning 'Rome'.

Romaine
(alt. Romina)
French, meaning 'from Rome'.

Romola
(alt. Romilda, Romily)
Latin, meaning 'Roman woman'.

Romy
Shortened form of Rosemary, meaning 'dew of the sea'.

Rona
(alt. Ronia, Ronja, Ronna)
Nordic, meaning 'rough island'.

Ronat
Gaelic, meaning 'like a seal'.

Rong
Chinese, meaning 'martial'.

Roni
Hebrew, meaning 'joyful'.

Ronli
Hebrew, meaning 'joy is mine'.

Ronnie
(alt. Roni)
English, meaning 'strong counsel'.

Roro
Indonesian, meaning 'nobility'.

Rory
Irish, meaning 'red king'.

Rosa
Italian, meaning 'rose'.

Rosabel
(alt. Rosabella)
Contraction of Rose and Belle, meaning 'beautiful rose'.

Rosalie
(alt. Rosale, Rosalia, Rosalina)
French, meaning 'rose garden'.

Rosalind
(alt. Rosalinda)
Spanish, meaning 'pretty rose'.

Rosalyn
(alt. Rosaleen, Rosaline, Roselyn)
Contraction of Rose and Lynn, meaning 'pretty rose'.

Rosamond
(alt. Rosamund)
German, meaning 'renowned protector'.

Rose
Latin, from the flower of the same name.

Roseanne
(alt. Rosann, Rosanna, Roseann, Roseanna)
Contraction of Rose and Anne, meaning 'graceful rose'.

Roseclere
English, meaning 'bright rose'.

Roselyn
English, meaning 'beautiful rose'.

Rosemary
(alt. Rosemarie)
Latin, meaning 'dew of the sea'.

Rosetta
Italian, meaning 'little rose'.

Rosie
(alt. Rosia)
Shortened form of Rosemary, meaning 'dew of the sea'.

Rosita
Spanish, meaning 'rose'.

Rowa
Arabic, meaning 'lovely vision'.

Rowan
English, meaning 'rowan tree'.

Rowena
(alt. Rowan)
Welsh, meaning 'slender and fair'.

Roxanne
(alt. Roxana, Roxane, Roxanna)
Persian, meaning 'dawn'.

Roxie
Shortened form of Roxanne, meaning 'dawn'.

Ruana
Persian, meaning 'soul'.

Rubena
(alt. Rubina)
Hebrew, meaning 'behold, a son'.

Ruby
(alt. Rubi, Rubie)
English, meaning 'red gemstone'.

Ruchira
Indian, meaning 'bright'.

Rumer
English, meaning 'fame'.

Ruslana
Russian, meaning 'lion'.

Rusty
American, meaning 'red headed'.

Ruth
(alt. Ruthe, Ruthie)
Hebrew, meaning 'friend and companion'.

Ruzgar
Turkish, meaning 'wind'.

Ryann
American, meaning 'great queen'.

Long names

Alexandria
Bernadette
Christabelle
Constantine
Evangeline
Gabrielle
Henrietta
Jacqueline
Marguerite
Wilhelmina

R

S Girls' names

Saada
African, meaning 'helper'.

Saadiya
Arabic, meaning 'bringer of good
fortune'.

Saba
(alt. Sabah)
Greek, meaning 'from Sheba'.

Sabi
Arabic, meaning 'lovely lady'.

Sabina
(alt. Sabine)
Latin, meaning 'from the Sabine
tribe'.

Sabiya
Arabic, meaning 'born in the
morning'.

Sabra
Hebrew, meaning 'to rest'.

Sabriel
American, meaning 'God's hero'.

Sabrina
Latin, meaning 'the River Severn'.

Sachet
Hindi, meaning 'conciousness'.

Sachi
Japanese, meaning 'child of bliss'.

Sada
Japanese, meaning 'pure'.

Sadella
American, meaning 'fairytale
princess'.

Sadie
(alt. Sade, Sadye)
Hebrew, meaning 'princess'.

Sadira
Persian, meaning 'lotus tree'.

Sadzi
American, meaning 'one with a
sunny nature'.

Safa
Arabic, meaning 'innocent'.

Saffi
Danish, meaning 'very wise'.

Saffron
English, from the spice of the
same name.

Safia
Arabic, meaning 'pure'.

Safiya
Arabic, meaning 'sincere friend'.

Sagara
Hindi, meaning 'from the ocean'.

Sage
(alt. Saga, Saige)
Latin, meaning 'wise and
healthy'.

Sagira
Egyptian, meaning 'small one'.

Sahar
Arabic, meaning 'dawn'.

Sahara
Arabic, meaning 'desert'.

Saheli
Indian, meaning 'beloved friend'.

Sahiba
Indian, meaning 'maiden'.

Saira
Arabic, meaning 'wanderer'.

Sakari
Native American, meaning 'sweet
child'.

Sakura
Japanese, meaning 'cherry
blossom'.

Sally
(alt. Sallie)
Hebrew, meaning 'princess'.

Salome
(alt. Salma)
Hebrew, meaning 'peace'.

Salva
Latin, meaning 'wise woman'.

Salwa
Arabic, meaning 'provider of
comfort'.

Sam
(alt. Sammie, Sammy)
Shortened form of Samantha,
meaning 'told by God'.

Samantha
Hebrew, meaning 'told by God'.

Samara
(alt. Samaria, Samira)
Hebrew, meaning 'under God's
rule'.

Sanaa
Arabic, meaning 'brilliance'.

Sandra
(alt. Saundra)
Shortened form of Alexandra,
meaning 'defender of mankind'.

Sandy
(alt. Sandi)
Shortened form of Sandra,
meaning 'defender of mankind'.

Sangeeta
Hindi, meaning 'musical'.

Sanna
(alt. Saniya, Sanne, Sanni)
Hebrew, meaning 'lily'.

Santana
(alt. Santina)
Spanish, meaning 'holy'.

Sapphire
(alt. Saphira)
Hebrew, meaning 'blue
gemstone'.

Sarah
(alt. Sara, Sarai, Sariah)
Hebrew, meaning 'princess'.

S

Sasha
(alt. Sacha, Sascha)
Russian, meaning 'man's defender'.

Saskia
(alt. Saskie)
Dutch, meaning 'the Saxon people'.

Savannah
(alt. Savanah, Savanna, Savina)
Spanish, meaning 'treeless'.

Scarlett
(alt. Scarlet)
English, meaning 'scarlet'.

Scout
French, meaning 'to listen'.

Sedona
(alt. Sedna)
Spanish, from the city of the same name.

Selah
(alt. Sela)
Hebrew, meaning 'cliff'.

Selby
English, meaning 'manor village'.

Selena
(alt. Salena, Salima, Salina, Selene, Selina)
Greek, meaning 'moon goddess'.

Selma
German, meaning 'Godly helmet'.

Seneca
Native American, meaning 'from the Seneca tribe'.

Sephora
Hebrew, meaning 'bird'.

September
Latin, meaning 'seventh month'.

Seraphina
(alt. Serafina, Seraphia, Seraphine)
Hebrew, meaning 'ardent'.

Serena
(alt. Sarina, Sereana)
Latin, meaning 'tranquil'.

Serenity
Latin, meaning 'serene'.

Shania
(alt. Shaina, Shana, Shaniya)
Hebrew, meaning 'beautiful'.

Shanice
American, meaning 'from Africa'.

Shaniqua
(alt. Shanika)
African, meaning 'warrior princess'.

Shanna
English, meaning 'old'.

Shannon
(alt. Shannan, Shanon)
Irish Gaelic, meaning 'old and ancient'.

Shantal
(alt. Shantel, Shantell)
French, from the place of the same name.

Shanti
Hindi, meaning 'peaceful'.

Sharlene
German, meaning 'man'.

S

Sharon
(alt. Sharen, Sharona, Sharron, Sharyn)
Hebrew, meaning 'a plain'.

Sashi
Hindi, meaning 'moonbeam'.

Shasta
American, from the mountain of the same name.

Shauna
(alt. Shawna)
Irish, meaning 'the Lord is gracious'.

Shayla
(alt. Shaylie, Shayna, Sheyla)
Irish, meaning 'blind'.

Shea
Irish Gaelic, meaning 'from the fairy fort'.

Sheena
Irish, meaning 'the Lord is gracious'.

Sheila
(alt. Shelia)
Irish, meaning 'blind'.

Shelby
(alt. Shelba, Shelbie)
English, meaning 'estate on the ledge'.

Shelley
(alt. Shelli, Shellie, Shelly)
English, meaning 'meadow on the ledge'.

Shenandoah
Native American, meaning 'after an Oneida chief'.

Sheridan
Irish Gaelic, meaning 'wild man'.

Sherry
(alt. Sheree, Sheri, Sherie, Sherri, Sherrie)
Shortened form of Cheryl, meaning 'man'.

Sheryl
(alt. Sherryl)
German, meaning 'man'.

Shiloh
Hebrew, from the Biblical place of the same name.

Shirley
(alt. Shirlee)
English, meaning 'bright meadow'.

Shivani
Sanskrit, meaning 'wife of Shiva'.

Shona
Irish Gaelic, meaning 'God is gracious'.

Shoshana
(alt. Shoshanna)
Hebrew, meaning 'lily'.

Shura
Russian, meaning 'man's defender'.

Sian
(alt. Sianna)
Welsh, meaning 'the Lord is gracious'.

Siara
Arabic, meaning 'holy and pure'.

Sibyl
(alt. Sybil)
Greek, meaning 'seer and oracle'.

Siddhi
Hindi, meaning 'spiritual powers'.

Siddiqa
Arabic, meaning 'righteous friend'.

Sidera
Latin, meaning 'luminous woman'.

Sidney
(alt. Sydney)
English, meaning 'from St. Denis'.

Sidonie
(alt. Sidonia, Sidony)
Latin, meaning 'from Sidonia'.

Siena
(alt. Sienna)
Latin, from the town of the same name.

Sierra
Spanish, meaning 'saw'.

Signa
(alt. Signe)
Scandinavian, meaning 'victory'.

Sigourney
French, meaning 'daring queen'.

Sigrid
Nordic, meaning 'fair victory'.

Sigrun
Scandinanvian, meaning 'won a secret victory'.

Siham
Arabic, meaning 'like an arrow'.

Sihar
Arabic, meaning 'enchanting'.

Sika
African, meaning 'wealthy woman'.

Silja
Scandinavian, meaning 'blind'.

Silver
English, meaning 'precious metal'.

Silwa
Arabic, meaning 'like a quail'.

Sima
Arabic, meaning 'prize'.

Simcha
Hebrew, meaning 'joy'.

Simin
Iranian, meaning 'silvery woman'.

Simone
(alt. Simona)
Hebrew, meaning 'listening intently'.

Sinead
Irish, meaning 'the Lord is gracious'.

Siobhan
Irish, meaning 'the Lord is gracious'.

Sippora
Hebrew, meaning 'birdlike'.

Siren
(alt. Sirena)
Greek, meaning 'entangler'.

Siria
Spanish, meaning 'glowing'.

S

Sisika
Native American, meaning 'like a bird'.

Sitara
Indian, meaning 'morning star'.

Sive
Irish, meaning 'good and sweet girl'.

Skye
(alt. Sky)
Scottish, from the island of the same name.

Skyler
(alt. Skyla, Skylar)
Dutch, meaning 'giving shelter'.

Sloane
(alt. Sloan)
Irish Gaelic, meaning 'man of arms'.

Socorro
Spanish, meaning 'to aid'.

Sohalia
Indian, meaning 'the moon's glow'.

Sojourner
English, meaning 'temporary stay'.

Solana
Spanish, meaning 'sunlight'.

Solange
French, meaning 'with dignity'.

Soledad
Spanish, meaning 'solitude'.

Soleil
French, meaning 'sun'.

Solveig
Scandinavian, meaning 'woman of the house'.

Sona
Arabic, meaning 'golden one'.

Sonia
(alt. Sonja, Sonya)
Greek, meaning 'wisdom'.

Sophia
(alt. Sofia, Sofie, Sophie)
Greek, meaning 'wisdom'.

Sophronia
Greek, meaning 'sensible'.

Sorano
Japanese, meaning 'from the heavens'.

Soraya
Persian, meaning 'princess'.

Sorcha
Irish Gaelic, meaning 'bright and shining'.

Sorrel
English, from the herb of the same name.

Soyala
Native American, meaning 'born in the winter solstice'.

Sparrow
English, meaning 'like the bird'.

Spencer
English, meaning 'administrator'.

Spring
English, meaning 'born in the season'. Also from the name of the season.

S

Sroda
African, meaning 'respected'.

Stacey
(alt. Stacie, Stacy)
Greek, meaning 'resurrection'.

Star
(alt. Starla, Starr)
English, meaning 'star'.

Stella
Latin, meaning 'star'.

Stephanie
(alt. Stefanie, Stephani, Stephania, Stephany)
Greek, meaning 'crowned'.

Sue
(alt. Susie, Suzy)
Shortened form of Susan, meaning 'lily'.

Sukey
(alt. Sukey, Sukie)
Shortened form of Susan, meaning 'lily'.

Suma
English, meaning 'born in the summer'.

Sumi
Japanese, meaning 'elegant and refined'.

Summer
English, from the season of the same name.

Suna
Turkish, meaning 'swanlike'.

Sunday
English, meaning 'the first day'.

Sunny
(alt. Sun)
English, meaning 'of a pleasant temperament'.

Suri
Persian, meaning 'red rose'.

Surya
Hindi, from the god of the same name.

Susan
(alt. Susann, Suzan)
Hebrew, meaning 'lily'.

Susannah
(alt. Susana, Susanna, Susanne, Suzanna, Suzanne)
Hebrew, meaning 'lily'.

Svea
Swedish, meaning 'of the motherland'.

Svetlana
Russian, meaning 'star'.

Swanhild
Saxon, meaning 'battle swan'.

Swarna
Indian, meaning 'golden one'.

Sybil
Greek, meaning 'seer'.

Sydney
English, meaning 'wide meadow'.

Sylvia
(alt. Silvia, Sylvie)
Latin, meaning 'from the forest'.

S

T

Girls' names

Tabia
Egyptian, meaning 'talented'.

Tabita
African, meaning 'graceful'.

Tabitha
(alt. Tabatha)
Aramaic, meaning 'gazelle'.

Tablita
Native American, meaning
'wearing a tiara'.

Taffy
Welsh, meaning 'much loved'.

Tahira
Arabic, meaning 'virginal'.

Tai
Chinese, meaning 'big'.

Taima
(alt. Taina)
Native American, meaning 'peal
of thunder'.

Taini
Native American, meaning 'born
at the time of the returning
moon'.

Tajsa
Polish, meaning 'princess'.

Taka
Japanese, meaning 'honourable'.

Talia
(alt. Tali)
Hebrew, meaning 'heaven's dew'.

Taliesin
Welsh, meaning 'shining brow'.

Talise
(alt. Talyse)
Native American, meaning 'lovely
water'.

Talitha
Aramaic, meaning 'young girl'.

Tallulah
(alt. Taliyah)
Native American, meaning
'leaping water'.

Talor
Hebrew, meaning 'touched by
the morning dew'.

Tama
Japanese, meaning 'as precious as
a jewel'.

Tamara
(alt. Tamera)
Hebrew, meaning 'palm tree'.

'Bad girl' names

Delilah
Desdemona
Jezebel
Lilith
Pandora
Roxy
Salome
Scarlett
Tallulah
Trixie

Tamatha
(alt. Tametha)
American, meaning 'dear Tammy'.

Tamika
(alt. Tameka)
American, meaning 'people'.

Tammy
(alt. Tami, Tammie)
Shortened form of Tamsin, meaning 'twin'.

Tamsin
Hebrew, meaning 'twin'.

Tandra
African, meaning 'beauty mark'.

Tani
Japanese, meaning 'valley'.

Tanika
American, meaning 'fairy queen'.

Tanis
Spanish, meaning 'to make famous'.

Tanya
(alt. Tania, Tanya, Tonya)
Shortened form of Tatiana, meaning 'from the Tatius clan'.

Tao
Chinese, meaning 'peach'.

Tara
(alt. Tarah, Tera)
Irish Gaelic, meaning 'rocky hill'.

Tasha
(alt. Taisha, Tarsha)
Shortened form of Natasha, meaning 'Christmas'.

Tatiana
(alt. Tayana)
Russian, meaning 'from the Tatius clan'.

Tatum
English, meaning 'light-hearted'.

Taura
Latin, meaning 'like a bull'.

Tawny
(alt. Tawanaa, Tawnee, Tawnya)
English, meaning 'golden brown'.

Taya
Greek, meaning 'poor one'.

Taylor
(alt. Tayler)
English, meaning 'tailor'.

Tazanna
Native American, meaning 'princess'.

Tazara
Arabic, meaning 'elegance'.

Tea
Greek, meaning 'goddess'.

Teagan
(alt. Teague, Tegan)
Irish Gaelic, meaning 'poet'.

Teal
English, from the bird of the same name.

Tecla
Greek, meaning 'fame of God'.

Tegan
Welsh, meaning 'pretty'.

Tehila
Hebrew, meaning 'song of praise'.

Teigra
Rumantsch, meaning 'tigress'.

Teja
Indian, meaning 'radiant'.

Tekli
Polish, meaning 'glory of god'.

Telyn
Welsh, meaning 'harp'.

Temima
Hebrew, meaning 'perfect'.

Spelling options

C vs K (Catherine or Katherine)
E vs I (Alex or Alix)
G vs J (Geri or Jerry)
N vs NE (Ann or Anne)
O vs OU (Honor or Honour)
S vs Z (Susie or Suzie)
Y vs IE (Carry or Carrie)

Temperance
English, meaning 'virtue'.

Tempest
French, meaning 'storm'.

Teresa
(alt. Terese, Tereza, Theresa, Therese)
Greek, meaning 'harvest'.

Terra
Latin, meaning 'earth'.

Terry
(alt. Teri, Terrie)
Shortened form of Teresa, meaning 'harvest'.

Tessa
(alt. Tess, Tessie)
Shortened form of Teresa, meaning 'harvest'.

Tevy
Cambodian, meaning 'angel'.

Thais
Greek, from the mythological heroine of the same name.

Thalia
Greek, meaning 'blooming'.

Thandi
(alt. Thana)
Arabic, meaning 'thanksgiving'.

Thea
Greek, meaning 'goddess'.

Theda
German, meaning 'people'.

Thelma
Greek, meaning 'will'.

T

Thema
African, meaning 'queen'.

Theodora
Greek, meaning 'gift of God'.

Theodosia
Greek, meaning 'gift of God'.

Theora
Greek, meaning 'watcher'.

Thisbe
Greek, from the mythological heroine of the same name.

Thomasina
(alt. Thomasin, Thomasine, Thomasyn)
Greek, meaning 'twin'.

Thora
Scandinavian, meaning 'Thor's struggle'.

Thu
Vietnamese, meaning 'born during autumn'.

Thy
Greek, meaning 'untamed'.

Tia
(alt. Tiana)
Spanish, meaning 'aunt'.

Tiara
Latin, meaning 'jewelled headband'.

Tien
Vietnamese, meaning 'fairy child'.

Tierney
Irish Gaelic, meaning 'Lord'.

Tierra
(alt. Tiera)
Spanish, meaning 'land'.

Tiffany
(alt. Tiffani, Tiffanie)
Greek, meaning 'God's appearance'.

Tigerlily
English, meaning 'an orange flower with black spots'.

Tiggy
Shortened form of Tigris, meaning 'tiger'.

Tigris
Irish Gaelic, meaning 'tiger'.

Tilda
Shortened form of Matilda, meaning 'battle-mighty'.

Tillie
(alt. Tilly)
Shortened form of Matilda, meaning 'battle'mighty'.

Timea
American, meaning 'honour God'.

Spring names
April
Andromeda
Cerelia
Ceres
Kelda
May
Primavera
Verda
Verna

T

Timila
Indian, meaning 'musical instrument'.

Timothea
Greek, meaning 'honouring God'.

Tina
(alt. Teena, Tena)
Shortened form of Christina, meaning 'anointed Christian'.

Tipper
Irish, meaning 'a well'.

Tira
Indian, meaning 'arrow'.

Tirion
Welsh, meaning 'kind and gentle'.

Tirzah
Hebrew, meaning 'pleasantness'.

Titania
Greek, meaning 'giant'.

Toby
(alt. Tobi)
Hebrew, meaning 'God is good'.

Tomoko
Japanese, meaning 'intelligent'.

Toni
(alt. Tony)
Latin, meaning 'invaluable'.

Tonia
(alt. Tonja, Tonya)
Russian, meaning 'praiseworthy'.

Topaz
Latin, meaning 'golden gemstone'.

Topper
English, meaning 'excellent'.

Tori
(alt. Tora)
Shortened form of Victoria, meaning 'victory'.

Tosha
Swahili, meaning 'satisfaction'.

Totole
Native American, meaning 'star'.

Tova
(alt. Tovah, Tove)
Hebrew, meaning 'good'.

Tracy
(alt. Tracey, Tracie)
Greek, meaning 'harvest'.

Tress
English, meaning 'long hair'.

Treva
Welsh, meaning 'homestead'.

Trianna
American, meaning 'gracious'.

Tricia
Shortened form of Patricia, meaning 'aristocratic'.

Trilby
English, meaning 'vocal trills'.

Trina
(alt. Trena)
Greek, meaning 'pure'.

Trinh
Vietnamese, meaning 'pure'.

T

Trinity
Latin, meaning 'triad'.

Trisha
Shortened form of Patricia, meaning 'noble'.

Triska
Slavic, meaning 'silver'.

Trista
Latin, meaning 'sad'.

Tristan
Celtic, mythological name meaning 'tumult'.

Triveni
Indian, meaning 'where the sacred rivers meet'.

Trixie
Shortened form of Beatrix, meaning 'bringer of gladness'.

Trudy
(alt. Tru, Trudie)
Shortened form of Gertrude, meaning 'strength of a spear'.

Tullia
Spanish, meaning 'bound for glory'.

Tumani
Swahili, meaning 'hope'.

Tunder
Hungarian, meaning 'fairy'.

Tuyen
Vietnamese, meaning 'angel'.

Tuyet
Vietnamese, meaning 'snow'.

Twilight
English, meaning 'dusk'.

Twyla
(alt. Twila)
American, meaning 'star'.

Tyler
English, meaning 'tiler'.

Tynan
Irish, meaning 'dark'.

Tyra
Scandinavian, meaning 'Thor's struggle'.

Tzeitel
Hebrew, meaning 'princess'.

Tzila
Hebrew, meaning 'shadow'.

Tzipporah
Hebrew, meaning 'bird'.

Autumn names

Autumn
Cedar
Demetria
Hazel
Juniper
Octavia
September
Theresa
Tracey
Willow

T

U

Girls' names

Uald
(alt. Ualda)
German, meaning 'brave'.

Udaberri
Basque, meaning 'spring'.

Udara
Basque, meaning 'summer'.

Udaya
Indian, meaning 'dawn'.

Udela
(alt. Udele)
English, meaning 'prosperous'.

Uditi
Indian, meaning 'rising sun'.

Uheri
Swahili, meaning 'fortunate'.

Ujjana
African, meaning 'youthful'.

Ujjwala
Indian, meaning 'lustrous'.

Ula
(alt. Ulla)
Celtic, meaning 'gem of the sea'.

Ulrika
(alt. Urica)
German, meaning 'power of the wolf'.

Ulani
American, meaning 'cheerful'.

Uldwyna
English, meaning 'special friend'.

Ulf
German, meaning 'wolf'.

Ulfah
Arabic, meaning 'familiar'.

Uli
(alt. Ulka)
German, meaning 'mistress of all'.

Ulima
Arabic, meaning 'astute'.

Ulla
German, meaning 'willpower' and Irish, meaning 'fill up'.

Ultima
Latin-American, meaning 'last'.

Ululani
American, meaning 'divine inspiration'.

Ullva
German, meaning 'wolf'.

Ulyana
Russian, meaning 'youthful'.

Names from nature

Acacia
Amaryllis
Bryony
Dahlia
Dawn
Holly
Hazel
Juniper
Primrose
Skye

Uma
Sanskrit, meaning 'flax'.

Umatilla
Native American, meaning 'princess'.

Umay
Turkish, meaning 'hope'.

Umaymah
African, meaning 'young mother'.

Umeko
Japanese, meaning 'plum blossom'.

Umeno
Japanese, meaning 'a field of plum-trees'.

Umia
African, meaning 'ladybird'.

Umika
Indian, meaning 'goddess'.

Umina
Australian, meaning 'sleep'.

Umm
Egyptian, meaning 'mother'.

Una
Latin, meaning 'one'.

Undina
Latin-American, meaning 'waves'.

Undine
Latin, meaning 'little wave'.

Unelina
Latin-American, meaning 'bear'.

Unice
Greek, meaning ' victorious'.

Unique
Latin, meaning 'only one'.

Unity
English, meaning 'oneness'.

Unn
Norwegian, meaning 'beloved'.

Unna
German, meaning 'woman'.

Unne
Norwegian, meaning 'love'.

Uny
Irish, meaning 'together'.

Upala
Indian, meaning 'jewel'.

Upama
Indian, meaning 'comparison'.

Ura
Indian, meaning 'heart'.

Urania
Greek, meaning 'divine'.

Urano
Japanese, meaning 'coast'.

U

Urbane
Israeli, meaning 'courteous'.

Urbania
Greek, meaning 'divine'.

Urice
Hebrew, meaning 'light'.

Uriela
Hebrew, meaning 'God's light'.

Urika
American, meaning 'useful'.

Urilla
American, meaning 'the Lord is my light'.

Urit
Hebrew, meaning 'light'.

Urja
(alt. Urjitha)
Indian, meaning 'energy'.

Urse
Scandinavian, meaning 'bear'.

Ursula
Latin, meaning 'little female bear'.

Urvi
Indian, meaning 'earth'.

Usagi
Japanese, meaning 'bunny'.

Usha
Indian, meaning 'sunrise'.

Ushakiran
Indian, meaning 'sun's rays'.

Ushas
Indian, meaning 'dawn'.

Ushi
Chinese, meaning 'ox'.

Usoa
African, meaning 'dove'.

Uta
German, meaning 'prospers in battle'.

Utano
Japanese, meaning 'a field full of song'.

Uttara
Indian, meaning 'imperial daughter'.

Uvatera
African, meaning 'God help us'.

Uzuri
Afgan, meaning 'beauty'.

Uzziye
Hebrew, meaning 'the strength of God'.

Short names

Bea
Bo
Fay
Jan
Jo
Kay
Kim
May
Mia
Val

U

Girls' names

Vada
German, meaning 'famous ruler'.

Vafara
(alt. Vafarah, Vaphara, Vafaria, Vafarya)
French, meaning 'brave'.

Vailea
(alt. Vaileah, Vaileigh, Vailee)
Polynesian, meaning 'of the talking waters'.

Valbourga
(alt. Valah, Valla)
Swedish, meaning 'great mountain' and German, meaning 'defensive ruler'.

Valda
(alt. Walda, Welda)
Teutonic, meaning 'ruler'.

Valdis
(alt. Valdiss, Valdys, Valdyss)
Norse, meaning 'goddess of the dead', based on the mythological goddess of the same name.

Vale
Shortened form of Valencia, meaning 'strong and healthy'.

Valeda
(alt. Valedah, Valayada, Valyda)
Latin, meaning 'strong woman'.

Valencia
(alt. Valancy, Valarece)
Latin, meaning 'strong and healthy'.

Valene
(alt. Valeen, Valeane, Valine, Valien, Valyn)
Latin, alternative of Valentina, meaning 'strong and healthy'.

Valentina
Latin, meaning 'strong and healthy'.

Valentine
Latin, from the Saint of the same name.

Valeny
(alt. Val, Valenie)
American, meaning 'hard'.

Valeria
Latin, meaning 'to be healthy and strong'.

Valerie
(alt. Valarie, Valery, Valorie)
Latin, meaning 'to be healthy and strong'.

Valeska
(alt. Waleska)
Slavic, meaning 'magnificent ruler'.

Valetta
(alt. Valeda, Valeta, Valletta)
Latin, from the place of the same name.

Valia
(alt. Vallie)
Shortened form of Valerie, meaning 'to be healthy and strong'.

Valiant
(alt. Valiante, Valeant, Valeante)
English, meaning 'brave'.

Valkyrie
(alt. Valkry, Valkri,)
Scandinavian, meaning 'selector of the slain'. In Norse mythology the Valkyries were maidens who led those slain in battle to Valhalla.

Valma
(alt. Valmai)
Welsh, meaning 'mayflower' and Finnish, meaning 'a devoted protector'.

Valonia
(alt. Vallonia, Vallonya)
Latin, meaning 'of the valley'.

Valterra
(alt. Valterrah, Valyonia, Valteira)
American, meaning 'from strong earth'.

Vanda
(alt. Vahnda, Vannda, Vanora)
German, alternative of Wanda, meaning 'tribe of vandals'.

Vandana
Sanskrit, meaning 'worship'.

Famous female singers

Amy (Winehouse)
Billie (Holiday)
Elaine (Paige)
Ella (Fitzgerald)
Etta (James)
Judy (Garland)
Julie (Andrews)
Leona (Lewis)
Lily (Allen)
Nina (Simone)

Vandani
Hindi, meaning 'honourable' or 'worthy'.

Vanessa
(alt. Vanesa)
English, from the *Gulliver's Travels* character of the same name.

Vanetta
(alt. Vanettah, Vaneta, Vanitta)
Greek, alternative of Vanessa, meaning 'like a butterfly'.

Vangie
(alt. Vangy, Vangey, Vangee)
Greek, alterative of Evangelina, meaning 'good news'.

Vani
Hindu, meaning 'voice' and Italian, alternative of Ann.

Vania
(alt. Vaniah, Vanea, Vanya)
Russian, alternative of Anna, meaning 'grace'.

Vanity
Latin, meaning 'self-obsessed'.

Vanmra
(alt. Vanmrah)
Russian, meaning 'a stranger' or 'foreigner'.

Vanna
(alt. Vannah, Vana, Vanae)
Cambodian, meaning 'golden woman'.

Vanora
(alt. Vannora, Vanorey, Vanory)
Scottish, meaning 'from the white wave'.

Vanthe
(alt. Vanth, Vantha, Vanthia)
Greek, alternative of Xanthe, meaning 'blonde'.

Varana
(alt. Varanna, Varanne, Varann)
Hindi, meaning 'of the river'.

Varda
(alt. Vardah, Vardia, Vardina)
Hebrew, meaning 'rose'.

Vardina
Hebrew, alternative of Varda, meaning 'rose'.

Varouna
(alt. Varounah)
Hindi, meaning 'infinite'.

Varsha
(alt. Varshah)
Hindi, meaning 'from the rain'.

Vartouhi
(alt. Vartoughi, Vartoughie, Vartouhie)
Armenian, meaning 'as lovely as a rose'.

Varvara
(alt. Vara, Varenka, Varina)
Russian, Spanish and Czech alternative of Barbara, meaning 'foreign'.

Vasanti
(alt. Vashtie, Vasanta, Vasantah)
Hindi, meaning 'spring'.

Vashti
Persian, meaning 'beauty'.

Vasta
(alt. Vassey, Vasey, Vasie)
Persian, meaning 'beautiful'.

Vasteen
(alt. Vastien)
American, meaning 'capable'.

Vaughn
(alt. Vaun, Vawn, Vaunne)
English, meaning 'loved one'.

Vayu
(alt. Vayyu)
Hindi, meaning 'air'.

Veda
Sanskrit, meaning 'knowledge and wisdom'.

No-nickname names
April
Beth
Dana
Joy
Jude
June
Karen
May

302

Vedette
(alt. Vedetta, Vedeah)
French, meaning 'scout' and Italian, meaning 'sentry'.

Vedi
(alt. Vedy, Vedee, Vedea, Vedeah)
Sanskrit, meaning 'wise'.

Vedis
(alt. Vedisse, Vedys, Vidis)
German, meaning 'forest spirit'.

Vega
Arabic, meaning 'falling vulture'.

Velda
German, meaning 'ruler'.

Velika
(alt. Velyka, Velicka, Velycca)
Slavic, meaning 'great'.

Vella
American, meaning 'beautiful'.

Velma
English, meaning 'determined protector'.

Venice
(alt. Venetia, Venita)
Latin, from the city of the same name.

Venus
Latin, from the Roman goddess of the same name.

Vevina
Scottish, meaning 'pleasant lady'.

Vera
(alt. Verla, Verlie)
Slavic, meaning 'faith'.

Verda
(alt. Verdie)
Latin, meaning 'spring-like'.

Verena
Latin, meaning 'true'.

Verity
Latin, meaning 'truth'.

Verna
(alt. Vernie)
Latin, meaning 'spring green'.

Verona
Latin, from the city of the same name.

Veronica
(alt. Verica, Veronique)
Latin, meaning 'true image'.

Veruca
Latin, meaning 'wart'.

Vesta
Latin, from the Roman goddess of the same name.

Vicenta
Latin, meaning 'prevailing'.

Vicky
(alt. Vicki, Vickie, Vikki, Vix)
Shortened form of Victoria, meaning 'victory'.

Victoria
Latin, meaning 'victory'.

Vida
Spanish, meaning 'life'.

Vidya
Sanskrit, meaning 'knowledge'.

Vienna
Latin, from the city of the same name.

Vigdis
Scandinavian, meaning 'war goddess'.

Vilina
Indian, meaning 'dedicated'.

Villette
(alt. Vyllet)
French, meaning 'little town'.

Vina
(alt. Vena)
Spanish, meaning 'vineyard'.

Vinata
Indian, meaning 'humble'.

Viola
Latin, meaning 'violet'.

Violet
(alt. Violetta)
Latin, meaning 'purple'.

Virgie
Shortened form of Virginia, meaning 'maiden'.

Virginia
(alt. Virginie)
Latin, meaning 'maiden'.

Virika
Indian, meaning 'brave one'.

Visala
Sanskrit, meaning 'celestial'.

Vita
Latin, meaning 'life'.

Vittoria
Variation of Victoria, meaning 'victory'.

Viva
Latin, meaning 'alive'.

Viveca
Scandinavian, meaning 'war fortress'.

Vivi
Latin, meaning 'alive'.

Vivian
(alt. Vivien, Vivienne)
Latin, meaning 'lively'.

Vivien
French alternative of Vivian, meaning 'lively'.

Vonda
Czech, meaning 'from the tribe of Vandals'.

Vova
Russian, meaning 'famous ruler'.

Vyomini
Indian, meaning 'divine'.

Vyra
American, meaning 'truth'.

 **Girls' names**

Wadd
Arabic, meaning 'beloved'.

Wade
English, meaning 'to cross a river'.

Wafa
Arabic, meaning 'devoted'.

Wahalla
Scandinavian, meaning 'immortal'.

Waheeda
Arabic, meaning 'the one and only'.

Wainani
Hawaiian, meaning 'beautiful water'.

Wakanda
Native American, meaning 'one with magical powers'.

Walad
Arabic, meaning 'new born'.

Walburga
German, meaning 'fortress ruler'.

Waleska
Polish, meaning 'beautiful'.

Walker
English, meaning 'one who walks in forests'.

Wallis
English, meaning 'from Wales'.

Walta
African, meaning 'like a shield'.

Wan
Chinese, meaning 'gentle one'.

Wanda
(alt. Waneta, Wanita)
Slavic, meaning 'tribe of the vandals'.

Wapeka
Native American, meaning 'skillful'.

Washta
Native American, meaning 'good'.

Wauna
Native American, meaning 'singing snow goose'.

Wava
English, meaning 'way'.

Waverly
Old English, meaning 'meadow of aspens'.

Wawa
Native American, meaning 'small girl'.

Wealote
Native American, meaning 'princess'.

Wednesday
American, from the day of the week.

Wendy
English, meaning 'friend'.

Wenopa
Native American, meaning 'two moons'.

Wesley
English, meaning 'one of the western meadow'.

West
English, meaning 'from the west'.

Wharton
English, meaning 'from the river'.

Whisper
English, meaning 'whisper'.

Whitley
Old English, meaning 'white meadow'.

Whitney
Old English, meaning 'white island'.

Whoopi
English, meaning 'excited'.

Wido
German, meaning 'warrior woman'.

Wihe
Native American, meaning 'younger sister'.

Wijdan
Arabic, meaning 'sentiment'.

Wilda
German, meaning 'willow tree'.

Wileen
Teutonic, meaning 'defender'.

Wiley
English, meaning 'from the willows'.

Wilfreda
English feminine form of Wilfred, meaning 'to will peace'.

Wilhelmina
German, meaning 'helmet'.

Willene
(alt. Willia)
German, meaning 'helmet'.

Willia
Shortened form of Willene, meaning 'helmet'.

Willow
English, from the tree of the same name.

Wilma
German, meaning 'protection'.

Wilona
English, meaning 'desired'.

Wilva
Teutonic, meaning 'determined'.

Wind
American, meaning 'windy'.

Winda
Swahili, meaning 'great huntress'.

Winema
Native American, meaning 'female chief'.

Winetta
American, meaning 'peaceful'.

Wing
Chinese, meaning 'glorious'.

Winifred
Old English, meaning 'holy and blessed'.

Winnie
Shortened form of Winifred, meaning 'holy and blessed'.

Winola
German, meaning 'charming friend'.

Winona
(alt. Wynona)
Indian, meaning 'first born daughter'.

Winslow
English, meaning 'friend's hill'.

Winta
African, meaning 'desired'.

Winter
English, meaning 'winter'.

Wisal
Arabic, meaning 'love'.

Wistar
German, meaning 'respected'.

Wisteria
English, meaning 'flower'.

Wova
American, meaning 'brassy woman'.

Wren
English, from the bird of the same name.

Wyetta
French, meaning 'fiesty'.

Wylie
American, meaning 'coy'.

Wynda
Scottish, meaning 'of the narrow passage'.

Wynne
Welsh, meaning 'white'.

Wyss
Welsh, meaning 'fair one'.

Names with positive meanings

Belle – Beautiful
Blythe – Carefree
Felicity – Happy
Lakshmi – Good
Lucy – Light
Millicent – Brave
Mira – Wonderful
Rinah – Joyful
Sunny – Sunshine
Yoko – Positive

X Girls' names

Xabrina
Latin alternative of Sabrina,
meaning 'from the Sabine tribe'.

Xadrian
American, meaning 'from the
Adriatic sea'.

Xalvadora
Spanish, meaning 'saviour'.

Xanadu
African, meaning 'of the exotic
paradise'.

Xandra
Greek alternative of Alexandra,
meaning 'defending men'.

Xannon
American, meaning 'ancient
goddess'.

Xantara
American, meaning 'Earth's
protector'.

Xanthe
(alt. Xanthe)
Greek, meaning 'blonde'.

Xantho
Greek, meaning 'golden haired'.

Xanthippe
Greek, meaning 'nagging'.

Xara
Hebrew alternative to Sarah,
meaning 'princess'.

Xava
American, meaning 'new house'.

Xaviera
Arabic, meaning 'bright'.

Xaverie
Greek, meaning 'bright'.

Xema
Latin, meaning 'precious'.

Xena
Greek, meaning 'foreigner'.

Xenia
Greek, meaning 'foreigner'.

Flower names

Daisy
Flora
Heather
Hyacinth
Iris
Lily
Poppy
Primrose
Rose
Violet

Xenobia
Greek, meaning 'from Zeus'.

Xenosa
Greek, meaning 'stranger'.

Xexila
Spanish, meaning 'blinded by her own beauty'.

Xilda
Celtic, meaning 'tribute'.

Ximena
Greek, meaning 'listening'.

Xin Qian
Chinese, meaning 'happy'.

Xing
Chinese, meaning 'star'.

Xiomara
Spanish, meaning 'battle-ready'.

Xipil
Aztec, meaning 'from the fire'.

Xochitl
Spanish, meaning 'flower'.

Xola
African, meaning 'in peace'.

Xolani
African, meaning 'forgive'.

Xuan
Vietnamese, meaning 'born during sping'.

Xue
Chinese, meaning 'snow'.

Xuxa
Portugese, meaning 'queen'.

Xyleena
Greek, meaning 'forest dweller'.

Xylia
Greek, meaning 'from the woods'.

Xyza
Gothic, meaning 'from the sea'.

Summer names

August
June
Juno
Natsumi
Persephone
Soleil
Summer
Suvi

X

Girls' names

Yabel
Latin, meaning 'lovable one'.

Yachi
Japanese, meaning 'eight thousand'.

Yachne
Hebrew, meaning 'hospitable'.

Yadira
Arabic, meaning 'worthy'.

Yadira
Hebrew, meaning 'beloved friend'.

Yadra
Spanish, meaning 'mother'.

Yael
Hebrew, meaning 'mountain goat'.

Yaffa
(alt. Yahaira, Yajaira)
Hebrew, meaning 'lovely'.

Yafiah
Arabic, meaning 'one with high standing'.

Yair
Hebrew, meaning 'God will teach'.

Yaki
Japanese, meaning 'tenacious'.

Yakini
African, meaning 'honest one'.

Yakira
Hebrew, meaning 'precious'.

Yakootah
Arabic, meaning 'like an emerald'.

Yalena
Russian alternative of Helen, meaning 'light'.

Yama
Japanese, meaning 'one who comes from the mountain'.

Yamha
Arabic, meaning 'dovelike'.

Yamilet
Arabic, meaning 'beautiful'.

Yamileth
Spanish, meaning 'graceful'.

Yamilla
Arabic, meaning 'pretty one'.

Yamin
Hebrew, meaning 'right hand'.

Yaminah
Arabic, meaning 'proper'.

Yamka
Native American, meaning 'blossom'.

Yana
Hebrew, meaning 'the Lord is gracious'.

Yanira
Hawaiian, meaning 'pretty'.

Yang
Chinese, meaning 'from the sun'.

Yara
Brazilian, from the mythological mermaid.

Yardley
English, meaning 'of the fenced-in field'.

Yareli
Latin, meaning 'golden'.

Yaretzi
(alt. Yaritza)
Hawaiian, meaning 'forever beloved'.

Yarkona
Hebrew, meaning 'green eyed'.

Yasmin
(alt. Yasmeen, Yasmina)
Persian, meaning 'jasmine flower'.

Yasu
Japanese, meaning 'tranquil'.

Yavesly
American, meaning 'divine miracle'.

Yedda
English, meaning 'one with the beautiful voice'.

Yei
Japanese, meaning 'flourishing'.

Yeira
Hebrew, meaning 'illuminated'.

Yelena
Greek, meaning 'bright and chosen'.

Yemaya
African, meaning 'intelligent'.

Yen
Chinese, meaning 'desired one'.

Yepa
Native American, meaning 'winter princess'.

Yeraldina
Spanish, meaning 'ruled with a spear'.

Yeriel
Hebrew, meaning 'founded by God'.

Yesenia
Arabic, meaning 'flower'.

Yestin
Welsh, meaning 'just'.

Yetta
English, from Henrietta, meaning 'ruler of the house'.

Yeva
Hebrew variant of Eve, meaning 'life'.

Yi
Chinese, meaning 'bringer of happiness'.

Yin
Chinese, meaning 'silvery lady'.

Yinah
Spanish, meaning 'victorious'.

Yitta
Hebrew, meaning 'gives off light'.

Ylva
Old Norse, meaning 'sea wolf'.

Ynes
French, meaning 'pure'.

Yo
Japanese, meaning 'positive'.

Yoki
(alt. Yoko)
Native American, meaning 'rain'.

Yolanda
(alt. Yolonda)
Spanish, meaning 'violet flower'.

Yonah
Hebrew, meaning 'a dove'.

Yoninah
Hebrew, meaning 'little dove'.

Yoomee
Native American, meaning 'star'.

Yordana
Bulgarian, meaning 'to flow down'.

Yori
Japanese, meaning 'reliable'.

Yoselin
English, meaning 'lovely'.

Yoshe
Japanese, meaning 'beauty'.

Yoshi
Japanese, meaning 'good'.

Yoshiko
Japanese, meaning 'good child'.

Yovela
Hebrew, meaning 'jubilee'.

Ysanne
Combination of Isabel and Anne.

Ysabel
English, meaning 'God's promise'.

Yuda
Indonesian, meaning 'war'.

Yue
Chinese, meaning 'moon'.

Yue-Yan
Chinese, meaning 'happy'.

Yui
Japanese, meaning 'elegant cloth'.

Yuki
Japanese, meaning 'lucky'.

Yule
English, meaning 'during Christmas time'.

Yuliana
Latin, meaning 'youthful'.

Yumi
Japanese, meaning 'short bow'.

Yumiko
Japanese, meaning 'child of the arrow'.

Yumna
Swahili, meaning 'fortunate'.

Yuridia
Russian, meaning 'farmer'.

Yusra
Arabic, meaning 'success'.

Yuuna
Japanese, meaning 'sun plant'.

Yvette
(alt. Yvonne)
French, meaning 'yew'.

Z Girls' names

Zaccai
(alt. Zaccae, Zakai, Zakae)
Hebrew, meaning 'pure' or 'just'.

Zada
(alt. Zayda, Zaida, Zayeda)
Arabic, meaning 'fortunate'.

Zafara
(alt. Zafarrah, Zaphara)
Hebrew, meaning 'singer'.

Zafira
Arabic, meaning 'successful'.

Zagir
(alt. Zagiry, Zagira, Zagirah)
Armenian, meaning 'like a flower'.

Zahar
(alt. Zahir, Zahyr, Zaher)
Hebrew, meaning 'dawn'.

Zahara
(alt. Zahava, Zahra)
Arabic, meaning 'flowering and shining'.

Zahiya
Arabic, meaning 'brilliant'.

Zaida
(alt. Zaide)
Arabic, meaning 'prosperous'.

Zaira
(alt. Zayra, Zayrah)
Arabic, meaning 'like a rose'.

Zaka
(alt. Zacca)
Swahili, meaning 'pure'.

Zale
(alt. Zael, Zayle)
Greek, meaning 'one who is as strong as the sea'.

Zalika
Swahili, meaning 'well born'.

Zaltana
Arabic, meaning 'high mountain'.

Zamara
(alt. Zamarrah)
Hebrew, meaning 'a female singer'.

Zambda
(alt. Zambdah)
Hebrew, meaning 'she mediates'.

Zamella
Zulu, meaning 'one who works to succeed'.

Zamia
Greek, meaning 'pine cone'.

Winter names

January
Neva
Neve
Perdita
Rainer
Tahoma
Winter

Zamir
(alt. Zameer, Zamyr)
Hebrew, meaning 'smart sovereign'.

Zan
Chinese, meaning 'supportive'.

Zana
(alt. Zanah, Zanna)
Hebrew, alternative of Susanna.

Zandra
(alt. Zan, Zondra)
Greek, meaning 'shy'.

Zane
(alt. Zaen, Zain, Zayn)
Scandinavian, meaning 'bold one'.

Zaneta
(alt. Zanetta, Zanita)
Hebrew, meaning 'a gracious present from God'.

Zaniyah
Arabic, meaning 'lily'.

Zannika
(alt. Zanicka, Zanyka)
Native American, meaning 'healthy'.

Zanoah
(alt. Zanoa)
Hebrew, meaning 'forgetful'.

Zara
(alt. Zaria, Zariah, Zora)
Arabic, meaning 'radiance'.

Zaria
(alt. Zariah, Zarya)
Slavic, meaning 'divine bride'.

Zariel
(alt. Zariele, Zarielle)
American, meaning 'lion princess'.

Zarina
African, meaning 'golden one'.

Zaylee
(alt. Zayley, Zaylie)
English, meaning 'divine'.

Zazula
Polish, meaning 'excellent'.

Zehara
(alt. Zeharrah)
Hebrew, meaning 'alight'.

Zehira
(alt. Zeheera, Zehyra)
Hebrew, meaning 'protected'.

Zela
(alt. Zelah)
Greek, meaning 'blessed with happiness'.

Zelda
German, meaning 'dark battle'.

Zelia
(alt. Zella)
Scandinavian, meaning 'sunshine'.

Zelma
German, meaning 'helmet'.

Zemirah
Hebrew, meaning 'joyous melody'.

Zena
(alt. Zenia, Zina)
Greek, meaning 'hospitable'.

Zenaida
Greek, meaning 'the life of Zeus'.

Zenda
Persian, meaning 'life'.

Zenon
Greek, meaning 'guest'.

Zephyr
Greek, meaning 'the west wind'.

Zetta
Italian, meaning 'Z'.

Zhen
Chinese, meaning 'precious'.

Zhenga
African, meaning 'queen'.

Zhenya
Russian, meaning 'noble'.

Zhi
Chinese, meaning 'healing'.

Zi
Chinese, meaning 'full of grace'.

Zia
Arabic, meaning 'light and splendour'.

Ziazan
Armenian, meaning 'rainbow'.

Zihna
Native American, meaning 'spins'.

Zillah
Hebrew, meaning 'the shade'.

Zinnia
Latin, meaning 'flower'.

Zirali
African, meaning 'the help of God'.

Zita
(alt. Ziva)
Spanish, meaning 'little girl'.

Zitkala
Native American, meaning 'small bird'.

Ziya
Arabic, meaning 'light'.

Zlata
Slavic, meaning 'golden'.

Zo
African, meaning 'spiritual leader'.

Food-inspired names
Anise
Candy
Cherry
Coco
Ginger
Honey
Meena
Olive
Saffron

Z

315

Bird names

Ava
Ibis
Oriole
Raven
Robin
Swift
Wren

Zoe
Greek, meaning 'life'.

Zola
Latin, meaning 'the earth'.

Zora
(alt. Zorana)
Slavic, meaning 'dawn'.

Zoraida
Spanish, meaning 'captivating woman'.

Zorina
Slavic, meaning 'golden'.

Zsa Zsa
Hungarian, meaning 'lily'.

Zoya
Greek, meaning 'life'.

Zula
African, meaning 'brilliant'.

Zulma
Arabic, meaning 'peace'.

Zurina
(alt. Zurine, Zurinia Zuryna)
Spanish, meaning 'white'.

Zuzana
Hebrew, meaning 'lily'.

Zuzu
Czech, meaning 'flower'.

Zyana
Aztec, meaning 'forever'.

Zyna
(alt. Zayne)
Arabic, meaning 'amazing'.

Zytka
Polish, meaning 'a rose flower'.

Powerful names

Aubrey
Allura
Inga
Isis
Lenna
Ulrika

Z